Design and the Digital Humanities

A Handbook for Mutual Understanding

Milena Radzikowska and Stan Ruecker

Bristol, UK / Chicago, USA

First published in the UK in 2022 by
Intellect, The Mill, Parnall Road, Fishponds, Bristol, BS16 3JG, UK

First published in the USA in 2022 by
Intellect, The University of Chicago Press, 1427 E. 60th Street,
Chicago, IL 60637, USA

Copyright © 2022 Intellect Ltd
All rights reserved. No part of this publication may be reproduced, stored in a retrieval system, or transmitted, in any form or by any means, electronic, mechanical, photocopying, recording, or otherwise, without written permission.

A catalogue record for this book is available from the British Library.

Copy editor: MPS Limited
Cover designer: Aleksandra Szumlas
Frontispiece image: Aleksandra Szumlas
Production managers: Faith Newcombe, Georgia Earl, Debora Nicosia
Typesetter: MPS Limited

Paperback ISBN 978-1-78938-358-4
ePDF ISBN 978-1-78938-359-1
ePUB ISBN 978-1-78938-360-7

Printed and bound by POD Worldwide

To find out about all our publications, please visit our website.
There you can subscribe to our e-newsletter, browse or download our current catalogue and buy any titles that are in print.

www.intellectbooks.com

This is a peer-reviewed publication.

Contents

Learning through making

Both design and digital humanities (DH) are best understood through the ways they learn their craft and the types of artefacts they create. Below and throughout this book you'll find carefully chosen exercises, some emergent from a 100-year-old tradition of how to teach visual literacy and design, and some pulled from DH curriculums across North America. These exercises are not intended to turn the reader (or the makers) into designers or digital humanists; though, if you complete them, you are likely to improve both your visual literacy and critical thinking. These exercises are meant to increase the depth of cross-disciplinary understanding and trust in the capabilities and expertise of the other.

Some of the exercises are best completed in a group or classroom setting, but many work well as solo activities. They are numbered for reference and, not necessarily, in terms of difficulty.

Check out the end of this book for a handy exercise outline.

What you'll need

Most of the exercises in this book can be done with simple office supplies. It will be handy to have a white board and some flip charts. Post-it notes of various colours and sizes are always useful to have around – to the point that they have become a cliché representation of design projects.

Additional materials:

- pencils (H or 2H);
- black and coloured markers (ideally various line thicknesses);
- tracing paper;
- sketchbook or at least some white blank paper;
- ruler;
- scissors;
- eraser; and
- paints or cut paper (various colours).

Sketchbook

Journaling and sketching is an important aspect of a visual education, and a fairly standard design tool. Designers use sketchbooks to record their ongoing learning process and development, as a tool for exploration when working through a design task (with notes, modifications, and critiques), as a source of historical and sociological information, and as a way to keep track of inspirational materials. There is no one prescribed format for a sketchbook, but it is important that it's a durable, bound book that you can easily carry with you. Whether or not it opens flat is a matter of personal preference.

Willingness to 'suck'

Depending on how you arrived here (thanks, by the way!), whether from an interest in or experience with the fine arts or design, or multiple degrees in the humanities, you're likely to find some of the exercises, more than others, challenging or even intimidating. If you've become accustomed to being 'an expert' in your discipline and producing high-quality work, the experience of 'sucking' can be somewhat traumatic. Try it anyway. Embrace the suck with pride in having leapt into the void.

We've both done it and we promise that it's worth it.

Acknowledgements

Parts of Chapter 3: 'Misunderstanding' have previously appeared in:

Michura, Piotr, Ruecker, Stan, Derksen, Gerry, Radzikowska, Milena, Dobson, Teresa and the INKE Research Group (2014), 'Documenting subjective interpretations of illustrated book covers for Lewis Carroll's *Alice's Adventures in Wonderland*', *Scholarly and Research Communication*, 5:2, pp. 1-11.

Radzikowska, Milena, Traynor, Brian, Ruecker, Stan and Vaughn, Norman, 'Teaching user-centered design through low-fidelity sketches', *Proceedings of the 4th Information Design International Conference*, Rio De Janeiro, Brazil, 9–12 September 2009, pp. 744–56, Rio De Janeiro: Brazilian Society of Information Design.

Ruecker, Stan and the INKE Research Group (2015), 'A brief taxonomy of prototypes for the digital humanities', *Scholarly and Research Communication*, 6:2, pp. 1-11.

Radzikowska, Milena, Ruecker, Stan and Rockwell, Geoffrey (2015), 'Teaching undergraduate design students using digital humanities research in the classroom', in A. Rowe and B. Sadler-Takach (eds), *Design Education: Approaches, Explorations and Perspectives*, Canada: A&D Press, pp. 37-44.

Parts of Chapter 5: 'Working better together' have previously appeared in:

Ruecker, Stan and Radzikowska, Milena (2008), 'The design of a project charter for interdisciplinary research', in *Proceedings of Designing Interactive Systems (DIS 2007)*, Cape Town, 25–28 February 2008, Published through the ACM, 2008 and available online.

Preamble: Identifying ourselves

Notes from our mutual admiration society

This book is written by two feminist practising design researchers (numbered among the founding members of the qLab at qcollaborative.com). Our work in design and digital humanities (DH) is reciprocally informed by our commitment to both. Our projects tend to be interdisciplinary and collaborative, marked by a passion to benefit others and informed by the last 15–20 years on teams with researchers from over 30 different fields.

We have had the great privilege of working on large, medium, and small national and international research teams, with students, industry partners, not-for-profit agencies, and scholars. Our work has been iterative and experimental – meant to challenge existing design conventions and explore unique alternatives to complex problems.

Much of our effort has been spent on the intersection of design and DH, although the last half of it has also seen us branching out so that one of our current interests is in how to use prototypes in research, first to formulate research questions, then to produce theories, and finally to test them. We have been thinking about the re-design of everything from the process of drug design to the monetary system to the university itself. We have even started to work on design for reconciliation in post-conflict zones, which involved a sometimes uncomfortable number of bullet-proof things like vests and vehicles. It was on that project where we coined the phrase: 'there's always room in the decoy truck'.

Land acknowledgements

This book was co-written by a refugee Canadian. The other still remembers the old homestead from three generations back, where the promise of a sod hut was better than staying in the UK. Both of us live and work on lands that have either been borrowed or stolen from the First Nations.

Dr Milena Radzikowska works at Mount Royal University, located in the traditional territories of the Niitsitapi (Blackfoot) and the people of the Treaty 7 region in Southern Alberta, which includes the Siksika, the Piikani, the Kainai, the Tsuut'ina, and the Iyarhe Nakoda. The City of Calgary is also home to the Métis Nation. Dr Stan Ruecker was born and raised on land that is located in the Treaty 6 Territory, the traditional territory of Cree Peoples, and the Homeland of the Métis.

Dr Stan Ruecker currently works at the University of Illinois at Urbana-Champaign, a land-grant institution, which acknowledges the historical context in which it exists. University of Illinois at Urbana-Champaign is located on the lands of the Peoria, Kaskaskia, Peankashaw, Wea, Miami, Mascoutin, Odawa, Sauk, Mesquaki, Kickapoo, Potawatomi, Ojibwe, and Chickasaw Nations.

We pay our respect to the First Nation and Métis ancestors of these lands and reaffirm our relationship with one another.

Thank you

Our biggest 'thank you' goes out to Margy MacMillan, Professor Emerita (Mount Royal University), information omnivore, and retired librarian for reading this text when it was at its roughest, and infusing it with clarity and confidence.

Introduction

For researchers in either design or digital humanities (DH) who are interested in productively working together on webpages, interfaces, and other tools, this chapter introduces our own twenty-year experience of this kind of interdisciplinarity, as well as some basic obstacles that need to be addressed before it can begin.

This book is organized into six chapters. Each chapter starts with a discussion, followed by a case study drawn from one of our research projects, and concludes with a set of exercises and classroom activities that are meant to provide you with a tangible view of what it's like to work with folks from one or both of these communities. Any individual exercise can be turned into a classroom activity or modified to accommodate collaboration. In fact, several visual examples used to demonstrate our exercises were completed by a group of volunteers from diverse disciplines, in a maker session hosted at Mount Royal University in October 2018.

We encourage members of both design and DH to embrace all parts of our book, not just the parts that are referring to the other side. We recognize that those designers and digital humanists who are reading our material are likely to be well versed in their own disciplines; however, we believe, it's better to know than not know what others believe to be true about you. As designers and DH scholars, we have worked on research projects with collaborators from Adult Education, Architecture, Archival Studies, Business, Chemical & Materials Engineering, Chemistry, Computer Science, Drama, Engineering Design, English Literature, French Literature, Gender Studies, German Literature, Health, Landscape Architecture, Library and Information Studies, Mechanical Engineering, Modern Languages and Cultural Studies, Parks and Recreation, Philology, Philosophy, Publishing, Sociology, and Stage Design. Many of the lessons we share with you here have been hard earned while on these projects. Thus, we have good reasons to believe that researchers outside design and DH can also benefit from the following text, especially those who are interested in working with colleagues in design or the humanities. Whatever your background or experience, thank you for sharing your time with us. We truly hope you find it worthwhile.

1

Selling the value of design

In 2005, Dr Stéfan Sinclair (of Voyant fame), Stan, and I crossed the Rocky Mountain Range from frosty Alberta to lush (at least for Canada) Victoria for the international digital humanities conference (ACH-ALLC 2005). We were on a mission – to sell the value of design to digital humanities (DH). Our pitch: identifying and describing one of the primary purposes of aesthetic quality in design – inspiring confidence. We were an interdisciplinary team of misfits. Stéfan, a professor in Humanities Computing at the University of Alberta, Stan (with a comb-shaped background in math, English, design, computing science, theology, and chemistry), and I – a modernist-trained designer from the international school. Our previous paper attempts at DH conversion had failed miserably. But we would not be deterred and, frankly, had gotten used to presenting to kindly roomfuls of three. Plus, we had the opportunity to spend a week basking in the sand-box brilliance of DH scholarship.

The day of our presentation we were pleasantly surprised to discover that we were scheduled to present in the big hall. Then, that we had standing room only.

Fourteen years, 70 design and DH projects, and over three dozen prototypes later, we have proof in the pudding for what we jazz-handed in Victoria: that these two intellectual traditions have a lot to offer each other in both research and practice.

Through this book, we are moving forward three of our long-standing agendas. First, we continue to argue that the twin interdisciplines of design and DH are natural allies, with much to be gained for researchers, students, and practitioners from both areas who are able to form alliances with those from the other. The fields share a common fundamental belief in the extraordinary value of interdisciplinarity, which in this case means that the training, experience, and inclinations from both areas naturally tend to align. The fields also share an interest in research that focuses on humanities questions and approaches, where the goal is to improve understanding through repeated observation and discussion. Finally, both design and DH tend to be generative in nature, with the ultimate end in many cases of designing and creating the next generation of systems and tools, whether those be intended for dealing with information or communication.

Second, we extend the assertion (proposed by Galey and Ruecker 2010) that the creation of an artefact can be, in and of itself, a way to formulate an argument about the creation of similar artefacts – a stark contrast to the way both disciplines have often been seen as not necessarily scholarly traditions in their own right, but in a service role to other scholarly disciplines. However, service is not research, and time devoted to service is time that could be spent producing a new prototype or carrying out a user study or writing an article.

And, third, we set out to share with you our experiences and emergent best practices for forming relationships, sharing intellectual trajectories, teaching, and doing research between design and DH. For all they have in common, design and DH also have significant differences. Their histories, practitioners, research archives, and traditions are distinct. The skillsets of the people involved have some overlap, but not much; just enough, in fact, to make misunderstandings more likely. They share some research methods, often in the form of those borrowed from other disciplines, but they also have their own emergent research methods and other scholarly activities. It is therefore useful to consider successful collaborations within a large terrain of shared interests but possible miscommunications.

Additionally, one of the most potentially difficult aspects of working with other scholars in an interdisciplinary manner is negotiating the problem of overlapping vocabulary between the disciplines. Some of the most potentially frustrating difficulties in any interdisciplinary collaboration can arise when the researchers are using terminology that seems identical but is in semantic and pragmatic terms quite different. Examples are often common words such as 'text' or 'image' which come with an entire multivalence of meanings, some of which may be subtext that is actually hard to articulate. In the case of design, for instance, 'text' is essentially a graphic object, perhaps more accurately and somewhat dismissively referred to as 'copy'. For DH, 'text' is at the heart of much of the endeavour, implying the cultural archive that is enshrined in the written word. While for designers, 'text' is a somewhat elevated term for 'content', for the digital humanist, the use of the term 'text' often implies a concession to the digital through not emphasizing the even more sacred words such as 'print' or 'the book'.

In fact, the conceptual ground is even more nuanced than this, in that 'text' does not just allow for the digital, but also suggests a certain disembodiment, implying that what is written can be disassociated from its medium. Formats such as HTML and XML, for instance, were intended to be 'cross-platform' or 'media-agnostic' so that the words could be easily transmitted and reassembled for readers using disparate technologies. Within DH, there is a contingent from book history who can sympathize with the heretical nature of these ideas for designers, who hold that at least arguably the instantiation of the prototype or addition needs careful attention from an intelligent hand.

To take another example, many fields are concerned with not only their data but also the way in which their data is organized. The common term, in this case, would be information design. The actual technical implementations of information design, and therefore what is understood about the phrase, vary dramatically between the fields. For computing science, for instance, data can take many forms but for several decades the default has been the relational databases where a rigid structure of fields contains information that fits appropriately in its respective location. In DH, on the other hand, relational tables are not always the best fit for containing useful information. Instead, various forms of text encoding have been applied: TACT, SGML and XML. For designers, whether information is stored in a database or an XML-encoded collection of files is more or less a matter of indifference. What is important is the visual form the data takes and the impacts that it has on its intended users, readers or audience. When a designer talks about information design, the digital humanist and computing scientist are liable to make fundamentally incorrect assumptions that may be delayed from coming to light because they are using the same words for different concerns. It is similarly necessary to disentangle a number of similarly overlapping terms such as structure, hierarchy, format, rhetoric, metaphor, sketch, prototype, publication, abstract, and attention to detail.

There are also a number of practical issues to be addressed. First of all, if you are a design researcher, why would you be interested in working with someone in DH as opposed to perhaps a colleague from English or Sociology or Computer Science? If you are a researcher in DH, why would you want to have a designer on your team? In either case, once you believe you want one, where would you find somebody? Is it possible to work with people at a distance? What does it mean to work with someone from the other field, and what does it not mean – that is, what are the assumptions from one field that need to be negotiated in working with another?

That the interdisciplinary approach to research can produce results that are profound and useful seems self-evident. One compelling argument is the proliferation of products and services that we deal with every day that are the result of researchers working across fields. The smart phone, for instance, brings together advances in computer hardware, materials engineering, industrial design and manufacturing. What we see on the phone is the work of visual communication designers, interaction engineers, computer programmers, experts in platforms and systems, and people who study user experience. There are components from security specialists, digital communications at multiple levels, and, of course, audio quality – since the thing has been, at the end of the day, sold as a telephone rather than a pocket computer. Which brings in the necessary expertise in business, marketing, and advertising that let everyone know the technology was available.

Given that interdisciplinarity can be useful, however, is not the same thing as saying that there are or indeed that there need to be interdisciplines, by which we mean fields that cannot exist without other fields. It might be reasonably the case, for instance, that people from within two or more disciplines get together over a topic of common interest, and see if a single research project could benefit from participation by diverse parties. Physics and Math, for instance, seem like a natural pairing, as do English and Film Studies. The objects of study overlap, and the research methods are similar, although we don't usually talk about research methods per se in the humanities, but instead about theoretical schools. A post-colonial approach to the novels of Jane Austen, for example, is not the same as a psychoanalytical approach, but neither is there a close parallel between the use of a semi-structured interview in psychology and a psychological study that uses a questionnaire with Likert scales.

When some of our colleagues talk about interdisciplinarity, what they are interested in are these kinds of paired disciplines. It is important, they feel, to have a disciplinary grounding to bring to the table. Otherwise they worry that interdisciplinary research may deteriorate into nothing more than dilettantism. Certainly that is a danger, especially in an era when it is nearly impossible to stay abreast of the research literature in even a single discipline. To voluntarily undertake to tackle more than one discipline suggests that once the literature review is done, there may be no time left for carrying out any original research. A much better strategy seems to be to bring to the table one person from each discipline.

We agree. Without a proper disciplinary grounding, there is always the danger that a researcher becomes simply a dilettante, and no one wants to spend too much time listening to a dilettante. However, we believe there is a further distinction to be made, in that some disciplines can operate more or less in isolation, while others require not just their own native approaches, but in order to be effective, they also need to communicate more widely. They need to take account of what is going on in companion fields of inquiry. Design and DH are examples of these kinds of interdisciplines. To put these two areas together produces a terrain that is multidimensional, because each has understood itself as interdisciplinary, but the outcomes in each case are different.

We often tell our students that DH has three faces: supporting humanities research with computers; taking computing as an object of humanities study; and producing computing artefacts such as software, interfaces, websites, multimedia objects, digital images, or video. Design, on the other hand, attempts to generate communicational artefacts, some of which might support humanities research, or may consist of computing artefacts of various kinds.

Additionally, there is a wide range of action-packed work being carried out by digital humanists across all the humanities, and the equally wide scope of work being done by researchers in design. And, putting the two together seldom results in a simple multiplication – but instead a proliferation – of research areas, since the result is an intersection rather than a union.

We acknowledge that not every research project in design can or should involve DH, and the converse is also true. However, the intersection between design and DH involves some core areas, including communication, typography, prototyping and visualization. Theorists from both areas can also treat the other as an object of study.

Further, while both fields have their own essential history, training, perspectives, venues for publication at both the national and international levels, and so on, both also imbricate – overlap – nicely with other fields. While it is possible to be a lone scholar doing design or DH, some key components of the research activity are more often than not central to the research pursuits within a given discipline. Even in cases where the components aren't central to another discipline, there is usually some disciplinary expertise that can be made available which will enrich the outcome.

Our approach in tackling the intricacies of interdisciplinary research conducted by design and DH is to discuss issues in the context of a variety of tried-and-tested research projects as well as classroom activities. The ultimate goal of the book is to provide both design and DH with a better mutual understanding, with the practical intention of working effectively together in ways that are productive and satisfying for everyone involved.

Famed DH scholar, Dr Susan Brown, has long championed design's cause, arguing that 'an algorithm has no impact without an interface' (Brown 2015: 81). Since first working with a designer on a DH project (that designer being, in fact, one of the co-authors of this text), Dr Brown has become one of design's passionate allies: 'design matters precisely because of those political implications and shaping impacts of which we can be only partially aware'.

1.1 The epistemological modes of knowledge production

We have described before – in fact, it seems like we are constantly describing – the ways in which different parts of the university produce new knowledge. Each of these is connected with a way of seeing the world: an epistemology. Since these ways of seeing the world are different from each other, the methods that are built from them create different kinds of knowledge, or at least they privilege different forms of knowledge, even if the results turn out to be the same.

For the physical sciences, the goal is to develop theories that produce hypotheses that can be tested without worrying much about who is doing the testing.

That is, the results should not depend on the subjectivity of the researchers. Most hypotheses in the sciences are of the cause-and-effect kind, where the theory predicts that variable Y is dependent on variable X. In setting up a test for the hypothesis, you should be able to tell by changing X whether or not Y changes. If it does, the theory has at least that much predictive value, and possibly more.

For the humanities, and much of the social sciences, the goal is to leverage the subjectivity of the researcher in the interests of producing an interpretation of the object of study. That is, different researchers are not just allowed to get different results from the same data – they are expected to. If there is any replication of results, that is just time and energy wasted. Here the goal is not usually to identify instances of cause-and-effect relationships (although it can be), but instead to turn a theoretical lens onto the object of study, and see what turns up. Because the theoretical lenses differ from one another, and the subjective thinking of the researcher differs from that of other researchers, the result should be a unique set of insights. By assembling all the sets of insights into one place – for example, in a section of the library – it is possible to see all the various ways that a particular object of study has been examined, and hopefully to add another way. A good percentage of DH research falls into this category.

The third mode belongs primarily to the fine arts. Here, the creative and expressive capacities of the individual researcher take precedence over everything else. The knowledge that is produced is usually instantiated in a work of art, which may in turn be subject to study using any of the other epistemological modes.

Finally, we have the mode that is most often used in design, as well as in the side of DH that proceeds by thinking through making. Here, the importance of the researcher's subjectivity again drops off, although not so far as in the sciences. In fact, how closely the two are inter-weaved – design and designer – depends on whether the two are positioned as correlative to the sciences or the arts: the perceived distance between design and designer becomes greater when viewed through a scientific lens and diminishes when viewed as one of the arts. It's important to note, however, that this binary is under challenge with a growing recognition that the positionality, experiences, and privileges of the designer have impact on what ends up designed. Neutral design simply does not exist.

1.2 Change is scary

There's an old adage that observes: you're friends for a reason, a season or life. Those who become your life-long friends are those with whom you share a common core. For DH and design that core is a passion for making. Sometimes digital humanists and designers make vastly different types of artefacts and, sometimes, they are the same in type but dramatically different in realization.

While the expertise required to produce material form is generally outside the scope of a humanities education, designers are trained specialists in manipulating it. Any graphical composition is constructed by, first, carefully choosing lines, shapes, tones, textures, colours, and the space these will occupy (the elements that are placed within a composition), then manipulating and arranging them within the space according to a set of principles (pattern, contrast, emphasis, balance, scale, harmony, rhythm, unity, and variety). Design elements describe the fundamental structure of any visual composition, while design principles govern the relationships created between the elements used within a design. Principles are used to visually group elements and units, differentiate elements and units from one another, establish a hierarchy of importance or priority, focus attention, direct the viewer's eye across the composition, create order and stability, and eliminate redundant elements. Each element can be selected, manipulated, structured, or organized well or poorly using some combination of the principles. Each element has both an internal quality – one that is inherent to it – and an external quality – one that is created by its interaction with other elements. How the relationship between elements and principles is constructed is dependent on numerous factors, and schools of thought regarding their application differ both across design sub-disciplines and between individual practising designers. Elements can be selected, combined, or manipulated, for example, in reference to and accordance with a particular art movement, or they can be manipulated according to the stylistic preferences of, or feedback from, a client or user. However, there are two interdependent goals, functional and interpretive, to the selection of elements, their manipulation and construction into units, and organization within a composition. Functional goals are most often related to the usability of the object as a whole, and to performance measures. Interpretative goals are most often related to establishing an intellectual and emotional connection with the user, a community or culture, the subject matter or domain, and/or the organization or company, while framing the composition as distinct or unique from its environment.

Whether deliberately or not, designers make choices regarding these building blocks the moment their pencil makes contact with paper. Furthermore, the choices they make and the visual quality of these choices impact how we interpret, use or avoid, and are affected by the design. Karvonen argues that 'beauty may be the decisive factor when wondering whether or not to trust a service enough to conduct business online' (2000: 86). Frascara supports this position, stating that visual design affects the user's immediate response of attraction or rejection to an artefact, the effectiveness of its communication, the length of perceptual time commitment, memorization of its message, the active life of the design, and how it impacts the quality of the environment within which it exists (2004: 3–32).

Since the rise of personal computing and graphical interfaces, many humanities scholars have been empowered to select, combine, and manipulate the elements of form in order to create artefacts through which their materials can be studied. In DH, distinctions between author/creator, critic, editor, and publisher are often blurred or even non-existent, and the urge to make is powerful. The Proceedings of the Old Bailey (https://www.oldbaileyonline.org) and The Bentham Papers Archive (http://www.benthampapers.ucl.ac.uk) are two famous examples of digital humanists as makers.

Over the past decade, DH scholars and designers have formed some notable partnerships that helped to define the territory of their interdisciplinary collaboration, sometimes working on web interfaces to text archives, on projects that combine text and images, or experimenting with interactive prototypes.

1.2.1 Territory of possible engagements

The No One Remembers Acronyms (NORA) project was a precursor to Metadata Offer New Knowledge (MONK). Funded by the Mellon Foundation, it was to provide access for humanists to state-of-the-art text-mining technologies. In this respect, it was infrastructure development more than research, but the goal of introducing new algorithms to the humanities, combined with the scale of the collections, necessitated some research into new approaches for the design of the human-computer interactions. For example, a team from the University of Maryland and University of Illinois designed an interface and used it to explore patterns of erotic language in Emily Dickinson's poetry (Plaisant et al., 2006). Once the system had lists of equal numbers of positive and negative examples (in this case, of ten or so poems that the experts had rated 'hot' and 'not hot'), it could identify features common to the poems in both sets, and use those to suggest other poems that might fall into either category. The experts could then analyse the features the system identified as well as the lists of suggested poems. They found it – it's there in what she left out and in the proximity or relationship of some words to others! Imagine if one hyphen speaks for your budding thoughts of kissing, but with three things have turned a trifle steamy. And also, of course, bees.

NORA was the work of an interdisciplinary team of researchers from five universities across two countries, with expertise in computer science, DH, design, visualization, and literary studies. In the course of the 18-month project, the designers on the team used a varied amplitude of their expertise. Our starting point was a spreadsheet-inspired interface with columns of numbers and texts. Colours and shapes had been used to highlight and group items and to segregate parts of an interface structured into three vertical panels.

For our re-designed version we worked within a very specific set of constraints. We were asked to retain the column panel structure and maximize how many items appeared on the screen before the user was forced to scroll down and view more. Consequently, we manipulated the colour palette, white space, geometric shapes, and typefaces and their treatments – the interface's visual form. We wanted to clarify what list items were meant to group together, remove unnecessary visual information and replace it with opportunity to rest the eye when scanning the lists, and reduce the aggressiveness of the visual choices. The final result has 10% more white space between the vertical clusters and horizontal items, much of that gained by removing cell outlines and changing the typeface from a serif (which appears as a slab serif because of low pixel fidelity) to a sans serif. We softened the colour palette, swapping red, black, and purple for saturation variants of green (cool) and pink (warm) – intending it to better match the objective of the colour coding which was to indicate items identified as not hot vs. those identified as hot (see Figure 1.1).

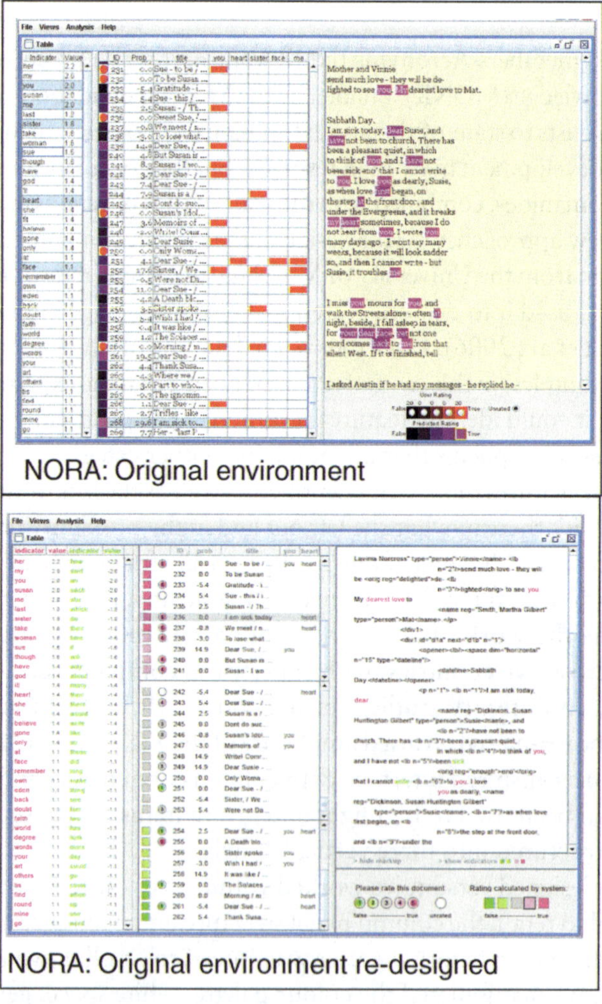

FIGURE 1.1: NORA project original environment (pre-designer intervention) and the re-designed alternative.

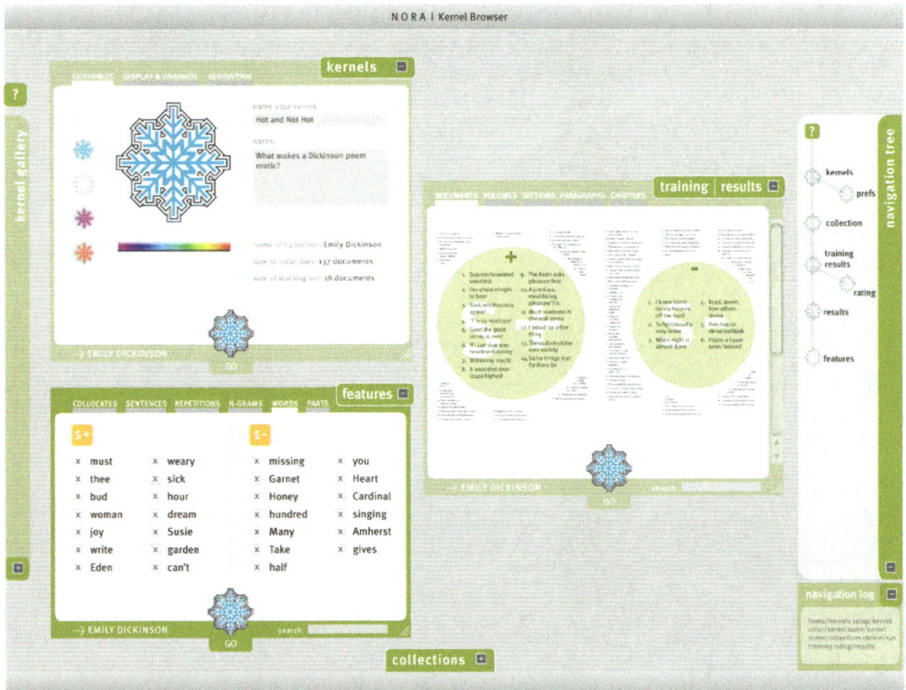

FIGURE 1.2: NORA palette interface.

Having accomplished the entry-level task that had been set before us, we now had the time and resources to experiment with a more disruptive alternative: the oil and water interface. The user would choose settings and develop a training set that became attached to a graphical object (Ruecker et al. 2011). We experimented with several alternatives for said object or kernel: cells, cogs, ferns, legos, snowflakes, and celestial orbits – items that could become more structurally complex as the user completed more and more of the text-mining process (see Figure 1.2).

The palette interface encountered several technical challenges to implementing a working prototype, sufficiently daunting that only a Flash video was ever produced. The display of countless titles in microtext and the fluid movement of that microtext on the screen were beyond the capability of desktop computing at the time. Since the project preceded the widespread adoption of touch-screen technology, the use of a drag-and-drop trigger for a complex algorithmic process would not have been readily recognized by typical users.

In our final design task for NORA we turned back to a table format, modified with some additional attention paid to layout, typography, colour-coding, whitespace, grouping, and hierarchy (see Figure 1.3). This alternative took advantage of some affordances that were relatively recent developments for use in prototyping,

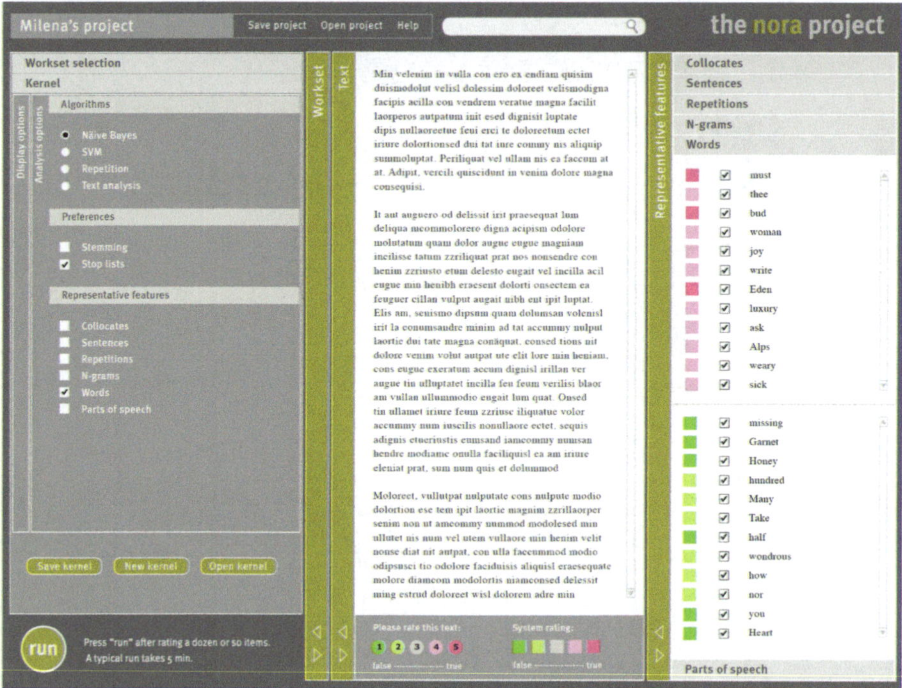

FIGURE 1.3: NORA window shutters alternative.

while at the same time relying primarily on programming assets that were readily available rather than hoped for at some indefinite point in the future (as was the case in the palette interface mentioned above). When attempting to work within the territory of experimental interface design, not only are there framed design research questions, but those questions are meant to be paramount. Contemporary technology is therefore not the logical limit of what is possible. In the case of the window shutters design, technical constraints (and the larger team's emphasis on a working prototype) directed and constrained the design.

The above-outlined example illustrates the diversity that's possible in the territory of how interdisciplinary teams can engage with designers and design expertise. On the one hand, all designers should come well-prepared to manipulate form in order to meet some predetermined set of objectives while respecting technical or functional constraints. On the other, some designers are capable of manipulating form while also engaging with design as a scholarly tradition in its own right – thinking through making in order to move the goalpost for what's possible and diversify the gene pool of ideas (Ruecker et al., 2008).

There's a range of possible engagements between the designer's expertise and the design task proposed by an interdisciplinary team – let's call this starting point,

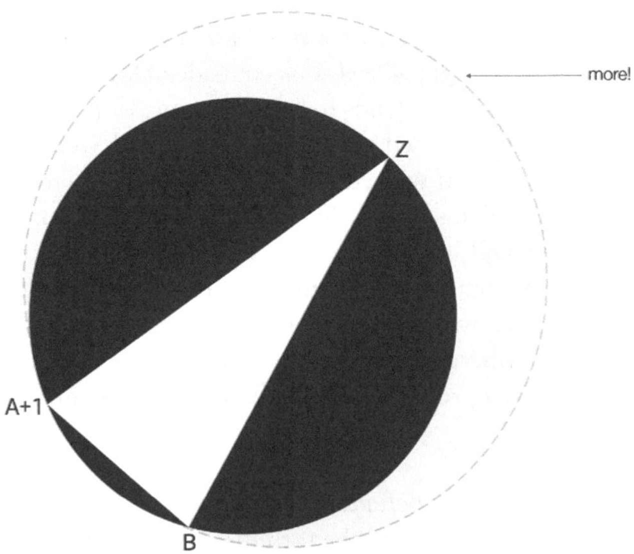

FIGURE 1.4: The territory of possible idea generation for design.

position A. Designers may examine position A and propose incremental change in form, perhaps content, in order to increase positive perception of that object. The new design takes the form of, what we've come to call, A+1. The first NORA re-design is a good example of an incremental-change (A+1) design (see Figure 1.4). A+1 tends to cost the least amount of money, time, and effort, involves fewest risks, and has the potential to produce immediate benefits for current users. However, A+1 is incremental change, not experimental research or its natural concomitant, disruptive design innovation. It does not pose any interesting or valuable questions, nor move the goalpost.

Alternatively, a designer may be approached by a researcher with some set of interesting research questions that might be well addressed by inventing a new system that involves a significant degree of change. We call this type of engagement, B: where a design will emerge out of a constellation of technology, data, processes, user engagement and feedback, and design methods. Design B is a deliberate shift away from common practice, and has the potential to benefit both the discipline of the initiating researcher and design.

If the objective is disruption, that's position Z – an attempt to intentionally shift the relationship between identity and current best practices. Z is design radical enough to be as far as possible outside the current bounds of discourse. It is meant to propose an actionable, ideal future.

Finally, there's Z+1. This area of design engagement is a dive outside of expected territory. While Z is bound by the knowledge, expertise, and past practices of the disciplines that make up the project team – Z attempts to subvert said practices while still keeping them in sight – Z+1 looks outside of known discourse towards what has been made invisible or tends to be under represented or, ideally, is counter to comfort. This idea is based on work by Rittel and Webber. In the 1960s, they proposed the concept of wicked problems (WPs) in design to challenge the notion that design problems are linear, with the proposed solution following a process of research and investigation. In contrast, they described a class of social system problems common to designers, which are ill-formulated, where the information is confusing, where there are many clients and decision-makers with conflicting values, and where the ramifications in the whole system are thoroughly perplexing. There are ten properties of wicked problems identified by Rittel and Webber (1973: 161–67):

1. Wicked problems have no definitive formulation, but every formulation of a wicked problem corresponds to the formulation of a solution.
2. Wicked problems have no stopping rules.
3. Solutions to wicked problems cannot be true or false, only good or bad.
4. In solving wicked problems, there is no exhaustive list of admissible operations.
5. For every wicked problem there is always more than one possible explanation, with explanations depending on the *Weltanschauung* of the designer.
6. Every wicked problem is a symptom of another, 'higher level', problem.
7. No formulation and solution of a wicked problem has a definitive test.
8. Solving a wicked problem is a 'one-shot' operation, with no room for trial and error.
9. Every wicked problem is unique.
10. The wicked problem solver has no right to be wrong – they are fully responsible for their actions.

Wicked problems are messy, unsettling, kinetic, ill-structured, and often vague. Thus, researchers will rarely, if ever, arrive at an agreed-upon definition of the problem. WPs aren't meant to have final solutions, only proposals or temporary arrangements: we work on these types of problems until we either give up, move on, or die. Then, hopefully, someone else will take over. Wicked problems have no single root cause, and seeking one 'correct' or 'true' answer isn't the objective.

Having stated the above, several of Rittel and Webber's WP characteristics cause us to break into a sweat. We believe that there is value to history and previous experience when tackling wicked problems. Each attempt at a WP extends our territory of understanding. The fact that wicked problems are constructed by the perceptions, beliefs, and values of the people working on them adds insight – diversity in experience is more likely to encourage a diversity of perspectives, expanding our pinprick-hole worldview into a lens. Finally, we maintain that mistakes are just as valuable as 'solutions'; mistakes are alternatives that may not be, for the moment, as valuable as other alternatives.

1.2.2 Moving the goalposts

Moving the goalpost is all about change. Experiments in change, rather than incremental iteration, have the potential to make interdisciplinary contributions, including back to design. While incrementation can be fun in practice, it holds no value to design researchers. But, it is well known that change of any kind, although it can be exhilarating, can also be challenging. Take for example an organization where employees are faced with a condition of positive change, both for the organization and for them. They may have had years of experience in doing their jobs and being evaluated according to a given set of criteria. Now, they will find themselves faced with a new set of tasks and revised evaluation criteria that are, at least to a certain extent, unknown. This circumstance puts pressure on the employees and the organization, and the question is whether or not the positive changes will be sufficiently beneficial to warrant the additional stress (Jansson 2013).

If we consider the humanities and the digital humanities as organizations, it is possible to understand that both are experiencing additional stress due to change. In the case of the Humanities, the agents of change are increasingly associated with DH in the form of the innovations they are producing. In DH, the stress arises from the pervasive nature of invention, where new practices, systems, data stores, standards, and also designs are an expectation of normal DH scholarly activity.

We first became aware of the problem during the communication process between digital humanists working on research teams as designers and digital humanists or computer scientists working as programmers (Ruecker et al. 2008). Recognizing that both groups routinely make significant intellectual contributions to a project (e.g. Mehta et; al., 2009), there is nonetheless often still a tendency for designers to imagine systems that initially strike programmers as too difficult, too unusual, or simply too odd, often perhaps unnecessarily so. There are several reasons for this tendency, which can be healthy in the sense that it implies the need for justification of choices that are off the current default, but can be less than useful in constantly challenging the need for innovation in design research.

First is that most modern programming languages come with libraries of design elements that are pre-programmed so that the development process is faster, easier, and less prone to error. To abandon these elements is therefore to make the programming process slower, harder, and more prone to error. However, for an experimental system, especially a system that is predicated on the need for interactive visualization, components that come 'out of the box' are less likely to provide evidence related to research questions about novelty of information presentation and use. For example, every interactive browsing tool needs a search component. However, not every experimental system requires one, since the need is already well established and does not need to be established anew with each new prototype.

Second is that the subset of computer science that comprises the academic programming community has a strong belief in the need to see a working system in order to properly understand and evaluate its potential. The alternative is 'vapourware' or designs that have not been realized as prototypes. Unfortunately, the result of this emphasis is that as little time as possible is spent on design, which represents a delay in the process of creating a working prototype. What can go unrecognized is that design and functionality are inextricably connected (e.g. Ruecker et al. 2007), so that studies attempting to isolate the two are often less useful and convincing than might otherwise be the case.

Third, as mentioned above, is that change itself is a source of additional stress, anxiety, and confusion. While this is true within the research team, it can be an even greater factor within the user community. For many Humanists, the scholarly effort spent on DH experiments is simply wasted effort, since it is clear that existing practices, systems, data stores, standards, and designs are sufficient to the task at hand, which is the hermeneutic or interpretive approach to the cultural objects of study, whether those be poetry, novels, plays, historical objects or documents, and so on. If there is a need at all for digital enhancements, then the process should consist of digital enhancements to approaches that have stood the various tests of academic rigour. Many Digital Humanists agree, and have focused their efforts on developing new systems that extend, for example, access to source materials.

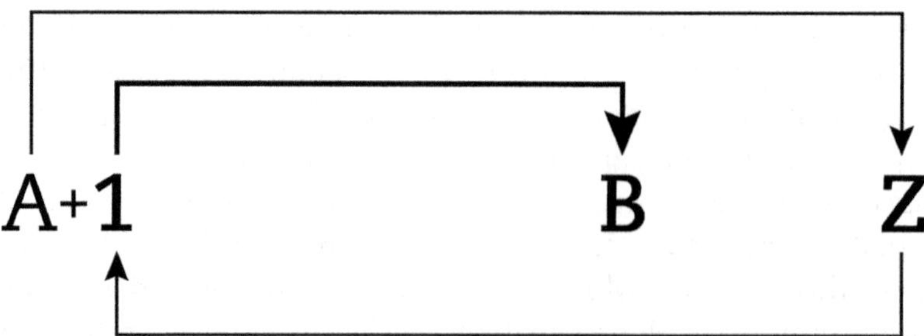

FIGURE 1.5: The design iteration process as illustrated through types of projects: A (the original design); Z (significant departure); A+1 (incremental change); and B (comfortable departure). First appeared in Milena Radzikowska, Stan Ruecker, and Stéfan Sinclair's 'From A to B via Z: Strategic interface design in the digital humanities', proceedings of the *International Association of Societies of Design Research* (IASDR) held in Brisbane, 2–5 November 2015.

Though often it is excitement about the possibilities afforded by change that initiates a project, it is fear of change (and its subsequent management) that drives it. A researcher interested in an experimental system consults potential users of the system in order to understand their current best practices. That's A. An interesting set of research questions might be addressed by inventing a new system that involves a significant degree of change – that's anywhere between Z and Z+1. Designers offer Z – an attempt to sufficiently shift the relationship between identity and current best practices – triggering a fight-flight response. In the process of considering Z, the scholarly community of Humanists and Digital Humanists alike has tended to shy back to A, changing the design requirements. The designer responds with incremental change (A+1), and the team spends some time, eventually recognizing its limitations, then asking instead for research in the area of position B. In terms of mental preparation for significant change, this is the ideal case, since everyone involved in the process has ownership of the idea.

We illustrate this process with reference to one of our past research projects: visualizations for decision support in the Oil Sands Project (please note that we dive even deeper into this project in Chapter 4).

Developed in the course of an industry partnership, the visualizations for decision support were an attempt to use methods from design and DH to make complex engineering models accessible to people with no university education. We were encouraged to explore experimental alternatives of the kind that could be implemented by our industry partner ten years in the future, and that were as different as possible from those discussed in existing literature on human-machine interface (HMI) design (as is shown in Figure 1.6).

As a point of radical departure, we designed position Z (see Figure 1.7). This design was focused on supporting users in decision experimentation. For every decision experiment, a new set of gears would appear, displaying the relevant variables and their relationships to one another. Both the nesting and the gear metaphor represent the relationship that exists between the different variables within the decision-making process. For example, a decision of whether or not to increase the production of one of the ice cream flavours does not occur in isolation, but is connected to numerous other factors. Users manipulated nested gears in the process of addressing their particular production question.

Our previous work on designing interfaces for decision support (e.g. Parades-Olea et al. 2008) had found that dates and times are important enough elements that they should be continuously present. Having time as a visual element would allow people affordances such as running the clock back to see when a particular decision had been previously made. It could also provide for overviews of details such as significant date ranges (e.g. planting, harvest). Once time was displayed in a

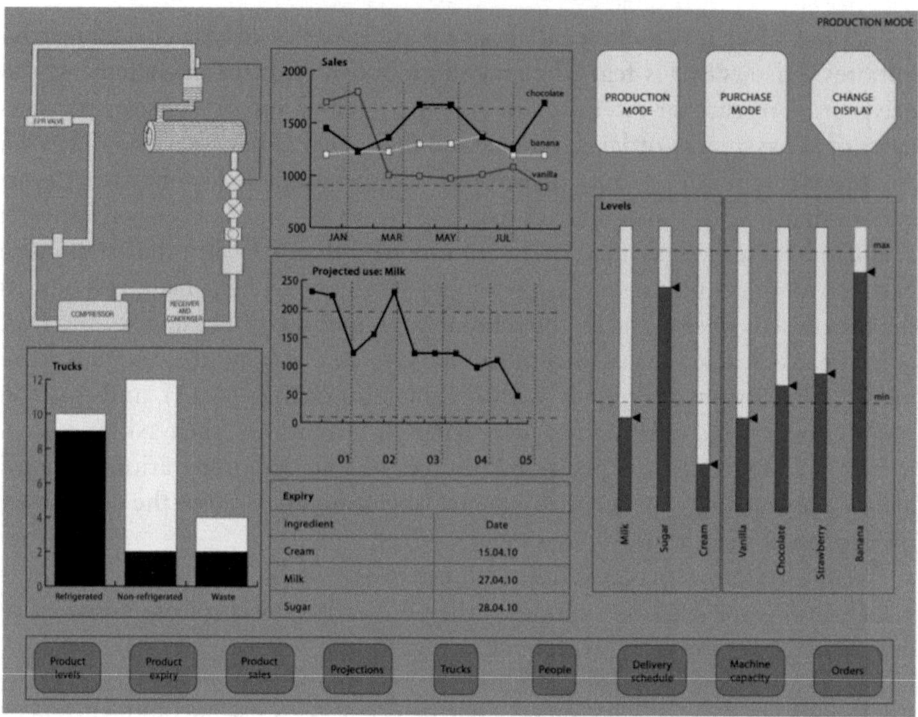

FIGURE 1.6: Position A for a decision support system based on Hollifield et al. (2008).

circular way, it seemed reasonable to indicate ranges of values through thickness of circular elements placed next to the calendar and clock.

From the perspective of programming a working prototype, the preponderance of rotating circular elements of varying thicknesses posed at the time a non-trivial challenge. People also responded with concern to the use of circular shapes to indicate scale, since they are more difficult to interpret and compare than rectangular shapes are. The result was Position A+1 for decision support (Figure 1.8), which uses conventional elements throughout. Its one innovation is in using discrete visual elements (the squares top right) to represent discrete variables (e.g. numbers of trucks).

In the received world of decision support, Position A+1 also includes the innovation of suggesting that the user might wish to modify some values in order to get and store alternative solutions for comparison (bottom right). The underlying systems are predicated on the idea that for a given set of values, there is only one optimal decision worth suggesting. So in order to make the prototype work, it would be necessary to allow it to make repeated runs that could be stored, rather than allowing for a range of values that resulted in the variations.

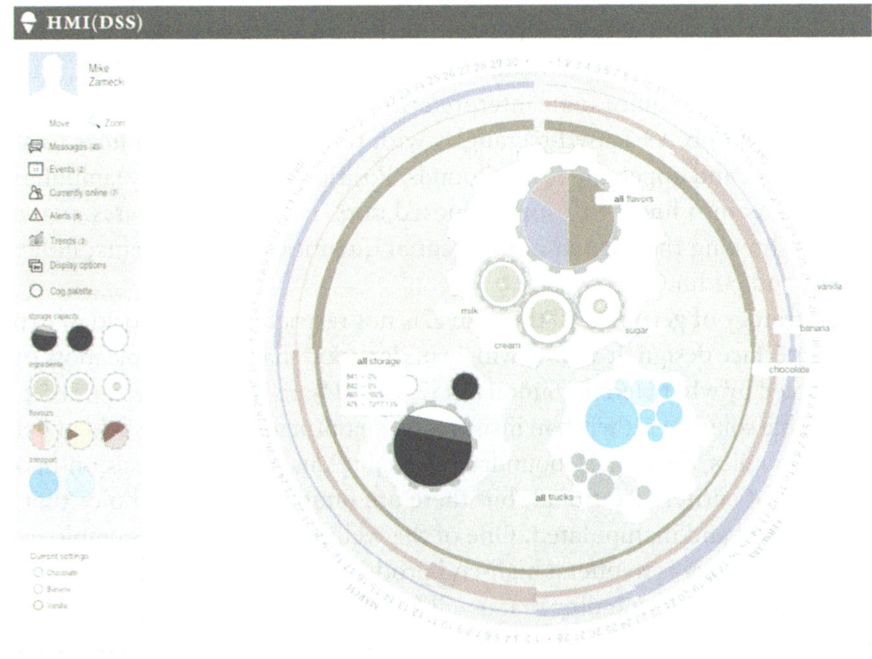

FIGURE 1.7: Position Z for decision support was based on a clockwork metaphor.

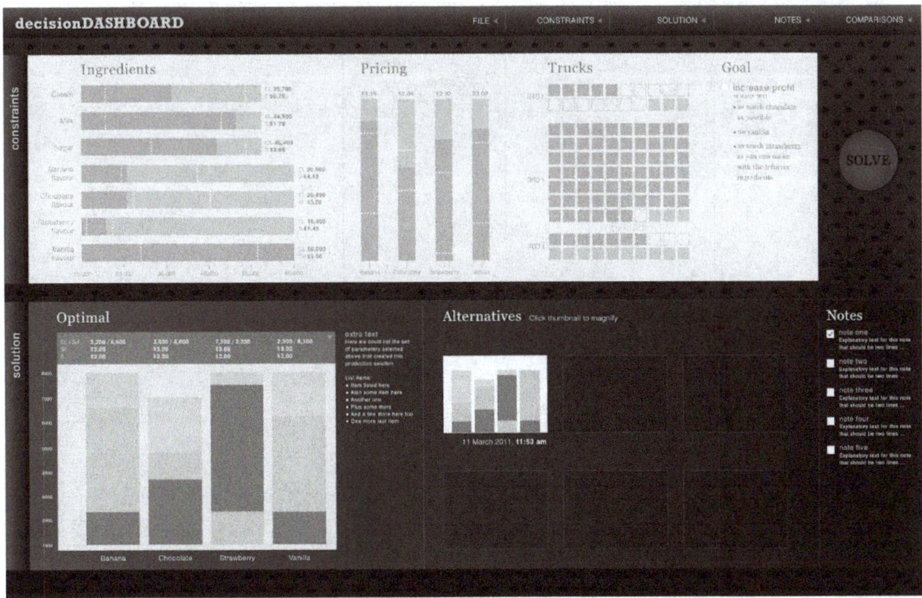

FIGURE 1.8: Position A+1 for decision support uses rectangular elements to convey quantity and to simplify comparisons.

The dissatisfaction with Position A+1 is that it seems pedestrian. The preponderance of blocks makes it difficult to understand where to begin first, and the overlapping areas require some interpretation before they make sense.

Where Position A+1 used rectangles with three superimposed lines to show current values and upper and lower bounds, Position B dramatically simplifies the visual display into lines with superimposed dots. It also incorporates a circular overview showing the current and potential quantities of ingredients, indicated by solids and outlines.

The strategy of getting to B through Z is not restricted to the world of experimental interface design. It is now widely understood that most people most of the time proceed by what Herbert Simon (1957) called 'satisfycing', meaning accepting a reasonable solution rather than insisting on an optimal one. In the field of behavioural economics, the term is 'bounded rationality', meaning that decision-making is usually not entirely irrational, but there are limits to rational choice that can be understood and manipulated. One of the well-known strategies employed by portfolio managers is to offer a high-end product that few customers are actually expected to buy, understanding that it will help to establish the bounds of discourse in such a way that the mid-range choice seems more reasonable, and the low-range one less satisfying than would otherwise be the case. Real estate agents routinely

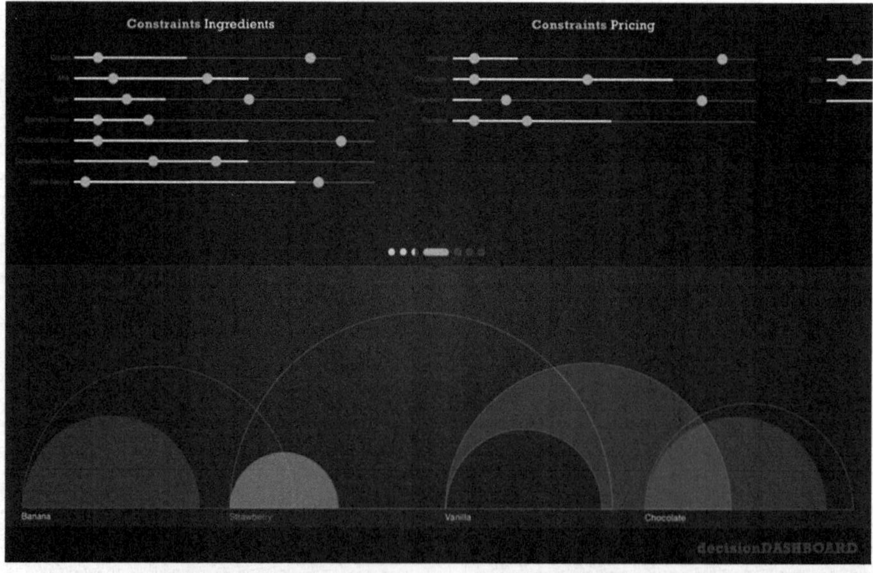

FIGURE 1.9: Position B for decision support has elements from Position Z and Position A+1. First appeared in Milena Radzikowska's 2015 unpublished Ph.D. thesis, 'Interface design to support human decision-making in the oil sands', at the University of Alberta, Edmonton.

follow a similar approach, showing high-end properties first so that the affordable lower-end ones are less attractive by contrast. However, as with many irrational human behaviours, knowing of their existence does not negate their effect, and the same can be said of the strategy we have come to recognize and use.

Though often unimplemented, Z and Z+1 hold much value in their own right – they aren't simply a means to an acceptable end (B). By spending time outside of 'known' territory, pushing boundaries of comfort, design now has the benefit of learning through making – more is possible! Z and Z+1 aren't lost effort.

1.3 What expertise looks like

1.3.1 Who are graphic designers?

Those who study design at a post-secondary level spend the majority of their time studying history, theories, processes, and methods that are specific to design. Depending on the focus of a particular program or institution (including whether it is located within or alongside fine arts, communications, or engineering) such study will include typography, semiotics and rhetoric, material culture, photography and/or printmaking, business and/or marketing, or social science or computing-emergent theories and methods. Students may specialize in graphic design (focusing on typography and the printed surface), communications design (focusing on the communication of ideas), industrial design (design for products or services), or user interface/user experience (UI/UX) (front-end interface design).

At least five accreditation levels exist for design. A certificate is a non-degree-granting programme of study, lasting from a few months to a year. An associate degree is a two-year degree at a college or university, while a bachelor's degree extends design study to four years and can result in a BA, BFA, or a BDes degree. There are also master of arts (MA), master of fine arts in graphic design (MFA), and master of design (MDes) degrees. For the MA, degree requirements include completion of a research or theoretical study (and lead to teaching at a K-12 level). MFA students tend to complete a creative dissertation or portfolio. MDes programs are either course-based with a major final project, or a mix of course-based requirements with a thesis or final paper. These degrees take from two to three years to complete, depending on the programs and graphic design schools. In Canada, the MDes degree is a terminal degree, while elsewhere Ph.D.s in Design do exist.

Design programs may be framed as majors in graphic design, communications design, communication arts, advertising design, visual design, visual communications, or visual communication design. Likewise, graphic designers working in industry are given a plethora of titles: graphic artist, art director, creative director, information designer, digital designer, visual designer, creative director, production artist, art manager, and web designer (this is an abbreviated list). Junior designers tend to be those with little to no professional experience and/or recent graduates. Senior designers, art designers, and creative directors have at least five years of experience and, typically, a design degree. Interface or web designers might have a graphic design-type background or might come from the computing sciences. This difference in origin tends to have a significant impact on the designer's skill set and type of expertise.

Since much of design (these days) is created on the computer, may be interactive or multimedia in nature, or employ motion graphics, designers usually also come pre-set with some technical skills. At a minimum those skills include some kind of layout, photo editing, and illustration package, and may include coding or, at the very least, experience with prototyping software. Designers tend to specialize, and specialties may include: typography, layout or desktop publishing, branding, advertising, interface or user experience design, product packaging, book or magazine design, logos, or data visualization.

1.3.2 Who are the digital humanists?

It is less clear that there is a simple trajectory for most scholars who enter DH. At the first graduate program in North America in DH at the University of Alberta, about half of the students came from typical humanities fields such as English literature, history, comparative literature, philosophy, and so on, while the other half came from the technical areas such as Computer Science and Engineering. A few also arrived from places in the Social Sciences, Business, and even Law. These combinations of previous backgrounds with emerging DH concerns lead to very fruitful outcomes and are much to be admired. However, in terms of background training and education, it is necessary to make some distinctions.

Those from the humanities will typically know a great deal about texts of some form, usually primary texts such as novels, plays, poetry, and historical documents of various kinds. They will usually be excellent readers, able to quickly and accurately extract the meanings of even the most complex sentences, and also to discern, explain, and debate the implications of larger patterns in the text. They have been trained extensively to do these things.

The scientists and engineers, however, will have worked largely with knowledge of the physical world. Their interactions with texts will have tended to be less interpretive or hermeneutic in nature than for the humanists. Instead, they will tend to understand what they read as being at face value, a simple means of trying to convey useful facts and theories about the way things work. The idea that different people would consider it necessary to read the same text from different theoretical lenses can be foreign and a bit repellent.

Like designers, however, many of these students will be comfortable with making and testing things, although, for the vast majority, the results will be some form of software or digital resource. The areas of possible overlap here would be the actual interface elements of the webpages or smart phone applications, but even then the non-designers and designers will tend to have very different training about how to go about the process and what is important at the end.

1.3.3 What expertise in collaboration looks like

One of the vexing central questions of interdisciplinary work is how to determine the degree to which the other people on the team can be relied upon to carry out their part of the project. This concern breaks down into several questions:

- How competent are they?
- What is their working style?
- Are they usually punctual in attending meetings?
- Do they tend to meet deadlines?
- Will they personally be doing the work or will they delegate it?
- If they delegate it, do they have good people working with them, and are they decent managers?

Another, perhaps strange, question is to what extent do they know what work is, in the sense of work on an interdisciplinary project. For many scholars, work consists primarily of communicating what they know to people who do not know it. At its best, this translates into engaging lectures about fascinating topics. At its worst, it degrades into a penchant for expressing opinions in public. In either case, it is of limited utility on an interdisciplinary project, where the goal is not primarily to inform each other, but is instead to knuckle down and get the various tasks completed.

Although it is not a very precise or accurate[1] indicator, life being what it is, the best method that we know for predicting future performance is looking at past performance. Specifically, take a quick look at the person's CV. For this purpose, you are less interested in the topics covered or the quality of the journals or conferences, although those are useful to know, and more interested in the patterns of collaborative work that are discernible.

If the publication list consists primarily of single-authored papers or presentations, then you probably are not looking at someone who has much practice in collaborative work.

If there are co-authored papers or presentations, but only with students, then you are likely looking at someone whose primary experience has been in delegation rather than collaboration.

If there is co-authorship with other professors in the same field, there is some possibility that things will go well, but working with colleagues in the same discipline is quite different from working with colleagues from another discipline. For one thing, the expectations around what constitutes a reasonable method and outcome tend to be relatively more homogeneous within a discipline than between disciplines. For another, the extra effort necessary to understand one another has largely already been accomplished during school for people who share a disciplinary background. For those who don't, the work still lies ahead.

At the next level, there are scholars who have co-authored with people from other disciplines. Now you are getting somewhere. You might want to check that gender, race, ethnicity (as a minimum bar) are well represented on the list, and that there is the mix of professors and students that makes you comfortable. Now is also the time to think about the depth and breadth represented in the work. If all the papers fall into the direct expertise of the person you are considering working with, that could be a warning sign that they are not very flexible in their thinking. This could be someone who other people work with, rather than a person who works with others. On the other hand, if the papers don't show a pattern of the person's expertise having been a valuable contribution, then you might be dealing with someone who doesn't pull their weight.

However, when everything is said and done, you can only learn so much from a CV. Typically, people join projects through endorsements from previous co-authors. Either someone has a colleague that they have learned to trust, or a student who is showing promise. It is also best practice to work first on a small project where the stakes are lower, in order to get a sense of how the collaboration will tend to work. It usually doesn't take long to see that someone skips meetings, misses deadlines, or produces inferior work.

Finally, it's worth saying a word about the social dimension of projects. Work is work, but at the end of the day, you want to have people around you that you enjoy spending time with. One of the stumbling blocks in our own experience has been the balance people place between the consumption of alcohol and food. For many, a drink is a chance to let their hair down a little and get to really know people. For others, a drink is a way to reduce both intelligence and social grooming, and they would rather everyone kept their hair up and enjoyed a good meal and some clever conversation.

1.4 Exercises: Meaning

1.4.1 Metaphors

What you'll need

- This exercise can be completed digitally or through analogue means. You will either need some software that will allow you to juxtapose images to one another or you can print them and combine through cut and paste.

Exercise type
Group or individual.

Choose one visual object or element and use it to create three different images. Each image should use the element as a metaphor, and each metaphor should be different from the others. Set up the metaphoric interpretation in three different ways by providing different contextual clues.

For example, you might choose an image of an elephant. That elephant near a donkey might form part of an image relating to U.S. politics, since the elephant represents one of the U.S. political parties and the donkey represents the other. Depending on which animal is dominant, you are making some kind of statement about the relationship between the parties.

In your next image, you might put the elephant next to a mouse, because we have the cultural idea that elephants are afraid of mice. So the metaphor there is one dealing with cowardice.

In your third image you might juxtapose the elephant with a clown, in which case you are making a metonymic reference to the circus. The purpose of this exercise is to demonstrate in practical terms that metaphor is not a code.

On the contrary, multivalency is a normal part of the use of images, just as it is a part of the use of words.

1.4.2 Object metaphors

What you'll need

- Physical or domestic objects.
- Camera.

Exercise type
Individual.

Take a common domestic object (garden tool, musical instrument, utensil), then place it in proximity to an object that has little to no typical relationship with the first. Alternatively, take the common object and place it in an environment that is unusual for it, but typical for another. This second scenario works best when the two objects resemble each other in some structural way (they're both round and small; they have the same colours). Take a photo of what you've created. Add a caption that is simple but wry or ironic.

1.4.3 Book cover design

What you'll need

- Novel.
- Bookstore.

- This exercise can be completed digitally or through analogue means. You will either need some software that will allow you to juxtapose images to one another or you can print them and combine through cut and paste.

Exercise type
Individual.

Choose any novel that you have read and enjoyed. Identify three different interpretations for the main point of the novel, and under the heading 'concepts', explain each of those interpretations in a short paragraph. Establish the reader profile in each case. This activity is intended to address the problem of visual interpretation of text.

But since dust jackets are also marketing tools, it is at least as important that your design address the issues of visual detection and attention. With that in mind, visit a bookstore and examine the interior in terms of the perceptual problems involved in drawing the attention of people to a given book. Look at colour differentiation among book covers of the genre you've selected. Are there prominent colours? Neglected colours? What kind of tonal palette is evident? Look for conventions in handling text for titles, author, and publisher's imprint. Are there systematic patterns in the designs that you can exploit or modify for your own benefit? Write your observations in a brief report of 500 words or less.

Then design three different dust jackets, each conveying one of the different interpretations of the novel, and attempting to draw on your bookstore observations. None of your covers should resemble published covers for that novel, although you are free to draw on literary critical theory for the various interpretations.

Example

You might choose to design dust jackets for the novel *Ulysses*, by James Joyce. *Ulysses* is a complicated modern novel, where the activities of the main character in Dublin parallel the activities of the hero in the Odyssey. People have interpreted *Ulysses* in various ways throughout the years. For some readers, it is a literary classic and part of the respectable canon of English literature. For other readers, it is a raunchy novel of the vernacular. The focus of the book might be the character Bloom. Or the focus might be the city Dublin. Joyce has suggested both, and other interpretations are also possible. Joyce also said in a letter about the novel: 'It is the epic of two races (Israel-Ireland) and at the same time the cycle of the human body as well as a little story of a day (life)'. Or in talking to an interviewer about the book: 'You catch the drift of the thing?' said Joyce. 'It's the struggle with Proteus. Change is the theme. Everything changes – sea, sky, man, animals. The words change, too'.

The purpose of this exercise is to get experience in moving from the concept to the visualization of the concept, while at the same time reinforcing the idea that the choices made by the designer during the visualization are key to conveying the concept at various levels of granularity. For example, at the large scale, is the novel tragic or comic or something else? At the smaller scale, is the image itself pleasant or disturbing? What ideas can you hope to convey with the various covers to a given demographic, and how clearly can these ideas be conveyed? What emotions can you hope to elicit in the readers as you are able to understand them, and what are the methods best used to elicit emotion for those readers?

Connections to design research

Book cover design per se falls more neatly into the category of design practice than design research, but the concept of visual positioning and the visual interpretation of text is an ongoing concern of everyone in visual communication design.

Connections to design practice

The design of print materials such as dust jackets, CD covers, video boxes, and so on is a well-established industry. These designs are often constrained to a high degree by marketing requirements, publishing house standards, management opinion, and so on. To be able to create effective design communication under these professional conditions is difficult, and requires a flexible approach coupled with the ability to cooperate with a team.

1.4.4 Hindsight is 20/20: Tinkering with the past

What you'll need

- Access to research resources.

Exercise type
Individual. Share with a group.

Select an area of design, and within that area a single design intervention that has been developed and implemented in the past. The intervention can be in the form of the development or introduction of a new or modified analogue or digital product, a change in processes or systems, or a communication campaign (government or industry). Your task is to write an essay and create an accompanying class presentation describing this intervention and its logical alternatives.

The essay and presentation should address the following topics:

- describe the problem the intervention was intended to solve (it may prove useful to explicitly outline more than one tier to the problem, in the sense of looking, for example, at the technical, political, and cultural levels; it could also be interesting to examine contemporary perceptions vs. analyses at some historical remove);
- critique the intervention in terms of its effectiveness (be sure to specify your evaluation criteria, and be prepared to justify your choices and omissions);
- within the historical context, suggest at least one reasonable alternative that was not implemented; and
- provide a rationale for your alternative design solution or solutions, indicating strengths and weaknesses in comparison to the actual intervention.

The essay should be approximately 1,200 words in length, with an accompanying 30-minute class presentation (to be followed by a brief discussion). It is not necessary to choose an intervention that was successful, nor is it advisable to present your alternative in an uncritical manner. Attempt insofar as possible to provide a reasoned and balanced description of the relevant terrain. Since there is an inevitable speculative component to this assignment, please endeavour to reduce the degree of speculation through the provision of some corroborating evidence for each of your basic assertions.

Factors to keep in mind

The shifting paradigms: design as engineering, as ornament, art, style, function, economics, and the design of production. National identities. The cultural context provided by design itself, as well as art, science, technology, philosophy, religion, ideology, literature, economics, politics, cultural history, or any other relevant aspect; and the operational and cultural impacts of design.

1.4.5 History down and across (exercise by Jorge Frascara)

What you'll need

- Access to research resources.

Exercise type
Individual. Share with a group.

Diachronic analysis

Each person works on the transformation through time of a subject relevant to design. Proposed subjects (others can be added):

- history of the notion of planning;
- history of the notion of functionality;
- history of the notion of style;
- history of design methods;
- history of the relation between design and business;
- history of the relation between design and art;
- history of the relation between design and technology/ideology as expressed by objects, environments, and customs;
- history of the design of the work space;
- history of the design of the entertainment space (from the Roman Colosseum to Las Vegas);
- history of the design of the leisure space;
- history of the design of the school space; and
- history of the design of transportation.

Synchronic analysis

Each person prepares a presentation about one of the possible key years to investigate: 1851 (The Great Exposition); 1874 (Le salon des refusees); 1889 (Paris Expo); 1914 (WW1); 1919 (Bauhaus); 1933 (Nazism); 1948 (the Cold War); 1951 (the Festival of Britain); 1956 (American consumerism, Italian neorealism, the Hungarian revolt and French existentialism); 1967 (Montreal Expo, Vietnam, Flower-power, the space race, Las Vegas); 1968 (the students revolution, the Czech revolt, Disneyland); 1983 (Reaganism); 1998 (?). This presentation should identify a key concept to lead the discussion: i.e. 1851 and the notion of progress; or 1874 and the notion of avant-garde. Other years and central events may be proposed. A context is to be provided by discussing the year in design, art, science, technology, philosophy, literature, economics, politics, cultural history, or any other relevant aspect.

1.4.6 Visual comparison and contrast

What you'll need

- Access to research resources.

Exercise type
Individual. Share with a group.

Choose either a person or an event that interests you. Create a dossier about that person or event, in which you describe them as completely as you can. Then you will be randomly paired with a colleague who will also have a dossier about a person or event. Together you will determine what the people or events you have chosen have in common with each other, and in what characteristics they differ. Each of you will then independently prepare a poster that visually communicates these similarities and differences.

Example

You might find, for instance, that you are talking about Mother Teresa and General H. Norman Schwarzkopf. Although at first glance they might seem to be quite different people, they nonetheless share many characteristics: both were responsible for managing people in life and death situations. Both were personally authoritative. They both wore uniforms. And so on. In terms of differences, one is a woman and the other a man. One is a general and the other a nun. And so on.

One key here is to understand the people or events in as great a depth as possible, so that the comparisons can reach beyond stereotypes and hopefully provide some interesting insights into both sides of the comparison, without wandering into the realm of what is conceptually untenable.

A second key is that the idea of providing 'insights' suggests that you are sufficiently knowledgeable about your audience to understand what they currently think or believe, so that you can know what is going to be interesting or unusual for them. This knowledge is a non-trivial factor both to obtain and to use.

Purpose of the exercise

One purpose for this exercise is to practice researching a person or event. A second purpose lies in communicating research results at the conceptual level with another student. The ultimate purpose of the assignment is to create a piece of visual communication that must in some way convey a complex message of similarity and difference to an audience that is as clearly understood as possible.

Connections to design research

This assignment provides some background into the area of organizing complex visual information to convey precise meaning for a particular user demographic. Since visual communication design is a form of intervention in the public space, design researchers are very interested in the means by which complexity can be adequately managed.

Connections to design practice

As a practical exercise, this project relates to the design of information materials in a number of domains, such as government, law, public health, commerce, and so on, where it is necessary to find means of constructing visual materials that provide clear information on topics that might be of crucial significance.

NOTE

1. These are, perhaps amusingly, related to the terms of art 'precision' and 'recall'. These are important concepts in the library world, and therefore also in much of DH. They have to do with search hits. If every hit you get is one you want, you have perfect precision. If you get all the hits that are in the collection, you have perfect recall. However, you can get a perfect score on precision with only one document, provided it is a good one. But if you have many good documents in the collection, your recall is poor. You can conversely get a perfect score on recall if you get a hit on every document, although your precision might be pretty bad if they aren't all documents you want. Most search engines attempt to get the best of both worlds with document ranking, so the most precise hits come first on a list with a long tail.

2

Creating understanding

For people from either field who desire a better understanding of the other field, this chapter discusses how designers and digital humanists think of themselves and what they are doing.

Before we get too far ahead of ourselves in tackling the three agendas described earlier, we need to outline some constraints to our discussion. If you google 'design', you'll quickly discover scores of disciplines and ways to practice. Similarly, 'DH' is a complex scholarly activity with as many sub-disciplines as there are humanities, plus all the intersections of computing and technology and sometimes also the fine arts and social sciences, their systemic use, as well as the reflection on their application. Some guide rails are in order.

2.1 Defining DH

Digital humanities (DH) have three main branches. In the first branch, computing is used to facilitate research on humanities questions, in some cases by providing better access to materials, in others by providing software tools that support the analytical processes used by humanities scholars. In the second branch, computing itself serves as the object of study, and the physical, cognitive, technological, interpersonal, and cultural aspects of computing are subjected to analysis. In the third branch, humanities computing is generative, and scholars produce and disseminate new materials (e.g. software, primary and secondary texts, and metadata) in electronic forms.

One of the threads that held the international DH community together for many decades starting in 1980s is a listserv, called Humanist, operated by Dr Willard McCarty. In a famous post to vol 18, no 718, under the subject 'Nomenclature', another DH celebrity, Dr Melissa Terras, approached the vexed question 'what is DH' directly.

Date: Tue, 19 Apr 2005 08:59:28 +0100
From: Melissa Terras
Subject: Nomenclature
Dear Willard and all,
I've been doing some reading around the field of 'Humanities Computing' and I would like to ask members of Humanist about what they feel certain names for our 'discipline' imply.

There seems to be various ways of referring to what we do – both in teaching, and research: Humanities Computing, Computing in the Humanities, Digital Humanities, Humanities Informatics, Cultural and Heritage Informatics, Digital Resources in the Humanities, Digital Resources for the Humanities, Literary and Linguistic Computing, etc.

I would like to explain what the wordings of these different names suggest to me, and ask members of Humanist what their thoughts are, which they prefer to use to describe what they do, and if there are any that I have missed.

Humanities Computing: A complex juxtaposition of two distinct (and wide) academic fields, which is almost an oxymoron, but makes a researcher in the area appear to be straddling across two fields equally. This can raise problems when trying to pigeonhole where the discipline fits (which is important for teaching programs, and for funding streams?) but nevertheless, gives the impression of an equality between the two, whilst being Computing specifically applied to the Humanities. Because it is also two academic terms, it seems to imply that this is a field of academic research, and less geared towards the heritage industry or wider world.

Computing in the Humanities: Similar to Humanities Computing, although this seems to be a little reduced in its strength, given that it only refers to computing that is happening within the humanities (whilst the above term could imply any computational technique which may be applied to the humanities).

Digital Humanities: By removing the 'computing' element, and replacing this with digital, it seems to me to remove the process or techniques of manipulating digital objects, and suggests that this is scholarship in the Humanities which merely relies on digitized objects, or on making things digital. It seems less strong a term than Humanities Computing to me, as it implies that you do less with the digital objects: I see digital as being slightly pejorative in this sense. Is this just me?

Humanities Informatics: Again, this has removed computing and focused on informatics which is the management of information and thus meaning that this is the management of Humanities data, and/or information. Is this a less strong term? Or a more focused one? Informatics also covers management and storage of information – but is it a wide enough computational term to embrace the type of research that goes on under our weirdly shaped umbrella? Would certain types of 'Humanities Computing' be 'Humanities Informatics', and some not? is it a specialism?

> Cultural and Heritage Informatics: By not mentioning Humanities or Computing, this to me disassociates from any academic field and seems to be more applied in its focus within the Cultural and Heritage Industry. This may be an 'applying for funding thing' as it gives the air of being more practical and focused than just general terms. A political term for our field, to be used in certain funding situations, or to explain how it can be applied?
>
> Digital Resources in the Humanities: Suggests that the people involved are solely interested in creating resources for the humanities – which may imply they are not using advanced computational techniques to manipulate them (or is this just a bias?) Are we only about the creation of resources, or about the use, manipulation, development, and theorizing about them too?
>
> Digital Resources for the Humanities: Similar to the Digital Resources in the Humanities, but there is something different in that in/for distinction. 'In' would imply to me that the producers are working within the confines of the Humanities, 'For' suggests that it is anyone making digital data producing, in this case, a resource that can be used in the Humanities – or do I read too much into it?
>
> Literary and Linguistic Computing: A term used historically which now doesn't encompass all that the wonderful world of using computing in the arts and humanities can offer.
>
> Am I reading too much into the language used in these terms – or are my hunches applicable? Do readers of Humanist have a favoured term? Do we even need a term that covers all that we do to define ourselves, or are we happy with these amorphous labels? I would be interested in hearing what anyone had to say.

It probably won't be surprising to learn that people have had a lot to say, both directly in response to this post and in discussions continuing over the ensuing years in many conference rooms, journal papers, books, as well as less formally in meetings around coffee tables and bars. For several years, the Day of DH project asked people who signed up how they defined DH, resulting in hundreds of wonderful short descriptions of the field and how the people who are doing it understand it, as well as what they and others are trying to do.

At the 2011 conference of the Modern Language Association, DH philosopher Stephen Ramsay famously proposed that digital humanists were people who made things, rather than used, for instance, the software tools that others had already made. A controversial proposition from what was fast becoming the old guard, it was roundly rejected by the many scholars who rightly felt that their own use of software, whether home-grown or not, was leading to insights that they wanted to talk about with their peers. One of us was in the room at the time, and it was clear that Dr Ramsay was playing the devil's advocate, but he was also indulging, as philosophers will do, in some thinking out loud. Or perhaps, as he would describe in a subsequent paper about DH methods, this was part of a larger research program of 'screwmeneutics' or 'the hermeneutics of screwing around' as a way of increasing understanding of a topic.

2.1.1 What do digital humanists do?

Although used everywhere in the academy, interpretive or hermeneutic inquiry is the primary mode of activity in the arts and humanities, as well as in much of the social sciences. It is also the approach most commonly used by readers in all professions. Interpretive inquiry involves iteratively identifying and analysing patterns in whatever materials are being examined. The goal of each analysis is not to find a single best answer or one right interpretation, but instead to enrich the object of study. By identifying and applying a new perspective or approach, the researcher acquires a new theoretical 'lens' that reveals new insights.

For people like Dr Stephen Ramsay, those lenses are most effective when they are tailored specifically for the project at hand. His students in English literature learn computer programming and write, as he does, one-off pieces of hacked-together code that only need to serve the purpose of the moment before being discarded. Trying to make them usable or even understandable for other scholars is not just beside the point, but actually misses the point altogether.

In other parts of DH, however, researchers are attempting to create new tools for assisting other scholars with various forms of hermeneutic inquiry. Traditionally, this is where design has had one of the biggest roles to play, since the systems and their interfaces must somehow be accessible to people who did not write them. Those people are DH researchers who use the tools, and also people who take humanities approaches to studying aspects of computing in culture.

Arguably one of the most useful categories of tools is interactive visualization. Typically, when we think of visualization in the service of research, we expect to see forms that provide the researcher with a visual representation of statistical data, often near the final stage of the activity. However, in developing interactive prototypes for use in the hermeneutic process, we often aim instead to create visual models that support the direct iterative investigation of texts, images, videos, and so on, without translating them into statistics first.

Data remains a central concern of DH, although not everyone would agree with the reductive nature of the term, when what is being signified are actually cultural objects like books. That said, decades of effort have been put into the creation of digital texts, images, videos, and especially their associated metadata. There are a wide range of approaches to modelling, producing, and storing metadata, but among the most popular formats are databases (such as MySQL) and Extensible

Markup Language (XML). DH projects that involve text encoding will nearly always reference the guidelines of the Text Encoding Initiative (TEI).

While access to digital forms of data is transforming, or arguably has already transformed, the humanities, we still have some work ahead of us in terms of what is possible in supporting scholars working with these materials. As a result, many have argued that a core activity in DH is in creating new prototypes and new tools. The argument is that this is a research activity: that we learn by making and by theorizing about making.

Many of the prototypes and tools being made are concerned with text analysis, which is the automated process of generating patterns about text in support of hermeneutic inquiry. Since making the patterns understandable is a central concern, a great deal of recent attention has been paid to visualization, and in particular interactive visualization that allows for an exploratory approach to the materials.

For the tools to be most useful, the data is standardized in some way, the tools work together, and are capable of accessing the data in whatever form it takes. Interoperability has therefore become an increasingly important concern in DH.

Finally, some tools draw on algorithmic processes that are quite sophisticated, and DH is always eager to identify and use technologies emerging from adjacent disciplines. An example is the adoption of text mining, with projects such as D2K and NORA, or SEASR and MONK.

Although no longer available, these projects were attempts to, first of all, allow regular non-programmers to sequence a pipeline of text analysis components, and second of all, to do it within a graphical user interface instead of a command line. Take, for instance, all of the plays of Shakespeare, and ask the question: 'what is it with these plays and blood?' One approach would be to get an electronic edition and search it. However, there is a lot of blood in there that doesn't appear using that word. Lady Macbeth herself talks about the problem of not having Spot Shot™ available at the time, and worrying that in trying to wash up, she would 'the multitudinous seas incarnadine, making the green one red'.

It's clear to a reader what is going on there, but a bit tricky to find with a standard string search. So we can imagine making a pipeline: divide the plays into words; stem the words by cutting off prefixes and suffixes; lemmatize the words by comparing them to a database that understands 'blood' and 'bleed' and may be also 'blud' or 'blude' as the same base word; do some semantics work that shows 'incarnadine' is suspect, especially so close to 'red'; then reassemble everything; and run the search, showing the results in context, perhaps using the KWIC concordance invented in 1959 by H. P. Luhn (http://drc.usask.ca/projects/archbook/concordance.php).

So that is the underlying technology (D2K and SEASR), and the interfaces were placed on top of them, with different strategies in NORA and MONK. NORA took the approach of providing a sequence of vertical shutters that could be opened and closed to free up the screen real estate for each task. MONK similarly provided a sequence, but was much more customizable in terms of the items that could be put into the pipeline by the user.

Some of the issues we had to address were the extent to which these interfaces should be, or even could be, accessible and friendly to first-time users, like Google search, or would require training and experience to use, like the Adobe Creative Suite. The question hinged to some extent on how often we could reasonably expect people to use the systems. If the answer was something like once annually, tied to some specific phase of a particular project, then it might be too much to expect people to have to relearn a complex environment. If the answer was that people would pick up the system and make it part of their regular toolkit, then a more complex approach could be used.

Another question was whether or not it was going to be important for literary scholars, who are for the most part not mathematicians, to understand the various underlying algorithms that were being used in techniques like semi-supervised classification using Naive Bayes or Support Vector Machines. As opposed to, for example, clustering – which sounds an awful lot like classification to a literary scholar, but is really a completely different algorithm. If it were crucial, then the interfaces should probably make that knowledge available; if not, then a link to a textbook or two might be sufficient. In the end, the team at Northwestern, led by Dr Martin Mueller, produced a written tutorial that could be found within the system.

A third topic that had to be addressed was what kind of data the system could use. The literary scholars on the team who made that decision had an unshakeable conviction that the results would be at least unreliable and misleading, and probably even invalid, if the texts had not been carefully curated and properly ingested. As a consequence, the systems had a large database of available texts, but adding to that database was not a trivial process.

Neither NORA nor MONK survives. What we do have instead are tools like Voyant, developed by Dr Stéfan Sinclair and Dr Geoffrey Rockwell. Voyant has many virtues. It combines a wide range of tools into a single interface. It can be used with any kind of data that the scholar wants to load. It is available online, so it does not require any particular expertise to install and run. It is also connected to a book (*Hermeneutica*) that provides the kind of background discussion that Dr Martin Mueller understood as being crucial for digital humanists using tools designed by others.

No discussion of design and DH would be complete without a few words on the topic of research through making, or more specifically, research through design. First proposed by Christopher Frayling of the Royal College of Art in London, the principle is that designers create new knowledge primarily by making things. For Frayling, design knowledge resides in three locations: people, processes, and artefacts. Therefore, the proper subjects of study for design researchers are: designers, design methods, and designs. The designs, or artefacts, could be anything from communications to objects to systems and protocols.

Subsequent discussions of research through design have expanded the discourse to suggest that the designs might not necessarily be intended to result in a commodity of any kind. Instead, they might be created specifically for the purpose of thinking about some larger topic or even concept. In that case, the prototypes will typically include features that would not be useful for a production system, and exclude features that would be necessary. The knowledge created with the prototypes, however, will hopefully be useful to a wider range of designers who need to make decisions on projects that are intended to produce a commodity.

2.2 Defining design

For many, design is synonymous with ornament, style, decoration, or pattern. In this way, the shadows made by leaves on a wall are sometimes, erroneously, described as a design instead of a beautiful pattern in light and dark. Identifying naturally occurring phenomena as design places nature or the divine in the role of active creator, with the potential consequences that all perceived entities then become design. Designers attempt to construct an initial, substantial narrowing of the field by defining design as the result of some kind of planned human activity, thus positioning naturally or non-intentionally occurring phenomena (independent of their aesthetic value or perceived intentionality) outside the design field.

Sometimes, design is described as pretty pictures, relegating its value solely in terms of the quality of its form (or its aesthetics). Though form quality is an important concern to designers, most would argue that aesthetics are not the primary focus of their work but are, in fact, subservient to a wide range of other factors (the functionality or usability of the artefact, for example). Most late twentieth-century designers (and many of the twenty-first) consider form after considering function.

This discussion – of form vs. function – has its origins in the tensions that emerged out of industrial manufacturing at the end of the nineteenth century. As mass manufactured products became more widely and more cheaply available, their visual and production quality came under increased critique. Many considered such products to be overly decorated in an attempt to make them appear more familiar and to mask their manufactured origins. In a counter movement, Morris, Image, Macmurdo, Ruskin, and others argued for a celebration of natural forms, a truth to materials, and a return of the artisan (both designer and creator) (Meggs, 2011: 162). Two schools of thought emerged: one that argued for a revival of classical forms and one that argued for a return to agrarian regional design. Thus, the idea that form follows function emerged, based on Sullivan's 'Form ever follows function' (Sullivan 1896). While form follows function promotes form's subservience to its use and purpose, Weitz proposes that when we consider 'Form ever follows function', neither come first but both exist in a delicate balance, created through equal emphasis (2013: n.pag.). Form ever follows function allows designers to begin the design process with a random connection, emotion, or experience – imagine the seemingly impossible – then figure out how to make it functional (Weitz 2013: n.pag.).

In an attempt to extend Weitz's argument, we propose that aesthetics have function: that form and functionality are so intricately intertwined that it is impossible to speak of one independent of the other. While Sullivan's (and Weitz's) statements suggest a positive value to both form and function (good form follows good function), our argument relies on the notion that when form exists, so does some kind of function, and vice versa. Whether they exist for good, and what kind of good they exist for, calls for subsequent interrogation and are central concerns for design.

Returning to the central theme, it is more accurate to describe design as a series of sub-disciplines and professions, all with a diverse set of practices, tools, and traditions. Most design fields have a rich history, with ongoing theoretical developments and debates. Most offer and require extensive and specialized training, either institutionalized or through practicum. Some design fields have an extensive academic underpinning and have made valuable multi- and cross-disciplinary partnerships, while others are squarely grounded in industry practice.

FIGURE 2.1: This sentence, developed by John Heskett, explains the four ways design can manifest: as the field or discipline, the process(es) used to achieve an outcome, the physical plan, and the finished product. (Diagram by Jennifer Windsor).

With its close relationship to drawing, design has also been described, more simply, as the plan or sketch for something to be created or constructed at a later date, as well as to 'plan out in the mind'(Merriam-Webster). Frascara's definition of design focuses on it as action – the product as a final step of a journey (often called design process):

> to invent, to project, to program, to coordinate a long list of human and technical factors, to translate the invisible into the visible, and to communicate.
>
> (Frascara 2004: 2)

Rand's definition highlights a view of design as a discipline in service to the needs of others, a view that has gained much prominence and buy-in over the past twenty years:

> Graphic design – which fulfils aesthetic needs, complies with the laws of form and the exigencies of two-dimensional space; which speaks in semiotics, sans-serifs, and geometrics; which abstracts, transforms, translates, notates, dilates, repeats, mirrors, groups, and regroups – is not good design if it is irrelevant.
>
> (Rand 2014: 9)

Simon's definition attempts to encompass all the above-mentioned definitions: to design is to '[devise a] course of action aimed at changing existing situations into preferred ones' ([1969] 1996: 111). While for Simon design is a science and the pursuit of design a scientific activity, Buchanan roots design in the humanities: a contemporary form of rhetoric. The scientific perspective focuses on the empirical study of the effects of design activities and artefacts on people. The rhetorical perspective sees design products as 'vivid arguments about how we should lead our lives' (Buchanan 2001: 194). Thus, design practice and scholarship, according to Buchanan, should act as facilitators who 'organize conversations and debates about the values of a community and how those values may be implemented with productive results'. Simon's position on design stands in contrast to that of Buchanan, together offering a useful snapshot on contemporary design. Cross (1982) argues that design is neither science nor humanities, but its own category, with its own, designerly, ways of knowing.

DiSalvo (2012: 15–16) argues that design possesses three characteristics, regardless of whether you support Simon's, Buchanan's, or Cross's views. Design's first characteristic is that its practice extends the professions of design, independent of whether that practice is defined as design or enacted by a designer (though it still remains a human activity). An activity becomes design when a deliberate and intentional approach has been taken to the creation of a product or service that shapes the environment. DiSalvo's second characteristic for design is that its practice is normative: 'design attempts to produce new conditions or the tools by which to understand and act on current conditions' (2012: 16). Thus, design acts have an ethical, moral, and political dimension, whether practising designers recognize or position it as such. Finally, the practice of design provides an experiential (tangible) accessibility to human ideas, beliefs, and capacities for action. Even though the process and materials may be different depending on the specific design sub-field, the end result – accessible tangibility – remains constant.

2.2.1 Is there such a thing as 'good design'? If so, what is it?

It strikes us that DiSalvo's characteristics pose a number of critical questions for designers, those who think about design, and those who engage with designed artefacts. How do we determine whether a design is intentional? Is this a binary characteristic, based solely on whether it is a deliberate, human act? Or, can the level and type of intentionality vary, be subsequently discussed or evaluated? Do characteristics act upon one another? If we agree with DiSalvo that all design has a political, moral, and ethical dimension, is there an – assumed – connection between it and intentionality? Do we question designers about the political, moral, or ethical position held, demonstrated, or supported through their design? Or should we? Furthermore, as design has 'accessible tangibility', should as well the positionality of its intention?

Is design – like literature – relative, subjective, or agnostic? Are there no value distinctions in design; can anything be called good design, as long as it is intentionally created by human beings, it is normative, and tangible? Or is design value subjective; is its evaluation a purely personal matter? Is there a greater truth about good design that, while it exists, our subjective value systems prevent us from knowing it? Is good based on usefulness or functionality; and are usefulness and functionality only valuable through tangible, measurable outcomes? Are all opinions on design created equal, or are some more valuable than others? Ones, for example, emergent out of a designerly expertise and capable of building a valid case for an evaluation?

There is a value judgement – sometimes unspoken and at times transparent – placed within the definitions of design outlined at the start of this chapter. Consider in Frascara, for example, a designer does not merely invent, translate, and communicate, she must do so well. Rand, Simon, and Buchanan are more direct, describing good design as one that is 'relevant' (Rand 2014: 9), that creates 'preferred' states (Simon [1969] 1999: 111), and that argues for better ways to 'lead our lives' (Buchanan 2001: 194). Rams believed that design could not be measured in a finite way; instead of a quantifiable metric, he proposed ten features of good (product) design: innovation, usefulness, aesthetic value, understanding, unobtrusiveness, honesty, endurance, thoroughness, environmental friendliness, and simplicity (Lovell et al., 2011).

Building on these definitions, we propose not only that good design does exist, but that we should consider two additional characteristics to the three outlined by DiSalvo and ten developed by Rams: good design as nourishing and good design as veracious.

Nourishing design leaves a mark in our memories and hearts: it plants a seed, then grows. It is 'not an expression of my beautiful soul' (a phrase sometimes used by University of Alberta's Dr Gary Kelly). It challenges, but through that challenge it is of use. Design at its best is transformative; it combines aesthetics, emotional engagement, and functionality to spur metamorphosis and growth.

Veracious design is transparent about its origins, positionality, and privilege. It acknowledges that all design is iterative – it can always be subject to critique, contextual development and change. Thus, through its welcoming of iteration, veracious design becomes accountable.

Having dedicated several pages to defining good design, permit us to end this section by describing its opposite. Bad design at its best is merely frustrating, dull, or unpleasant. It is the itch at the back of your throat. It is an obstacle instead of an enabler; it is useless and self-serving. At its worst, bad design causes harm; it creates negative outcomes or situations. It obscures or deceives. Consider the following example: the painting of pink fracking drill bits as a breast cancer fundraiser. In 2014, Susan G. Komen partnered with Baker Hughes, a leader in hydraulic fracturing equipment, to raise breast cancer awareness among (mostly male) oil field workers. Baker Hughes donated $100,000 to the Foundation, then painted 1,000 drill bits used in fracking the specific shade of pink trademarked by Susan G. Komen (Levine 2014). Given the carcinogenic nature of fracking chemicals, the cost involved in painting pink these many drill bits, and the cost of the Baker Hughes' marketing campaign (versus the monetary benefit to breast cancer awareness and research), this becomes silly, if not ethically questionable.

2.2.2 Why design matters

That design matters – that it exists, that it will have an impact, and that this impact can be positive – has, more recently, entered the multi-disciplinary discourse. Fuller acknowledges that 'objects, devices, and other material entities have a politic – that they engage in the arrangement and composition of energies, allow, encourage or block certain kinds of actions' and points out that 'these concerns have also more recently been scrutinized by the interdisciplinary area of science and technology studies' (2008: 7). In 2007, we argued that 'research interests in graphic design and presentation find a new relevance and weight, not only as a contributing factor in the design of computer interfaces and visualization systems, but also as an area of study in their own right'. The contributions possible by design are increasingly being recognized as valuable, the 'significance of the visual is sufficiently evident [...] that aesthetic factors become intrinsically woven with issues of functionality' (Ruecker et al. 2007: n.pag.). For the humanities, Brown champions design's cause, arguing that 'an algorithm has no impact without an interface' (2015: 81), adding that design's importance to DH, while an 'uncomfortable truth for many digital humanists' will, according to Cohen, determine whether a 'resource will be useful and used' (Cohen 2008: n.pag.). In particular, the critical analysis of design, argue Galey and Ruecker, 'positions us in a potent space between the past and the future. Failing to recognize design as a hermeneutic process means failing to understand how our inherited cultural record actually works' (2010: 421).

Critical design

In the late 1960s, Sottsass declared that design 'is a way of discussing society, politics, eroticism, food and even design. At the end, it is a way of building up a possible figurative utopia or metaphor about life' (cited in Dormer 1993: 5). Antonelli (2015: n.pag.) traces the history of critical design to predating the Radical Design defined by the Italian movement of the 1960s. He argues that architecture and design have, at different points in the past, 'raised red (never white!) flags and creatively proposed corrections under different manifesto umbrellas'. The 1964 First Things First Manifesto, for example, published by Ken Garland and 20 other designers, photographers, and students, was a reaction against trivial production and mainstream advertising. It called on designers to 'focus efforts of design on education and public service tasks that promoted the betterment of society' (Garland 2015: n.pag.). Forty-five years earlier, Walter Gropius called for a unification of the arts with craft through an artistic revolution of a sort,

> Let us therefore create a new guild of craftsmen without the class-distinctions that raise an arrogant barrier between craftsmen and artists! Let us desire, conceive, and create the new building of the future together. It will combine architecture, sculpture, and painting in a single form, and will one day rise towards the heavens from the hands of a million workers as the crystalline symbol of a new and coming faith.
>
> (cited in Dempsey 2002: 130).

In 2000, the First Things First Manifesto was re-written and re-published, once again encouraging designers to seek 'pursuits more worthy of our problem-solving skills'. The manifesto singles out 'cultural interventions, social marketing campaigns, books, magazines, exhibitions, educational tools, television programs, films, charitable causes and other information design projects' dealing with the environment, and social and cultural crisis as particularly deserving of design attention (Garland 2002, pp. 5-32). In the 1990s, *Colors*, a Benetton magazine launched by Tibor Kalman and Oliviero Toscani, featured thematic, multi-language issues on topics ranging from AIDS and victims, to touch, water, and prayer. It was powerful, well-crafted, antagonistic design, though also called opportunistic by its critics (e.g. Giroux, 2015). Adbusters, a Canadian-based not-for-profit organization founded in 1989, has launched numerous international campaigns, including Buy Nothing Day, TV Turnoff Week, and Occupy Wall Street. Its anti-consumerist and pro-environment publications are known for their subvertisements (spoofs of popular ads).

The term 'critical design' first appears in Dunne's *Hertzian Tales: Electronic Products, Aesthetic Experience and Critical Design* (2008b), then in Dunne and Raby's *Design Noir: The Secret Life of Electronic Objects* (2001). In *Hertzian Tales*, Dunne's interest lies in using design research to draw our critical attention to the 'hidden social and psychological mechanisms' of designed artefacts (2008b: xvi). Dunne builds on work by Ezio Manzini in which he envisions two roles for the future designer: the designer using her or his skills to imagine alternative futures in ways that can be communicated with the public, and the designer as strategist, directing industry to work towards achieving these futures (Dunne 2008b: xvii). The goal becomes to look beyond commercial and marketing activities, and construct opportunities for democratic conversation about what kinds of future people really want from design (Dunne 2008a). For Dunne, design cannot be divorced from people, and people's mental lives (Dunne 2008b: 148), making our conversations about technological developments essential for an informed debate about design's possible implications (Dunne 2008a).

Some of those who advocate for critical design have turned to critical theory to support their approach (Bardzell et al. 2012: ff.). Critical theory is a massive tradition (Adams, 1992), with both 'a narrow and a broad meaning in philosophy and in the history of the social sciences' (Bohman 2013: n.pag.) According to the Frankfurt School, 'a theory is critical to the extent that it seeks human emancipation' (Horkheimer 1990: 246). Numerous critical theories have been developed, in connection to various social movements. In both its broad and its narrow definition, critical theory has as its aim to 'explain and transform all the circumstances that enslave human beings' (Bohman 2013: n.pag.) Critical theorists have intentionally sought to distinguish their approaches to those practised by the natural and social sciences and combine the differences found in the poles of philosophy and the social sciences to seek human emancipation (Horkheimer 1990: 244). Since critical theory no longer concerns itself, solely, with the fine arts and literature, but also with current popular and consumer culture, there is much potential in appropriating (or re-thinking) a critical theory vocabulary to explore relationships between an artefact's features and qualities, the structures of users' experiences, and the contexts within which the relationships between artefact and users are created, experienced, and maintained. All the while, it is argued, designers can preserve their commitment 'to socially good and richly fulfilling aesthetic experiences' (Bardzell et al. 2012: 289). Critical theory is seen as offering resources designers can use to create artefacts that engage the public in challenging existing sociocultural norms and structures. The body of work produced by Bardzell, Bardzell and colleagues in Feminist human-computer interface (HCI), interactive criticism, and critical HCI (extensively cited in this book) is notable in this area. HCI, when seen as an interventionary field in particular, when we do more than react to inventions or empirically derived user needs, when we are 'proactive to imagine and support lifeworlds in which technologies play positive social and cultural roles' (Bardzell et al. 2008: 1136), appears a natural fit with critical theory.

Dunne and Raby, however, argue that critical design is not related to critical theory or the Frankfurt School but is, instead, critical thinking, 'not taking things for granted, being skeptical, and always questioning what is given' (2014: n.pag.). While critical design often deals with larger and more complex issues, all good design is in fact critical design because 'designers start by identifying shortcomings in the thing they are redesigning and offer a better version' (Dunne and Raby 2013: 35).

Design practice that aims to improve the current state of human existence appears to share much in common with critical theory. Both appear to agree that social transformation can be achieved 'only through interdisciplinary research that includes psychological, cultural, and social dimensions, as well as institutional forms of domination' (Bohman, 2013: n.pag). For Dunne, critical design is a 'synthesis between theory and practice, where neither practice nor theory leads' (Dunne 2008b: xvii). It is an opportunity for designers to engage in the social, cultural, and ethical implications of the artefacts they help create. Balsamo supports such engagement, arguing that '[d]esigners serve as cultural mediators by translating among languages, materials, and people to produce – among other things – taste, meaning, desire, and coherence' (2011: 11). Thus, design work can be profound when designers embrace the notion that '[t]hrough the practices of designing, cultural beliefs are materially reproduced, identities are established, and social relations are codified. Culture is both a resource for, and an outcome of, the designing process' (Balsamo 2011: 11). Thus, approaching the study of interfaces for DH? specifically, through the lens of critical design may lead us to challenge the design notions and expectations that have been established within these domains, and provoke new ways of thinking about these objects, their use, and how they impact the surrounding environment. This may be in the form of imagining desirable future states for such systems, or through imagining the 'undesirable things – cautionary tales that highlight what might happen if we carelessly introduce new technologies into society' (Dunne and Raby, 2014: n.pag).

In many ways, by being seen as having coined the term 'critical design', Dunne and, subsequently, Raby have come to stand for it. Malpass, in his doctoral work, challenges the idea that Dunne and Raby are critical design and poses, instead, that the Dunne and Raby critical design exists within a much broader context of critical design practice that can be traced back to Radical Design in the Italian tradition, mentioned earlier, Anti-Design, New Design and Conceptual design, and critical practice in HCI (Malpass 2012: 20). Malpass is concerned that critical design is seen as a novelty or as quasi art:

> the danger is that critical design becomes overly self-reflexive and introverted. As it gathers in popularity, there is a risk of it becoming a parody of itself and its usefulness as part of a larger disciplinary project is undermined. There are already utterances of critical design being, 'design for design's sake', 'design for designers' or perhaps more appropriately 'design for critical designers'.
>
> (Malpass, 2012: 6)

Critical design is subject to iterative design like any other intentioned artefact. Aside from Malpass' proposal of a taxonomy for critical practice in product design, work has also taken place on challenging both speculative and critical design's perceived lack of political accountability. Prado and Oliveira question the validity of a (critical) discipline 'that consistently dismisses and willingly ignores struggles other than those that concern the intellectual white middle classes–precisely the environment where SCD comes from' (2014: n.pag). In their harsh and deeply important criticism, they call out critical designers for depicting 'a dystopian universe where technology comes to paint a world in which their own privileges of their own reality are at stake, while at the same time failing to properly acknowledge that design is a strong contributor to the complete denial of basic human rights to minorities, right here, right now' (Prado and Oliveira 2014: n.pag). They accurately, to our minds, describe CD as primarily focused on white, middle-class, cisgendered, and heterosexual needs (and possible futures). When imagining either utopian or dystopian technological futures, do we consider that those future artefacts 'will most probably be manufactured in China, Indonesia or Bangladesh'?

The work in Feminist HCI comes closest to considering issues of race, gender, and privilege; however, even this area – more thoroughly discussed below – fails to adequately acknowledge its own, narrow position. Prado and Oliveira (2014: n.pag) still believe that design's powerful language 'is perfectly positioned to provide relevant social and cultural critique', but to achieve such relevance it must be 'held accountable for its political and social positions' and 'escape its narrow northern European middle class confines'. The only way it can gain relevant accountability is by being accountable and by diversifying beyond its limited, privileged starting points.

What do designers do?

Design is concerned with the envisioning, planning, and creation of artefacts whether material or virtual, and includes many sub-disciplines. The focus of this book is on design for digital media, specifically human-computer interface (HCI) design and interactive visualization. Designers propose solutions to problems. They do so by considering those who are affected by the problem (and are, therefore, the intended audience or users of the solution), the context(s) within which the solution will be implemented, its purpose, the content (textual and graphical), and the affordances and constraints of the media in which it will be executed. Some designers develop a plan for the solution that is then executed by those in other disciplines. For example, an interface designer may create a series of sketches for a new web interface that will, subsequently, be implemented by a programmer. Some designers both develop a plan and implement its execution. For example, a book designer may design all aspects of the book, then implement the design, and submit the files to a printer. Another type of design activity involves style-based projects, where the objective is to apply an appropriate form to the content (creating a brochure layout, for example). Systems, service, or experience design attempts to understand and create various aspects of complex environments, how they intersect, the inputs and outputs, the constraints and affordances.

Design research has been described using a variety of taxonomies. Forlizzi et al. (2009) interviewed a dozen design researchers and have applied three different prepositions to indicate the emergent sub-groups: for, through, and on. In research for design, the results are theories, methods, and knowledge that can, at least in some instances, be leveraged by designers to improve their work. Supporting research for design is research through design, which feeds insights from design projects back into research for design, and research on design, which studies designers and the design process, ideally to also contribute back to research for design.

Design is a fundamentally interdisciplinary area, since it operates at a level distinct from the particular content domain that is chosen for any given use case. A systems designer, for instance, might work in any field where a system is involved, ranging from transportation to healthcare to multi-modal industry. Similarly, a communication designer may work on any material, media, or technology used to communicate any kind of information, ranging from printed novels to digital systems for visualizing XML-encoded court records.

Design research also functions in conversation with a topic area, but is in some ways agnostic about which topic area is chosen. A systems design researcher can ask research questions about systems design in any area where there are systems; a communication design researcher can ask research questions about communication design in any context where communication is involved.

2.3 What is publishable?

For researchers working in conventional disciplines, part of graduate training is to begin to understand what the community of practice considers publishable. Although the preferences will vary somewhat from journal to journal or conference to conference, in general the warrant is clear: this kind of work is the kind that we do, and is done the way we do it, and this other kind of work is not.

For interdisciplinary fields like design and DH, the landscape is more complicated. The researcher has the opportunity to contribute within their own conventional field, within the design or DH publication infrastructure, or within someone else's conventional field. In all but the first case, the instincts developed during grad school may not help very much, and may in fact unnecessarily constrain what the researcher tries to undertake. So it is necessary to do some additional learning when venturing out for the first few times.

To complicate matters even further, both design and DH are fields of practice as well as research, and it is not always clear where the line sits between the two. For some designers or digital humanists, it seems reasonable to assume that case studies are worth disseminating, and in fact much of the literature is dedicated to these instances where a project was carried out for other purposes than creating knowledge, and then the team who did the project reflects upon it and hopefully gains some new insight that is worth sharing.

Unfortunately, that mode actually seems to contribute very little to a workable body of knowledge in a field. Part of the problem is that if you are thinking in terms of data points, the case study essentially represents only one, and as evidence it has the weight of only one. It is not difficult to imagine all kinds of variations that would have been useful to consider as a way of providing additional insights or even just some context.

In fact, in design there have been attempts to develop a systematic way of capturing information about a case study so that different ones could be aggregated and compared. One example of this approach is Lim and Sato's (2001) Design

Information Framework (DIF), which provides an ontology of design knowledge that can serve as a template for recording salient features of any given case. The problem with attempts like these is with the implementation: no matter how easily and quickly it is possible to extract the relevant information from the case and put it in the system, nothing is easier or quicker than not doing it at all.

A better solution is therefore to undertake research where the primary goal of the project is new knowledge, and the things that get made along the way are designed to maximize their contribution to understanding. If that understanding produces a new model, a new way of understanding the conceptual structure of the topic, then we have something that should be publishable. If the model is also a theory, in the sense that it shows dependencies that can lead to hypotheses that can be tested, then the situation is even stronger. As de la Rosa et al. (2017) argue, in order to make this possible, it is useful to design a variety of things in any given research project, increasing, in essence, the number of data points that can be brought to bear as evidence.

If multiple experimental prototypes are the gold standard, or at least a high bar, then the opposite end of the spectrum is the practical project that is sufficiently excellent that it has embraced all of the current best practices, without extending beyond them or challenging them in any interesting way. Troubleshooting a photocopier, for example, is not a task that can usually be published (although we have to nod to the brilliant Lucy Suchman [1987], who did exactly that). For people who are still learning about working in interdisciplinary ways, and have had only limited prior contact with either design or DH, it is natural to ask the team members from either of those areas to, essentially, troubleshoot the photocopier.

In such cases, the mental model of the interdisciplines consists primarily of their practice mode. Designers are great with visual projects, so we will ask our design researcher to make our website; digital humanists are great with digital texts, so we will ask our DH researcher to encode our material in XML. While both of those tasks may need to be done, and done well, it is important to keep in mind that the scholar's job is to carry out research, produce new knowledge, and publish it. Neither of these tasks meets any of those criteria. It is therefore important to keep in mind that this instrumental use of researchers from either design or DH should be kept to a minimum. As an alternative, include in the budget some funds to hire people who are working in the practice rather than as researchers. The researchers will likely even know some to recommend.

2.4 Case study 1: How design students define themselves

Many of the definitions of design included in this chapter are the work of writers now resting in the great Barcelona Chair in the sky. But, how do newly minted designers define what they do? What role do they expect to play in their industry, their society, and their culture, and as co-makers of their discipline? As we briefly mentioned previously in this chapter, architecture and design (not to ignore artists, poets, performers, musicians) have, at different points in the past, 'raised red (never white!) flags and creatively proposed corrections under different manifesto umbrellas'. So we asked a group of 4th-year undergraduate design students from Mount Royal University (MRU) to share with us how they see themselves as information designers by penning and signing their own manifestos. Here are two of the results, reprinted with permission:

Five women, one MANIFESTO, 2017

Lucy Randal, Danielle Massee, Phoebe Davis, Jenny Masikewich, and Anye Juressen

We are critical thinkers, researchers, advocates, and innovators in our visual communication practice. By utilizing these skills holistically, we aim to address both design problems and popular assumptions to challenge the boundaries of information design. We are committed to keeping an open mind, welcoming criticism, minimizing bias, and always, always asking questions.

We are inspired by present and former practitioners of design who have developed powerful messages through research and iteration. By their example, we are challenged to view problems, both systematic and distinct, and develop informed solutions that provide opportunities for education and action. We commit to the release of our ideas for investigation and will act on criticism to improve the ability of a design to deliver this goal.

We determine that our beliefs of who we are, what we do, and who we do it for are intertwined. We work to understand our own positions and challenge our centrality, so that we value the perspective of others whose collaboration in design allow us to move past our own limitations. We can only ever fully understand our own experiences, yet by nature, design is collaborative, so we engage in our practice beyond individual reflection. We remember these values, but spend our efforts wisely in the practical world.

We are interested in understanding both the user and the distinctions among recipients. As such, there is a responsibility to never define or limit the 'user' to a single group or persona. We do not create to exclude people in language or form, but to remain aware of the potential limitations of imagery in public entry. Our design, then, is to embody inclusiveness in its access, practicality in its usage, and sincerity in its form. We the undersigned agree to uphold the following precept in our study and creation of design as communication.

We take on these responsibilities with weighted consideration to establish a standard of practice to inform our action and refer our judgement.

Design Manifesto, 2017
Orry Roth, Payton Glagau, Piper Goodfellow, and Lauren Piwek

This manifesto has been born of our dedication to explore intentional design: to provide an ethical review of our design process and outcomes.

We ground ourselves in industry practices; our focus of inspiration, ideation, and implementation is in pursuit of holistic outcomes. We strive to include both the individual and the community within each segment of our solution, with consideration towards leaving the world in a better state than we found it. We lead with a focus to expose meaning and, as truthfully as possible, make private issues public for the purpose of awareness and growth.

We apply cyclical thinking, to continuously critique and challenge our work as it unfolds with the intention of growth and forward momentum. We encourage actively challenging our assumptions and interrogating our design ideas as individuals, and as a collective towards developing concrete work. Each of us will commit to contribute as individuals, elevating the group collectively. As we abide by these words, we will hold each other accountable.

We are dedicated to a strong, multi-level awareness and understanding within each element of our practices. An awareness that is based in research, with the intention to help us anticipate how the outcome, and its parts, may contribute to its designated system and extended environment. We hold ourselves accountable in this way, to mindfully include diverse perspectives and explore our blind spots, in the hope that this inclusivity transcends unto the user experience.

We value engagement with as many audiences as possible, and therefore, value an end result which draws inclusion beyond those who align with the solution. We value user feedback as part of our engagement to help give direction for improvement on projects; users may have different values or thinking systems than us so they can help identify any issues we may not have interrogated enough or find improvements we may not have thought of. We demonstrate our work in a form that attains clarity and understanding for inclusive learning. We push for aesthetic quality within solutions that are both cohesive and enticing. We each support and pledge to uphold this system of values throughout our practice, as individuals, and as a group. This is our manifesto.

These students are optimistic, engaged in their sense of responsibility for their work and how it may impact others, and cognizant of their worth. Since the information design program at MRU is fairly evenly split between instruction in communication theory, design practice, and writing, our students tend to enter the program with more strength and interest in one of the three areas, and less so in the others. Some students have been well prepared for the study of visual form, while other students gravitate towards the written language. All must achieve a certain level of theoretical understanding and design and writing competency to become practising information designers. MRU's design program (like most others) privileges project-based studio instruction – classes have one session of three plus hours of contact time per week, with 12 to 20 students in each course section. We routinely engage not-for-profit agencies in classroom projects, being careful that the client's objectives do not overshadow the learning outcomes established for the class. It is a delicate balance, but one that provides a remarkable learning opportunity for the students. In 2012 we worked on visualization projects with researchers from the University of Alberta, in 2013 with HIV Edmonton, in 2014 with the MRU Daycare, and in 2017 with MRU's Geology department.

In addition, there are lecture components, where we provide some digested information that the students can attempt to remember and use (there's a core curriculum that hasn't changed much in the past 50 years of design instruction). To balance lecture-style instruction, we meet with students one-on-one or in small groups to discuss their projects. In-classroom critiques are an important component of most design teaching practice. Since iteration is critical to good design practice and foundational to design education, we pace projects in such a way as to enable multiple touch points, and opportunities for questioning and redirection, if necessary.

Our goal is to graduate practising information designers. Our students apply to our program, undergo an interview process, and, if successful, join a cohort of other ID students (between 40 and 50, depending on the year) who take a set of dedicated courses, eventually participating in a 4-year portfolio course, where they showcase their work to industry, friends, and colleagues. Between year 2 and 3, they must also complete a paid work term in the ID industry. While our program is fairly practice-focused, some of our graduates may (and have) continued in their academic study. Some of our courses, the fourth year critical design course for example, are specifically structured to meet the needs of those considering graduate study in design. Each student must reach a level of competency within the four cornerstones of information design:

1. *Everything communicates*: Though we cannot (and should not) control the behaviour of our fellow humans, what we create in design must serve a purpose, to some predefined community, within a particular context. In essence, we try to make things that exist for reasons that are outside of ourselves. When words, images, colours, or shapes are put together, they communicate. When they are changed, so is what they say. Nothing can be random or arbitrary.
2. *Iteration*: In every course, we aim to help students add to their information design toolbox. Depending on the specific course, that addition may be a theory, a tool, a way of working, a strategy, or a method. Iteration is part of

the design process – one of the more critical tools in design – that asks us to make, look, and re-make based on our observation. Sometimes the making and re-making emerges out of our own critical thinking and, sometimes, it's based on consultation, testing, or co-creation with pre-determined readers/users/communities. Most often, it's both.

3. *Critique*: At key intervals within the design process, designers seek feedback on their work, usually from colleagues, classmates, superiors, and, sometimes, from clients and others. In their most basic use, critique and iteration help designers improve functionality and target look-and-feel. When done well, critiques challenge assumptions, biases, and stereotypes; push against the status quo; clarify contexts of use; and raise expectations of quality, including accuracy, thoroughness of research, attention to detail, and justification of design choices.
4. *Service*: In information design, we aim to be of service to others: individuals and communities. Sometimes that service means identifying a problem, and attempting to address it using ID tools, methods, and practices. Other times, service means challenging existing systems, practices, attitudes, or behaviours. Other times still, it means telling meaningful stories emergent out of qualitative and/or quantitative data, using visual and textual means.

Whether we am teaching visual rhetoric, typography and layout, design history, feminist and critical design, interface and interaction, or material data, those four principles scaffold it all. What changes is the level of detail in our instruction, weight of expectations in my students' deliverables, and complexity level of the final design.

Design is an inherently (whether or not consciously or intentionally) political activity. As Winhall (2006) so smartly put it, design is political because it can have consequences, and sometimes serious ones. Design is also created and experienced contextually, within a particular historical, social, and cultural environment. However, with our near-global connectivity, design must also be considered outside of its direct cause and effect and grounded within a critical self-reflection. That's a lot to ask of undergraduate students, but ask we must. The information designers we graduate will be the makers and co-makers of things that engage (positively or negatively) with people and communities, that will serve or obstruct, that will support or challenge the status quo, and that will – unquestionably – reflect the ethics of their creator. The following illustrates how the social, political, and cultural contexts play out in our classrooms. Many years ago, I was teaching a class in digital layout. The students were tasked with designing a book cover and proposing a typographical system for a book that dealt with supporting women who had been diagnosed with breast cancer. One student presented a cover idea during critique that showed the close-up of a young woman's perfectly formed breasts. She was shown without a face and in soft, erotic lighting. Formally, the combination of text and image that created the cover's layout (balance, emphasis, size, texture, and colour) was very well constructed. However, to consider this design without the context of its subject matter and intended audience would have been irresponsible. As part of the critique, the student was asked to consider what it meant to depict a healthy breast on the cover of a book that dealt with the subject of breast cancer. They had to consider the impact/implications of such a decision. Without this discussion, the project would have been little more than a software-based exercise.

It is our job as design educators to sometimes shift and, other times, challenge the assumptions, world-views, perspectives, and belief systems of our students. Depending on the particular project's content (and the seniority of the students) such challenge may come in the form of 'questions for consideration' or, in the critical design class for example, in clearly outlined expectations to research and consider opposing viewpoints.

2.5 Exercises: Form and text

One of the principal (though not exclusive) jobs of designers is to manipulate form. This part of our skill set is perhaps one that's most misunderstood – considered as subjective expressions of our beautiful souls. Great form can look effortless – just enough perfectly-chosen stuff and nothing more. But great form can also be painstaking and intricate – rich with attention and detail.

So which of these approaches is good design? What makes one design perfectly minimalist, while another just plain boring; one design a journey of visual discovery, and another visual noise? The two examples of book covers you see in Figure 2.2 are vastly different in terms of visual complexity – sheer volume of stuff on the page – yet both are absolutely perfect in connecting form with meaning. One of our co-authors, Dr Susan Liepert, studied music and, specifically piano, for 12 years, starting while barely out of diapers. Besides her concert-level competence in piano performance, she has been trained to be an expert 'hearer' through exposure, practice, and theory, her relationship to sound becoming deep and complex while also second-nature. Designers are trained just like Dr Liepert, except their expertise is in 'seeing'.

The following exercise set is meant to expose you to some of the training critical to visual competency. Through each one you'll experiment with manipulating form.

FIGURE 2.2: On the left is a book cover for *Jaws* designed by Tom Lenartowicz. On the right is a book cover by Carlo Giovani for Jules Verne's *Journey to the Centre of the Earth*.

2.5.1 Abstraction through reduction

What you'll need

- Black pen.
- Sketchbook or white paper.
- Tracing paper (for self-care modification).
- Paints or cut paper.

Take an object (a tree, mug, building, lamp, vase of flowers) and draw it with as much detail as you can. Look at your drawing, then start another one, reducing what you see in your first drawing to simple forms. Do this several times until you've reduced the object into roughly geometric shapes. Finally, using cut paper, make simple, opaque geometric figures. The final image will be a pure geometric abstraction. Look at your work in sequence, as a series.

Self-care modification

If the idea of drawing from real life stresses you out, instead of abandoning the exercise, do this instead: find a photograph that has an object in it (avoid photos with lots of tiny details). Using one sheet of tracing paper, use your black pen to trace the image. For the first drawing, trace as much of the image as you're able. Then, continue the exercise as above, except create each new image by laying a new piece of tracing paper over top of the previous drawing.

Once you're done, ask yourself the following questions:

1. At what point in the sequence do you stop being able to recognize the original object?
2. How much or how little visual information do you need to still recognize the object for what it is?
3. Are some parts of the object more important for recognition to take place than others? For example, how much pig do you need to draw to tell that it's a pig, and are there some pig parts that are more 'piggish' than others?

Design isn't about accurate or detailed representation of reality. In fact, too much visual information can make it harder for us to discern what is most valuable, figure out how items group together, and the sequence in which the surface is meant to be read or understood. Excessive information becomes noise – for visual design it's the equivalent of trying to listen to a newscast in a buzzing coffee shop.

2.5.2 Abstraction through addition

What you'll need

- A printed photograph (portrait).
- Other images or collage material (optional).
- Scissors.
- Paints or markers.
- Camera.

Designers manipulate form in order to achieve some predetermined outcome. Even tiny adjustments can have a substantial impact on how we interpret what we're seeing. This exercise is an opportunity to experiment with changing form and observing the resulting emotional or intellectual transformations.

Begin with a printed photograph of a face. Paint or draw over it, cut and reassemble it, or partially merge it (using collage) with photographs of other faces or things. Once you're finished, re-photograph the end result, then print again. The end result should be surprising, perhaps grotesque. Your treatment may reflect any number of intentions, or reveal some subconscious view on the subject. If the original face is recognizable, the result may be satirical on the individual's character, politics, or personality. Try subverting how the person in the photograph is usually depicted. Try using a photograph of someone you despise, and place them into a 'loving' context.

2.5.3 Unexpected encounters

What you'll need

- Camera.

The ordinary, everyday world is full of rhythms, patterns, balance, unity, and contrast – an endless exhibition of similarities and dissimilarities. While navigating through your world, look for the following relationships (and capture compulsively on camera):

- Ordinary objects in unusual circumstances.
- Very different objects that happen to have a visual resemblance.
- Objects that are ordinary or ugly in meaning but strikingly beautiful in form.

FIGURE 2.3: Unexpected encounter by M. Radzikowska.

2.5.4 Poignant close-ups

What you'll need

- Camera.

Take advantage of the fact that a camera has a limited field of view. Look for damage and decay. Get close. Photograph so that context is excluded and you're left

FIGURE 2.4: Poignant close-ups by M. Radzikowska.

with an abstraction – texture, colour, and depth. Look at these objects without prejudice – focus on curiosity and wit, and capturing parts of the world that are often overlooked.

2.5.5 The black square problem

What you'll need

- Card-stock.
- High-quality, black markers, various thicknesses.
- Pencil and eraser.

Using four solid black squares, create a graphic image to express the meaning of the following four words: **structure, cunning, unease,** and **joy.**

Make 25 preliminary sketches for each word, then select the most effective solution for each, and execute it at a larger size (5 inches square). Using only four squares may seem very limiting, but the intent of this problem is for you to develop a vocabulary through the discovery of various two-dimensional design principles. The necessary principles include:

- *Framal reference*: The ways that shapes relate to the edges of the design space (border);
- *Touching*: Shapes can interact with each other by proximity (so close they touch);
- *Overlapping*: Shapes can overlap one another;
- *Cropping*: Shapes can bleed off the edge of the design space;
- *Illusory space*: The ways that shapes are arranged and/or manipulated can create a feeling of depth;

- *Contrast of elements* (size, direction, space, position); and
- *Positive and negative space*: shapes can be created between shapes (that's negative space).

Combining these principles can further expand a mere graphic vocabulary into a comprehensive, abstract graphic language, maximizing the possibilities for graphic expression.

Because design skills become more comprehensive by creating several solutions for a single problem, selecting the most effective solution is an important condition.

2.5.6 Typographic portraits

What you'll need

- Access to a typeface sample on your computer.
- Tracing paper.
- Regular paper.
- Black ink pens and a pencil.

Using an existing typeface as a starting point (feel free to start by tracing it), select one of the below concepts and carefully render your first name so that it expresses the concept you chose. You can modify the typeface as needed, but try to avoid simply adding images or graphics to communicate your idea. How you've rendered your name will communicate your idea. Consider typeface style, letter spacing, size, and use of upper and lowercase characters. Pay particular attention to the actual size and placement of your name in the rectangle (the name tag).

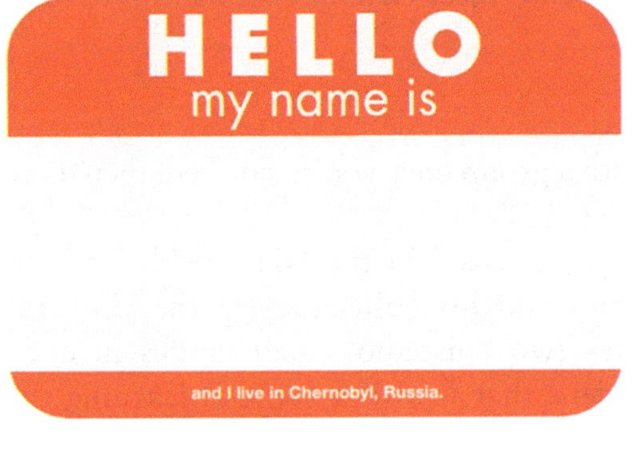

Hello, my name is ( ) and ...

- I live in Chernobyl, Russia
- I have an allergy
- I am accident prone
- I am a magician
- I have the hiccups

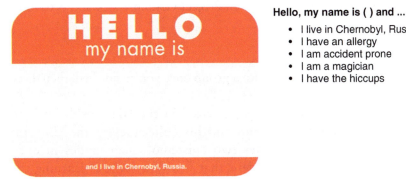

FIGURE 2.5: Typographic Portraits template (on the left) with options for topics (on the right).

FIGURE 2.6: From left to right, Obnoxious Family by Kirk Eberle, and Quaint System by Asfa Riyaz.

This exercise focuses on expressive (rather than functional) type design. Additionally, it's meant to challenge initial problem-solving impulses – usually oriented towards the literal – and push beyond this point, taking a more conceptual approach. The use of a name to express the solution represents a limited language for solving such a complex visual problem, yet the conditions of the problem dictate the art of implying or inferring. Subtle design decisions bring each solution to life.

2.5.7 Deformation

What you'll need

- Starter textual material: check out Project Gutenberg for access to full books (https://www.gutenberg.org).

Exercise type

Individual; consider sharing it with a group once you're finished, then discussing the deformation.

First proposed, or at least popularized in the DH world, by Victorian literary scholar Jerome McGann and his colleagues at the University of Virginia, deformation combines two epistemological modes in one exercise. It is a kind of theoretical lens that is also a form of learning through making.

The idea is that one way to get new insights into the object of study is to systematically change it in some way. A simple and effective introduction to the method

32 *Book I · Canto i*

3
Vpon a great aduenture he was bond,
That greatest *Gloriana* to him gaue,
That greatest Glorious Queene of *Faery* lond,
To winne him worshippe, and her grace to haue,
Which of all earthly thinges he most did craue;
And euer as he rode his hart did earne,
To proue his puissance in battell braue
Vpon his foe, and his new force to learne;
Vpon his foe, a Dragon horrible and stearne.

4
A louely Ladie rode him faire beside,
Vpon a lowly Asse more white then snow,
Yet she much whiter, but the same did hide
Vnder a vele, that wimpled was full low,
And ouer all a blacke stole shee did throw,
As one that inly mournd: so was she sad,
And heauie sate vpon her palfrey slow:
Seemed in heart some hidden care she had,
And by her in a line a milkewhite lambe she lad.

5
So pure and innocent, as that same lambe,
She was in life and euery vertuous lore,
And by descent from Royall lynage came
Of ancient Kinges and Queenes, that had of yore
Their scepters stretcht from East to Westerne shore,
And all the world in their subiection held,
Till that infernall feend with foule vprore
Forwasted all their land, and them expeld:
Whom to auenge, she had this Knight from far compeld.

---

of Bk I. By this badge, he symbolically bears the cross; cf. *HHL* 258–59 and II i 18.8–9. **2 deare**: implying also 'dire'. **his dying Lord**: cf. 2 Cor. 4.10: 'Euerie where we beare about in our bodie the dying of the Lord Iesus, that the life of Iesus might also be made manifest in our bodies'. **4 dead as liuing euer**: cf. Rev. 1.18 on John's vision of the resurrected Christ who tells him '[I] am aliue, but I was dead: and beholde, I am aliue for euermore'. The pointing may be either 'dead, as liuing euer', or 'dead, as liuing, euer'. Nelson 1963:147 notes that the paradox, 'Christ dead is Christ living', is the principal subject of Bk I. **5 scor'd**: painted or incised. **6 For soueraine hope**: i.e. to show the supreme hope. **hope** and **helpe** are linked alliteratively to indicate their causal connection. The knight's enemy Sansfoy curses 'that Crosse . . . | That keepes thy body from the bitter fitt' (ii 18.1–2). **7 Right faithfull true**: cf. Rev. 19.11: 'And I sawe heauen open, and beholde a white horse, and he that sate vpon him, was called, Faithful and true', which the Geneva Bible glosses: 'He meaneth Christ'. **Right**: upright, righteous (cf. Ps. 51.10); or it may function as an adverb. 'The faithfull knight' is his common tag, as in Arg. to cantos iv, v, and x. **8 too solemne sad**: too grave or serious; cf. Guyon who is 'Still solemne sad' (II vi 37.5) when he avoids pleasure in order to pursue his quest; and Arthur, 'somwhat sad, and solemne eke in sight' (II ix 36.8) in his desire for glory; and Una who is 'sad' (4.6) in mourning. **too** prepares for his encounter with Sansjoy. **9 ydrad**: dreaded.

Stanza 3
1 bond: obs. form of 'bound' (going); also bound by vow (cf. 54.3). **2–3** 'In that Faery Queene I meane glory in my generall intention, but in my particular I conceiue the most excellent and glorious person of our soueraine the Queene' (*LR* 32–34). On **Gloriana**, see II x 76.8–9, VI x 28.1–3, and 'Gloriana' in the *SEnc*. **Glorious** refers to Christ's cross (2.3) before being applied to the Queen. On her role in the poem, see Fruen 1987, 1994. **4 worshippe**: honour, renown. **5 earthly**: as distinct from his hope in Christ (2.6). **6 earne**: yearn, as 7 confirms. It also carries the usual sense, 'seek to deserve by merit'. **8 his new force**: either the force of the armour newly given him, or his unproven power in wielding that armour. The phrasing is scriptural: e.g. Col. 3.10.

Stanza 4
Until she is named at 45.9, Una is associated by the lowly **Asse** with Christ's humility (Matt. 21.5–6, from Zech. 9.9); by **more white then snow** with truth (in Ripa 1603:501, Verità is *vestita di color bianco*) and with faith (cf. x 13.1); and by her **vele** with the truth that remains veiled to the fallen. White and black are the colours of perpetual virginity and hence the Queen's personal colours (Strong 1977:71, 74). While the **lambe** associates her with innocence and with the sacrificial lamb of John 1.29, the king's daughter leading the lamb bound by her girdle is a traditional item in the legend of St George; see 'Una's Lamb' in the *SEnc*. Una riding an ass is a familiar Renaissance emblem, *asinus portans mysteria*, which symbolizes the true church; see Steadman 1979:131–37. As an allegorical enigma, see Nohrnberg 1976:151, 207–08, 268. On Una as Holy Church in relation to Elizabeth, see Perry 1997. **1 louely**: also 'loving' and 'worthy of love'. **him faire beside**: as she is fair and rides becomingly by his side. **beside**: indicating one meaning of her name, Lat. *una* (together), because her 'wondrous faith' is 'firmest fixt' (ix 17.4–5) in her knight; see 45.9*n*. Her place is taken by Duessa who rides 'together' with him at ii 28.1. **3 the same**: i.e. the whiteness of her garment. **4 wimpled**: lying in folds. Her 'widow-like sad wimple' is not thrown away until xii 22.3. **6 inly**: inwardly, in her heart; 'entirely' (E.K. on *SC May* 38). **9 in a line**: on a lead. Buxton, in the *SEnc* 724, concludes that this detail is purely pictorial, one of the very few where S. recalls an image he had seen. A woodcut in Barclay 1955 shows a lamb on a string; see the *SEnc* 706.

Stanza 5
1 innocent: in the religious sense, 'sinless', as the virgins who follow the lamb (Rev. 14.4); also 'undeserving of punishment' from which she seems to suffer. **2 vertuous lore**: i.e. in her knowledge of, and obedience to, moral doctrine. **3 Royall lynage**: see vii 43.3–9*n*. **5 from East to Westerne shore** asserts Una's claim to be the holy Catholic Church; see ii 22.7–9*n*. The Church of England claimed that its authority derived from the Apostolic Church before it was divided with the West ruled by Rome. Cf. Drayton's prayer that Elizabeth's empire might 'stretch her Armes from East in to the West' (1931–41:2.530). **6** In man's unfallen state, God 'gaue | All in his hand' (x 42.7–8) and commanded him to 'fil the earth, and subdue it' (Gen. 1.28). **7 feend**: Satan; called **infernall** because he comes from hell. **vprore**: revolt, insurrection; cf. the account of his rebellion at vii 44. **8 Forwasted**: utterly laid waste. **9 compeld**: called; with the stronger implication, 'forced to come'.

FIGURE 2.7: An example of a page from a scholarly edition (the Hamilton edition of Spenser's epic poem *The Faerie Queene*). Note the ratio of poetry (above the line) to scholarly gloss (2/3 of page below the line).

is to simply swap the genders of everyone in a novel, then read it in the new form. Other ideas include:

- Tinker with formality by, for example, changing all first names to last names or vice versa.
- Rearrange the order of chapters or sections to experiment with the effects of sequence.
- Introduce zombies.

2.5.8 The scholarly edition

What you'll need

- Manuscript.

Exercise type

Group; works well with students.

For this activity, divide folks into pairs with each pair having a designer – preferably a typographer – and a digital humanist – preferably one with a background in digitization and metadata. Give them a manuscript and have them create a page of a scholarly edition, complete with as much learned apparatus as possible.

A scholarly edition is a copy of a primary text, perhaps a novel or a play, that explains what the history of the text has been in terms of variations of words or phrases in different editions. Think of a Norton edition as a light-weight version of this kind of book. The learned apparatus provides footnotes, or perhaps notes in a scholar's margin to the side of the text, of some definitions of historical terms, alternative explanations from various scholars of difficult passages, and so on.

The goal here is to have them discuss what is the hierarchy of importance of the textual information, how it can best be conveyed, what needs to be there, and what can be left out.

It will work best if you also provide an example of a completed page in a scholarly edition from the same genre, although not necessarily from the same author.

You might also consider providing them with a copy of the Text Encoding Initiative (TEI) guidelines (http://www.tei-c.org/guidelines/). These are about the invisible encoding that goes into the metadata, so they may not make sense at first to the designer, but they are also a succinct description of what is important.

3

Misunderstandings

For readers who are ready to tackle the nitty gritty, this chapter discusses how some of the core terminology might prove to be an obstacle to researchers in the other field.

One thing that soon becomes apparent to scholars working in an interdisciplinary manner is that vocabulary is a pitfall. In fact, one of the most potentially difficult aspects to negotiate is the problem of overlapping vocabulary between the disciplines, where the words are the same but the meanings, whether denotative or connotative, are different.

For example, many fields are concerned with not only their data but also the way in which their data is organized. The shared term, in this case, would be information design. The actual technical instantiations of information design, and therefore what is understood about the phrase, vary dramatically between the fields. For computing science, for instance, data can take many forms, but for several decades the default has been the relational databases – where a rigid structure of fields contains information that fits appropriately in its respective location.

In digital humanities (DH), on the other hand, relational tables are not always the best fit for containing useful information. Instead, various forms of text encoding have been applied: TACT, SGML, and XML. So here we have two fields using the same word, and they are more often than not talking about different philosophies, approaches, and underlying technologies.

For designers, whether information is stored in a database or an XML-encoded collection of files is more or less a matter of indifference. What is important is the visual form the data takes. When designers talk about information design, they are almost always referring to how the information looks on the page or screen. The digital humanists and computing scientists at the table are liable to make fundamentally incorrect assumptions that may be delayed from coming to light because they are using the same words for different concerns.

3.1 Terms from DH

In addition to a number of instances where terminology is shared, causing potential confusion, it also can happen that there is domain-specific vocabulary that needs to be sufficiently understood by the other discipline. An example of vocabulary that is widely used in DH and also in design is data, by which we mean the raw material that will be turned into something interesting. Often for DH that is a text, while for design it can be a text, or numbers, or equally often an image or video. However, DH also uses a word not typically found in design, which is metadata. In the DH context, metadata consists of information that is developed and stored about other data. There is an inherent distinction, for example, between a novel by Jane Austen and the bibliographic entry that describes that novel or the semantic encoding embedded in the digital edition that identifies all the places where property is discussed – including those where the word 'property' does not appear.

For an unsuspecting designer beginning to work on a digital edition of Jane Austen's novel, the contents of the novel might appear to be the primary focus of attention, when in fact for the digital humanists the intelligent development and use of the metadata might be of equal concern – in which case the design activity will be at least potentially vastly more complex than it otherwise might seem. Similar concepts that need to be articulated include: metadata, structured data, linked data, federated data, hermeneutic inquiry, encoding vs. programming, text analysis, and interoperability.

EXAMPLE: PRIDE & PREJUDICE

Literary Data

Chapter 1. It is a truth universally acknowledged, that a single man in possession of a good fortune, must be in want of a wife.

However little known the feelings or views of such a man may be on his first entering a neighbourhood, this truth is so well fixed in the minds of the surrounding families, that he is considered the rightful property of some one or other of their daughters.

'My dear Mr. Bennet', said his lady to him one day, 'have you heard that Netherfield Park is let at last?'

Mr. Bennet replied that he had not.

'But it is', returned she; 'for Mrs. Long has just been here, and she told me all about it'.

Mr. Bennet made no answer. [...]

Metadata description using XML

<title>Pride and Prejudice</title>, <creator>Jane Austen</creator>, <first published>1813</first published>, <language>English</language>,

<form>Prose</form>, <genre>Romantic</romantic>, <literary period> Romantic</literary period>, <number of chapters> 61</number of chapters>.

Semantic Encoding using XML

Data: Chapter 1. It is a truth universally acknowledged, that a single man <property> in possession of a good fortune</property>, must be in want of a wife.

However little known the feelings or views of such a man may be on his first entering a neighbourhood, this truth is so well fixed in the minds of the surrounding families, that <property>he is considered the rightful property of some one or other of their daughters</property>.

'My dear Mr. Bennet', said his lady to him one day, 'have you heard that <property>Netherfield Park is let</property> at last?'

Mr. Bennet replied that he had not.

'But it is', returned she; 'for Mrs. Long has just been here, and she told me all about it'.

Mr. Bennet made no answer.

It is a matter of some discernment whether Mr. Bennet should also be tagged as property, but on the whole, perhaps not.

3.1.1 Text encoding

The DH community has spent several decades enriching text data with various markup languages. While many designers are familiar with HTML and CSS, very few will have experience with the use of Extensible Markup Language (XML).

XML has several strengths, which can all be construed as having an impact on its use in designs for interfaces intended to support text browsing and retrieval. Firstly, and perhaps most fundamentally, XML defines markup languages, which enable the taggers to attach human judgements to individual pieces of text within the document. This ability is a basic distinguishing feature of textual markup, which differentiates it from situations involving retrieval of unmarked text by allowing the potential for the user to retrieve from a given document at a passage level rather than at the granularity of the entire document. From an information exploration framework, passage-level tagging that can be resolved to a tree structure, as XML documents can, also allows for the possibility of internal document reorganization at the point of retrieval, so that individual researchers might be able to specify from a number of views of a particular document.

XML is also a highly flexible markup environment, by virtue of its realization as a grammar that can be used to define markup languages. In document retrieval terms, this flexibility means that individual markup projects are at liberty to identify the portions of each document that they deem significant (within the constraints of the ontology instantiated by the schema). An ontology in this context is a way of looking at the world. For example, in a particular text, we might look at it primarily from economic terms (as does Mrs Bennet). The schema that corresponds to that way of seeing the world would include tags like property, and also probably other tags such as transaction, debit, credit, debt, loans, savings, income, bad investment, and so on.

This means that a project is only limited by the way of thinking that has been used as a basis for its organizational system. One of the problems in accessing unmarked text is that documents, especially documents of any length (or, for that matter, the majority of documents of interest to scholars in the humanities) are not usually about a single topic. This problem is so widespread that the library science community has even coined the term 'aboutness' to simplify their discussion of possible approaches to the problem. In traditional document-indexing schemes, there is provision only for document-level indexing, with all the loss of detail and precision necessitated by that procedure. One level of improvement to this situation is provided by any textual markup scheme. But a more precise and potentially significant level of improvement is made possible where the markup scheme can be tailored for a particular document collection.

> **Aboutness of Pride & Prejudice:** satirical and social critique on social status, social expectations of women during the eighteenth century, prejudice, reputation, class, marriage, family, deceit, romance, language and communication, and principles (this is a short list).

XML is also largely platform independent, at least to the extent of maintaining its data in a comparatively portable ASCII-based format. There are some caveats to be made in the nature of the necessity for each platform to support a suite of XML-aware applications, without which the data is not particularly useful, but given the even more-rapid obsolescence of other electronic data, even this added degree of independence has a significant value. In the humanities, where the research paradigm includes a significant degree of continually revisiting source documents, there is a considerable incentive to create digital resources that can survive changing technologies, platforms, and programming languages.

Another advantage of XML is that it has been used as the basis for the **Text Encoding Initiative (TEI)** standard for document encoding. The TEI (and its affiliated intellectual brethren, the TEI-lite and the Dublin Core) have paid particular attention to the kinds of metadata that should be included in digital document headers. At the level of document retrieval, the information contained in the TEI header provides the kind of information that would traditionally have been available for printed material through a library cataloguing system. Perhaps needless to say, for electronic documents without TEI-style document headers, some other mechanism needs to be provided if the user is to be able to locate the document.

One of the primary limitations of XML is indicated by the form of the question: 'What does (or will)...'. There is a sense in which the use of XML in full-text retrieval situations is a largely unexplored territory. However, a few general comments can be made about the requirements for an XML-based retrieval engine.

Firstly, there needs to be some mechanism for putting the controlled vocabulary represented by the tag entity definitions into the hands of the searcher. This mechanism could take the form of a thesaurus, or a topic map, or a semantic representation such as an inference net. The difference would be that the contents of these mechanisms would be derived from the tagset, and perhaps the attribute values allowable on the tags, rather than from the explicit content of the text document. If a similar instrument is then developed for the content, the situation arises in which two distinct tools are interacting within the retrieval mechanism – one representing the tags and the other the textual contents. A third mechanism is also indicated, which includes some representation from both the others, in the form of instances of the content that has been interpreted in some manner through enclosure within a given tag (see Figure 3.1). There is also the possibility of creating extensions of the tag-content relationship, either through grouping tags into pragmatic clusters, or redefining tags within the context of the search paradigm of a given researcher, or creating analogies or links between tags.

Given the information grazing strategies that have been identified as characterizing the information-seeking behaviours of humanists, it might also be useful to generate as wide a range as possible of other tools, each of which could draw on the complex nature of the interrelated 'hidden' tag data (and tag attributes) and 'explicit' text content. For example, there may be some value in a mechanism that allows traversal by juxtaposition of thematically related elements, without the necessity of displaying entire documents.

As an example, take the Orlando project, which is an online history of women writers in the British Isles, heavily encoded in XML. A fairly straightforward example

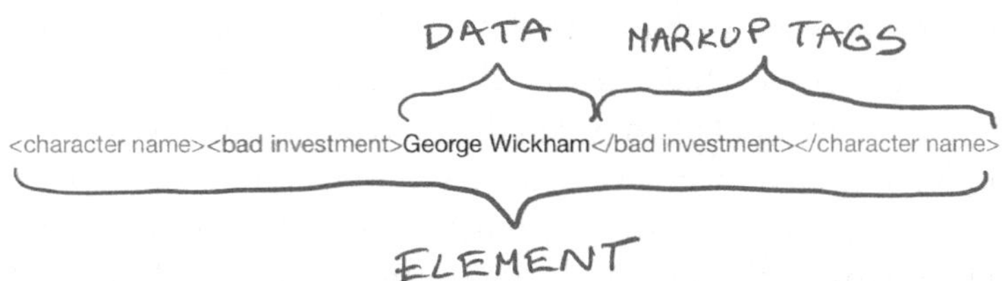

FIGURE 3.1: Nested tags and data contents.

from the Orlando textbase might be an instance where someone reading about the suffragette Annie Kenny being arrested in London asks 'what happened next?' The answer could involve the system having to exit the current document altogether, in order to perform a combination date and content retrieval, revealing for instance that her arrest was part of a mass arrest orchestrated by the suffragettes to draw public attention to the demographics of their movement (they wanted to indicate that they were not a fringe or pauper society, but had primarily middle-class and some noble members). Another useful tool might consist of a number of means for recording interaction histories, which the user could create and annotate and subsequently re-access.

Our typical approach in considering the design of systems for retrieval of XML-encoded documents in the humanities has three prongs:

1. a participatory design approach that attempts to incorporate the significant aspects of the domain of the end user – working with actual domain experts to discover their needs, desires, and obstacles;
2. some central organizing metaphor that allows the user to quickly establish a reasonably accurate mental model of the interface; and
3. an application of the principle of situated activity, in which the system provides means for the user to become involved in an environment that easily becomes (in Heidegger's terms) 'ready to hand'.[1]

3.1.2 Structured data

DH has been defined by some experts as fundamentally concerned with (in syntactic terms) the structuring, organization, and delivery of information, or (in semantic, or perhaps even pragmatic terms) knowledge management. It is therefore not unreasonable to say that many of the key issues in humanities computing involve our understanding of how various genres are structured.

In DeRose et al.'s 'What is text, really', the authors were attempting to formulate an ontology of text: they wanted to define what text *is*: how it can be understood as an existing object. Their hypothesis in the 1990 paper was that descriptive markup reflected a reasonable and defensible ontology – namely, that a given text consisted of an ordered hierarchy of content objects (OHCO). For example, in a novel we have chapters, and chapters contain paragraphs, paragraphs contain sentences, and sentences contain words and punctuation marks and perhaps even white space, if we want to get right down to the details. A play also has this internal nested hierarchy, consisting of acts, scenes, lines, words, etc.

Descriptive markup languages (like the tag sets that can be defined using XML) are also inherently hierarchical – the objects defined by the language need to be nested in order for the result to be resolvable into a tree structure, which is essential both for traversing the tagged document and allowing automated forms of checking for correct tag syntax. They distinguish descriptive markup from several other possibilities, the main alternative being procedural markup, where the user supplies typographic indicators (e.g. print this text in 14 pt Frutiger Bold, leave an additional 24 pts before the next line, and print that line in 10/12 Sabon). One of the advantages of descriptive markup is that it can be understood as platform-independent. By specifying that some string of text is a <heading1>, the decision as to how <heading1> text is going to be displayed can be left to the contingencies of the equipment at hand. The convergence of the practical necessities of a markup grammar like XML and the ordered hierarchy of content objects as an ontology of text seemed particularly fortuitous.

Subsequently, it became clear that not all text could be reasonably characterized as comprising an OHCO. Renear et al. (2004) reformulated their ideas in 'Refining our notion of what text really is' by arguing that although ordered hierarchies are not unknown, and perhaps even comprise a majority of textual instances, they are not of themselves complete. The primary spoke in the wheel of the OHCO is the problem of overlapping text hierarchies. For example, if someone revises a line by crossing out some of the words, but the revision breaks the boundaries of the previous hierarchy (if, for instance, the line crosses from the end of one sentence through the beginning of the next), then a scholar who wants to capture that revision in a markup language has the problem of one tag set crossing another. The standard solution to this problem is to incorporate into the document more than one encoding scheme.

An interesting historical side note comes from the scholars working on the Wittgenstein archive. Wittgenstein was a philosopher well known for his tendency for idiosyncrasy, complexity, and multiple revisions. One of Wittgenstein's anthologies (Wittgenstein, 1970) was in fact published posthumously from a collection of paper scraps found in a shoe box. As a result of the necessity of encoding this complex material, Claus Huitfield and the other members of the Wittgenstein group developed a markup language called MECS. By definition, MECS allowed its users to define overlapping content objects. However, it had the disadvantage that encoded documents could not be rendered into a tree structure. When things are organized as a tree, they can be quickly found by searching down the branches. With each choice, large portions of the tree can be set aside and not searched further.

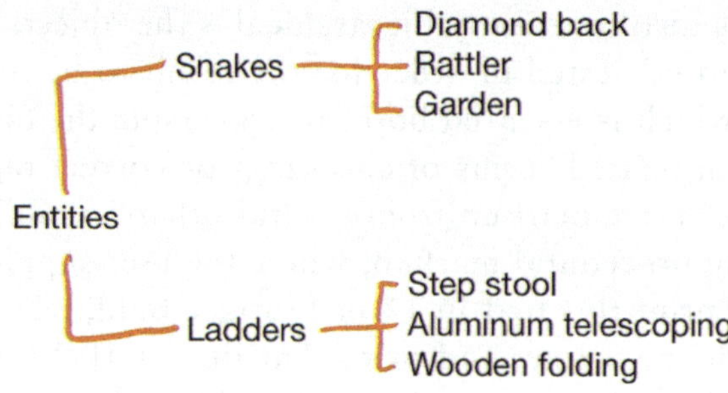

FIGURE 3.2: A tree showing snakes and ladders.

3.1.3 Federated data

For more than 30 years, the DH community has been working hard to create digital collections that are available to researchers around the world. Some of their colleagues and allies in this project are library and information scientists, archivists, and computer scientists, which is a good thing, because it has been nearly impossible to produce materials that share enough characteristics to be connected in any meaningful way.

The Text Encoding Initiative (TEI) is an international group that has been dedicated to helping this happen, and they have produced an excellent iterative series of guidelines for all manner of content, from manuscripts to letters to books, plays, poetry, and so on. However, guidelines are open to interpretation, and people from the humanities interpret for a living. The result, as we realized in Metadata Open New Knowledge (MONK), is that even among TEI-compliant collections, there is sufficient variation in how tags have been understood and applied that it was necessary to produce an ingestion mechanism that rendered everything down into a minimum set of tags that would be useful to the algorithms we were using (cf. Pytlik Zillig, 2009).

This is where federated data comes in. Rather than trying to rationalize all the various projects into a single, interoperable metadata format, federation proceeds on the principle that a new layer of metadata can be created that will allow cross-talk among collections.

One approach to federation is through the use of Resource Description Framework (RDF) triples. Triples are semantic units, of the kind that consist of two nouns linked by a verb. For example, 'tomcats are male felines'. So project A contains a semantic triple like that. Project B has 'Mrs Cheever owned a tomcat'. We can therefore federate those two projects, and the computer, without any additional human input, can recognize that 'Mrs Cheever owned a male feline'.

It sounds quite promising in theory, but of course in practice the variations in semantic domains are also significant, so that a third project, C, might have a triple about the promiscuity of a man in a novel: 'Fritz was a tomcat'. Then we can get 'Fritz was a male feline'. Which is somewhat misleading: triples are not necessarily very good with similes and metaphors.

3.1.4 Linked data: A brief historical foray into the Memex

Many people became aware of the concept of linking information in the early 1990s, when the internet, which had been around for decades, suddenly became the web. Two important factors were the emergence of personal computing equipment, which was becoming affordable and fashionable for civilians, and a graphical user interface. A third was that the information out on the web was linked up, so that it could be searched and navigated. However, the concept of linked data was not new: it goes back at least as far as Vannevar Bush, of Manhattan Project fame.

Bush's often-cited article 'As We May Think' is known to most scholars in DH, and almost none in design. It first appeared in the *Atlantic Weekly* right at the end of the Second World War. It is of a piece with its time, which is to say almost unreadably sexist by today's standards, but it is also full of the promise of hope, primarily through linked data.

Bush was calling for the scientific community to take stock of the internal changes it had experienced through participation in the war effort – changes that included vastly increased success through cooperation and information exchange – in the context of attempting to find some means to continue the best parts of that experience during peacetime. He begins by summarizing a number of areas where technical advances will be made, including improvements in printing, photography, and other mechanisms for capturing and publishing information. But the main problem to be addressed, he thought, was lack of adequate methods of access and organization of material, especially current technical research.

In short, he identified an information explosion, and wanted to suggest a mechanism that academics might use in dealing with it. His proposal was the Memex (Figure 3.3), which he saw as a desk that would be equipped with two basic mechanisms. One was a storage facility that would contain all the published material in the world. The other was a means whereby the operator of the Memex could connect pieces of the published material to create new anthologies. These anthologies or paths would constitute a record of the browsing activities of a scholar, and

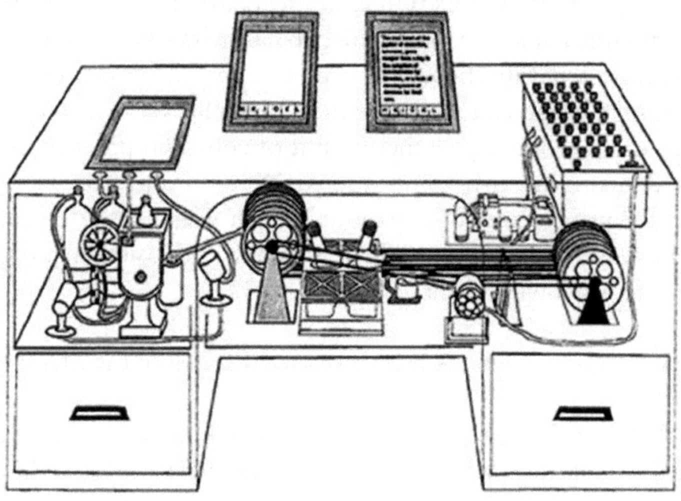

FIGURE 3.3: A sketch of the Memex (in *LIFE* 19:11, p. 123).

could be subsequently reused either by the same scholar or by others interested in the same topic. Bush even postulated the development of a new occupation, which he called 'pathfinder', for people who enjoy creating interesting anthologies.

At least three objections to the idea of the Memex are summarized by Miall (1998), who points out that in the first instance, the act of compiling excerpts from technical literature is not a primary form of intellectual activity in any domain, and may therefore have only limited usefulness to the working academic. Secondly, the principle of the Memex seems to indicate that the material will tend to be accessed out of context – an objection that probably holds more weight in the humanities than in the sciences, since the necessity of reading complete documents in context was identified long since (in fact, by Watson Boone 1994) as one of the information emphases of humanities researchers that tends to distinguish them from their counterparts in the sciences. The argument is that humanists of necessity include more contextual information in their articles since it is one of the functions of humanities scholarship to continually revisit and critically examine its own methods – a function that is less necessary in scientific circles, where methods are part of a more firmly established and acknowledged consensual domain. The third objection to the Memex is that by privileging one form of intellectual activity, it would tend to reinforce that form as an acceptable model of cognitive processes.

We would argue that, over time, the web slowly became the Memex, albeit a digital rather than a mechanical one: it combines a vast amount of information in a hyperlinked format and its readers have the ability to create and manage those links.

3.1.5 Conclusion

The list of DH terms covered here is too small by far to be of much practical application, but by focusing primarily on the concepts related to data, we hope to have captured at least some of the blind spots in the typical designer's education and experience. It would not be unreasonable to develop an entire book or database just on the topic of vocabulary in the arts, social sciences, and humanities, especially as it relates to the various theoretical lenses that are in play. There is also a tendency to use the names of scholars as a kind of shorthand, which in itself is somewhat unusual in design, although there are a few people who are mentioned in that way. An example is the Canadian guru of typographic design, Robert Bringhurst, whose book *The Elements of Typographic Style* (1992) is often referred to by his last name only.

3.2 Terms from design

Just as designers need to become familiar with terms specific to DH, so it is useful for those in DH to become aware of concepts specific to design. It is possible to divide those concepts into those related to design process, and those related to fundamental principles. An example of a common design process is critique, which can take several different forms, any one or more of which may be familiar to any particular design researcher. There are one-on-one critiques, desk critiques, group critiques, and public competitions. None of these would be considered a component of user studies, yet each of them can provide valuable feedback to the designer at nearly any stage of the process. Other terms include: visual material, design principles and elements, gestalt, typography, white space, and visual noise.

3.2.1 Sketches

Sketching is fundamental to many disciplines, including the fine arts (painting, printmaking, sculpture, and photography) and design (industrial design, interface design, visual design, and architecture). Sketches are used for initial idea generation through a process of repeated evaluation and refinement. Sketches are elaborated, explored, and, often, used as a means of communicating with others. Smith (2005: 3–5) gives a very thorough discussion on how important sketches are to architects as they can be used throughout the design process to capture and evolve ideas. They imply action and are immediately perceived to be imprecise. In a typical visual design curriculum, students are taught to sketch as though they were learning the fine arts. This approach is often called drawing, and involves a focus on detailed observation and development of rendering skills through the study of objects, materials, textures, and systems of perspective (NSCAD University 2008). We agree that learning how to produce accurate drawings from observation is a useful skill for information designers to have. However, for the purpose of a first-semester course, we argue that it is more important for students to gain competency in visualizing ideas and in communicating those ideas to others. Unfortunately, learning how to make rough drafts or outlines often falls on experience by doing, primarily through studio-based projects (Heller 2003; Resnick 2003), though some design programs are introducing additional courses focused on rapid idea development in a variety of drawing media (NSCAD University 2008).

Types of sketches

A number of sketching techniques exist, some well-established, such as concept mapping, and some less common, such as animated use sketches. Some sketches are created to experiment with composition – establishing content placement, balance, unity/variety, and hierarchy. Other types of sketches act as idea generation or brainstorming sessions in a visual form. Löwgren notes that through the process of sketching, ideas 'develop and grow in the conversation between eye and hand. Sketching is not merely a matter of documenting images that are already complete in the mind's eye. Thinking occurs, quite literally, in the manual actions involved in creating the sketch' (Löwgren 2004: n.pag.). Some sketches are graphical, where the viewer can clearly identify, for example, a logo, a menu bar, and a photograph of a person holding an apple. Other sketches are more abstract – geometric shapes and squiggly lines are used as representations of future content. Still other sketches are primarily textual, and take the form of concept maps or brainstorming sessions. Graphical sketches may include textual or interactive components in the form of annotations or sticky notes outlining content, layout, or interaction ideas (Landay and Myers 1996). Depending on the level of detail or complexity found in a sketch, it may function either as a designer's object of reflection or as a way to gather user feedback at various stages of a project.

Below are a few of the more common sketch types:

- *Concept maps*: Visual representations of ideas through networks consisting of nodes, links, and (often) text labels (Lanzing 1997);
- *Single or multi-page sketches*: Quick and loose drawings establishing the overall concept and direction of the design piece;
- *Storyboards*: Sketches arranged along a panel or series of panels;
- *Video sketches* (also called video prototypes) (Löwgren 2004): Scenarios that use sketches to enact and record the use of a design piece;

- *Animated use sketches* (Löwgren 2004): Movie scenarios, showing the use of an envisioned design, created using cut-out animation, primitive motion, and a simple soundtrack; and
- *Low-fidelity mock-ups* (Landay 1996): Sketches that include cut-up and glued components, post-it notes, and fold-outs.

Design sketches are meant to be quick, disposable, iterative (evolutionary), and lacking in detail. As long as the sketches are good enough that they capture the necessary elements, drawing skill is unnecessary. In fact, the appearance of a sketch – its looseness and energy – is intended to convey the invitation to the self and to others that this concept is open for people to criticize and suggest alternatives.

The quick and rough nature of sketches is what makes them such a powerful design tool. The design representations are ill-defined because the ideas themselves, at that particular stage of the process, are also ill-defined (Kavakli et al. 1998). Concept maps, single and multi-page sketches, and storyboards tend to embody most clearly these 'quick and rough' attributes, while video sketches, animated use sketches, and low-fidelity mock-ups tend to illustrate ideas that have gone through some level of refinement. Other, commonly used design process visualization tools such as interactive and non-interactive paper or digital prototypes tend to have undergone even more iteration.

3.2.2 Three forms of user-centred design

With respect to the degree to which a design methodology incorporates insights from the users, it is possible to establish a pair of difference poles within the terrain of reasonable practice. It has been a long-established principle in the computer science community, for example, that the systems development life cycle needs to include stages that involve relevant information being collected from the user by the programmer, designer, systems analyst, or project manager (depending on how far one wants to move up the hierarchy). In the watershed model of systems design, the primary phase for this data collection is during the definition of requirements, although additional input might also be sought during the design phase proper, and certainly end-user testing will occur at some point before the final applications are rolled into production. In the slightly more sophisticated spiral models of systems design, the process is clearly seen as iterative, with various checkpoints for user involvement and feedback.

The solicitation of user input in the watershed model might be established as one difference pole. Typically, in spite of what might seem at the theoretical level to be an adequate degree of user involvement in the process, a programming team working in COBOL on a mainframe in the 1970s or 1980s would have had almost no direct interaction with the final users of the system. One of our co-authors actually received a written reprimand from an immediate superior for contacting a manager from another division, the end user of the MIS reporting package the author had been assigned to develop. Conversations about user requirements with an actual user were seen as violating the chain of command to an extent that was essentially outside the bounds of contemporary discourse, at least in that environment. Although there are many good reasons for a well-established protocol for information exchange, including adequate record-keeping, project accountability, and the logistics of time and resource management, such procedures can have the disadvantage of rendering the user's actual requirements opaque to the people who need to try to address those requirements.

Moving further along the spectrum, a significant milestone could be placed at the point where interface designers are able to position themselves within the framework of 'human-centred design'. In recognizing not only that minimizing contact between application development staff and end users poses fundamental problems in application design, but also that genuinely useful communication activities in the form of intelligence-gathering methodologies are not straightforward, human-centred designers as early as the late 1960s have been looking to the social sciences for suggestions. By coupling such strategies as structured interviews, questionnaires, focus groups, participant observation, and video ethnography with an equally wide range of instruments for prototyping and end-user testing, human-centred designers have made a tremendous contribution to the design and development not only of a wide range of products (both analog and digital), but also of the culture of design. As human-centred design advocate Jorge Frascara has pointed out, through applying the principles of thinking as human-centred designers, we have come to realize that no one can design a chair that will enable someone to sit and work at a desk for 8 hours a day. What we need to re-design is not the chair, but rather work itself.

Still further along the spectrum, and in fact establishing the current difference pole, is the domain of participatory design, which seeks to expand to an even greater extent the kinds of information obtained from the end user. Participatory designer advocates such as Jeannette Blomberg or Elizabeth Sanders attempt to situate the activities of designers within the native environment of the end-user community, in order to attain as great a degree of empathy as possible with the full extent of the user's needs. Sanders (2004), in fact, goes so far as to say that she tries to understand what her clients 'dream'.

Our current approach to participatory design is to involve the designer and end user working together to as significant a degree as possible in order to obtain the most useful artefact. For example, one of us worked for several years on the design of a field sales management system for a Calgary-based sales management outsourcing company. The strategy with this client was to implement a participatory design approach to the system by working in the client's own office with a single representative staff member. The end user had the advantage of working both as a field salesperson and a field sales manager, which allowed us to capture both kinds of domain knowledge necessary to the system. The project coupled the user's domain knowledge to the design solution, and also to the dynamics of the development process, which were iterative to a high degree. The designer had no domain knowledge whatsoever in field sales theory or practice before beginning the project, and the end user had no previous experience with systems development or database design.

The procedure we adopted was to begin with a simple working prototype that was implemented very near the beginning of the contract. We both understood not only that the interface would change, but also that the data model would develop through what was essentially experimental use. This prototype was then iteratively expanded (and also iteratively reduced) through a series of modifications. At certain checkpoints, where a fairly stable version was running, we would pause development and the user would simply work with the system, documenting problems or insights until the development process would resume.

From a design perspective, it was important to clearly define expectations concerning the importance of full participation by the end user, in the sense that what we were trying to do was model his brain, his methods of working on the computer. We were saying, in essence: 'Whatever you are already doing, that's what we need to capture. We want to take what you know about field sales, your best practices, and make them a part of this system'.

Another aspect of this project was the paradigm of situated activity, which we established as the working framework for our efforts. The principle is discussed by ethnomethodologist Lucy Suchman in her book *Plans and Situated Actions* (1987). Suchman was studying people who were trying (and largely failing) to use the functions on a photocopier with a traditional step-wise list of instructions. Her conclusion was that people in general cannot be expected to formulate a plan and follow it. Plans are created only when situated action fails (an insight that strikes me as highly reminiscent of Heidegger's 'unreadiness to hand', which results in a cognitive shift out of Dasein and into reflection). Situated actions are the responses people make to their environment, doing 'what comes naturally'. Within that paradigm, our work on the field sales management system was intended to create an artificial environment, complete with its own affordances, constraints, and natural mappings, which would enable the user to do the right thing by doing the default thing.

An example is the process of establishing time commitments across a wide range of projects. Within the situated activity of the interface environment, the completion of a task is marked by pushing a button called 'done' immediately next to the text describing what needed to be done and its reminder date (the propinquity of the button and fields is an example of natural mapping). One effect of pushing 'done' is that the text field is cleared (and archived) along with the date. A more-or-less natural consequence of the now-empty field is the user's cognitive awareness of the necessity for filling it with the next task in that project that should be done, along with an appropriate reminder date for that task. Using such a system requires little awareness of a larger plan, but rather takes the form of simply doing what is 'ready to hand'.

3.2.3 Design thinking

We have to admit this is a bit of a buzzword of the past. Popularized in the early 2000s by industrial design firms such as the US-based IDEO, it was an attempt, at best, to suggest that designers have a way of thinking about things that is different from how most people in an organization have been trained and rewarded for thinking. At worst, it was just a marketing tool to sell more design to more businesses.

It is an echo of Nigel Cross's phrase 'designerly ways of knowing', which itself invokes the three kinds of logic, as defined by the bewhiskered philosopher Charles Sanders Peirce (1839–1914). Most people are familiar with deduction, where the process is to take what we already know and rearrange it until we know something else. The evidence is before us, dear Watson, if only we knew how to see it. Some may also recognize induction, which suggests that if a thing is true for one instance and can be shown to be true for any arbitrary number of instances plus one, then it can be shown to be true in all cases. Whereas deduction only gives the illusion of new knowledge – because we are all Watson and not Holmes – induction can actually produce some.

The third kind of logic is a questionable kind at best, but is necessary to account for things like how do people come up with new ideas, scientists with new hypotheses, writers with new novels, and so on. Called abduction, it has been embraced as the key mode of thinking of designers. In the design process, the use of abduction is sometimes called ideation, which is a word designed primarily to give English-speaking people outside the United States conniption fits.

In practical terms, design thinking implies that there should be particular administrative practices and structures in place for managing designers, since to treat them like the rest of the staff is going to result in poor performance and perhaps a marked lack of actual designers willing to work in the company. In impractical terms, it implies that anyone can be a designer, as long as they are sufficient in jazz hands. Actually, as Frascara (see Ruecker, 2018: 41) points out,

'Yes, anybody can be a designer. Of course, if you go five years to a design school, and you practice for 20 years, you can be a designer, but it takes more than reading one book'.

3.2.4 Reframing

Generally speaking, when people are assigned a task in writing, they may ask for some clarification, but they will attempt to accomplish the task. For designers, however, the situation is somewhat different. It is a part of the lore of the discipline that clients often ask for something they don't really want or need, and it is up to the designer to think through the situation from a broader perspective and suggest alternatives. In some respects, this is making a virtue out of necessity, since coming up with alternatives is one of the core skills of a designer, and you can't really stop them from doing it anyway. So you might as well embrace it. This is called reframing the brief.

A classic example provided by Wiseman and Sless (2006) had to do with a signage project for a hospital. Hospitals, like many public buildings, can be impossible for first-time users to navigate. They are labyrinths, with some sections open to civilians, others closed, and still others in some liminal zone where the public is welcome under certain circumstances but not others. In addition, the people who are doing the navigating are often not at their best, or they wouldn't be in a hospital to begin with.

Faced with this problem, Sless and his team decided to spend some time in the hospital themselves, getting some primary research done through observations, interviews, intercepts, and so on. What they determined was that the complexity of the system was such that no amount of signage would improve things: in fact, it was likelier to just add to the confusion. Instead, they noticed a particular volunteer at one of the entrances. He had drawn a rough map of the buildings, photocopied it, and whenever someone asked him for help, he would hand them a copy of the map and fill in the navigational details needed by that particular visitor.

The design project was therefore reframed, and what they created was a system to make sure that all the greeters had this tool and had been trained to use it. The original brief had called for signage. The actual problem was navigation. The solution was not, in the end, signage. This is reframing. Needless to say, not every client likes it or wants it to happen, but it is good for designers to have the opportunity to try it, and if at the end of the day, signage is what will help, they will produce it with more confidence for having thought about the larger situation and considered some alternatives.

3.2.5 Gestalt

You won't spend much time around designers before you hear mention of the Gestalt principles. Design is a field that is still in the process of developing its own ways of understanding the world and creating new knowledge (cf. Frayling 1993; Forlizziet al. 2009; Gaver 2012), but it has a long history of importing for practical purposes what people have figured out in other fields.

The Gestalt psychologists, for instance, were a group of scholars working in the 1920s in Germany who began to realize that people were capable of seeing a part of something and recognizing the whole (e.g. Koffka 1935). You've experienced the Gestalt phenomenon of Closure whenever you've looked at a magazine cover where the title is partially obscured by the image, yet you still know what the title is (Figure 3.4).

This was great news for visual communication designers, who either now had food for thought, or else suddenly had someone to point to as an authority whenever they used tricks like that.

Here is a summary of the principles that were of most interest to designers:

- *Proximity*: Things close to each other will typically be understood as belonging together;
- *Similarity*: Things that share attributes (e.g. colour, size, shape) belong together;

FIGURE 3.4: The Gestalt principle of closure doing its good work. In your mind.

- *Closure*: A partially obscured item or one with pieces missing will be perceived as a whole; and
- *Continuity*: People can easily fill in a complete line if they see a line with breaks in it.

They also provided some 'laws' that were less immediately useful for design, but which still bear thinking about. These include:

- *Symmetry*: When faced with an asymmetrical item, people will spend energy trying to find symmetry;
- *Past experience*: Two items seen in a short interval will tend to be grouped together;
- *Common fate*: Objects are perceived as lines that move along the smoothest path; and
- *Good gestalt*: Elements of objects tend to be perceptually grouped together if they form a pattern that is regular, simple, and orderly.

More work has been done since the 1920s, including some consideration of what principles should be applied to moving objects. For example, Kim (2007) studied the addition of time as a new element for the perception of grouping in video. In particular, he looked at six phenomena. The first three were inconclusive, but he found significant evidence to support the last three:

- *Motion proximity*: Frequent and regular movements;
- *Motion similarity by direction*;
- *Motion similarity by speed*;
- *Motion common-fate*: Parallel movement in replication for concurrent and harmonious movement;
- *Motion good-continuation*: A causative logic of motion relating to different linked circumstances; and
- *Motion closure*: Semantic summarization directed to completion.

There are also a variety of websites that discuss the Gestalt principles. Many include others that were not on the original list. For example, the Interaction Design Foundation in Denmark lists more than a dozen, including:

- common region;
- convexity;
- figure/ground;
- good form;

- familiarity;
- prägnanz;
- regularity; and
- synchrony.

3.2.6 Conclusion

For digital humanists working with designers, taking onboard this handful of terms and a few more, making them part of your working vocabulary, will go a long way towards improving the effectiveness of the daily conversations. It will also demonstrably indicate a respect for the domain knowledge of the people you are working with. That is a two-way street, of course, but you can only be responsible for the side of the street you are on.

3.3 Claim games

It is necessary to disentangle a number of similarly overlapping terms, such as text, image, structure, hierarchy, format, rhetoric, metaphor, sketch, project, prototype, publication, abstract, research, and attention to detail.

3.3.1 Research

Design and DH have both suffered in the past from being understood primarily as applied disciplines, meaning that research happened somewhere else and you went to design or DH when you needed a website. Thankfully, that perception has been rapidly changing, and both fields are now recognized as having their own contributions to knowledge.

However, there is still plenty of room for confusion. As a reminder of what we've covered in more detail earlier, Ruecker and Roberts-Smith (2018) have argued that there are at least four different ways that the university develops new knowledge. In the sciences, theories are pitted against one another in the cage fight of experiments, and winner takes all. The humanities, on the other hand, are happy to have multiple theories exist simultaneously. They don't have to co-exist harmoniously, or even have mutual awareness, as long as they all contribute to a richer understanding of the object of study. In the fine arts, the mode is primarily what we might call the exploratory expressive, where the goal is to capture some unique or at least unusual subjective understanding that can be communicated or shared. Finally, there are the generative disciplines, where the knowledge is primarily concerned with what does not yet exist.

Insofar as DH is about learning through making, it can be understood as a generative discipline, like design, computer science, engineering, synthetic chemistry, nanotechnology, and so on. However, DH also has deep roots in the humanities, where the aggregative mode predominates. Humanities scholars in fact seldom use the word 'research', since it has connotations for them that are not appropriate to the production and application of new theories that are not intended to compete or supplant the old ones, but instead to add new perspectives. There has consequently been a lot of debate over the years, arising largely from this mutual misunderstanding of what knowledge is and how it gets created. Coming from the humanities side, DH seems woefully 'under-theorized'. From the digital perspective, which is closer to design, knowledge is developed through new objects, processes, protocols, and so on. As Galey and Ruecker (2010) put it, a prototype is an argument.

So how do we get these two epistemological modes of knowledge production to become aware of each other in a way that respects and maintains both traditions, while at the same time allowing them to work together in creating new knowledge?

3.3.2 Projects and research projects

In the design world, a project is usually preceded by a brief that outlines the goals of the client, so that anything extending beyond those goals needs to be negotiated, in order to avoid scope creep. One of the first things many designers will do is challenge the brief, through a step in the design process called Reframing. The idea is that the client's goals and the opportunities that the designer sees are not necessarily immediately congruent, so it is only reasonable to check signals before the project begins.

The DH community has a similar sense of projects, in cases, for example, where the goal is to digitize a collection and populate it with metadata. In addition to being an academic task, this is also a management challenge, requiring the project leads to assemble a team that can carry out the often repetitive work over an extended period of time.

In the domain of academic research, design and DH both tend to guide the project by research questions rather than a brief. In addition, the design research approach is often to begin with experimental prototyping, as a means of quickly coming to understand some of the details of the question. This manner of proceeding can be uncomfortable at first for scholars from either field who are more used to the first way of working. The primary difference is that, rather than everything being mapped out in advance, the team will tend to find their way into the topic through iterative cycles of prototyping, analysis, and modelling.

3.3.3 Text

If ever there was a term that you would think is shared by multiple disciplines, it would be the word 'text'. Unfortunately, it is one of the more perilous ideas in terms of mutual misunderstanding. For most of the scholars in the humanities, and for many in DH, 'text' has valences that can be almost religious. They speak of clean text and corrupt text, of scholarly editions vs. mere reading editions, of canonical sources and errors in transmission. The library community even has a philosophical statement about what kind of text they are describing with their metadata. Called Functional Requirements for Bibliographic Records (FRBR), the description has four levels: work, expression, manifestation, and item. A work is the text in the head of the author; its expression is the text the author puts on the page; the manifestation is an edition that gets published; an item is the individual copy that a person can hold in their hand or read on the screen. Put more formally, using the correct verbs, a work is realized in an expression that is embodied in a manifestation that is exemplified in an item. All of which is to say that a lot of thought and effort has been put into the idea of a text.

For designers, on the other hand, text (or more often 'copy') is just another visual element, no more or less important than the images, figures, charts, or graphics on the same page, the lines and circles and boxes, the typeface and the white space. This absurdly cavalier attitude to the central object of attention and study can manifest itself in various ways, from the use of 'dummy' text like the notorious Lorem Ipsum – a chunk of fake Latin used by designers to 'show where the text will go' – to the much more dangerous anonymous version of the text just pulled from the web somewhere, God knows where, probably full of errors ranging from uncorrected optical character recognition ('dirty OCR') to simple lack of proper provenance. That the placeholder text will be replaced at some point with the real text just smacks of carelessness, if not actual disrespect, or perhaps callous ignorance about what is really important in this world. It is as though designers are in the habit of picking up humanist infants and swinging them around by one foot: not only is it ill-advised, but who does that?

The lesson here for designers is to be careful. The best approach is to get the text right in the first place, asking for the proper version and treating it with the respect it deserves at every stage of the process. Next best is to use the fake Latin, since, while it is offensive, it is not also potentially misleading. Taking the lead from the humanists in this matter will go a long way towards establishing yourself as a designer who is a colleague and peer to be taken seriously in your own area of expertise. The same can be said of humanists in the next section.

3.3.4 Image

In much the same way that the word 'text' is sacred to the Digital Humanists, designers tend to have a certain complex relationship with the word 'image'. Whether it is a photograph, illustration, diagram, exploded diagram, model, or doodle, the image is a fundamental unit of information and communication. While the humanities crowd were spending decades soaking themselves in words, the mathematicians in equations, the computer programmers in code, and so on, the designers were bathing in images, absorbing visual culture by surrounding themselves with it, selecting it, flipping through it, interrogating it in its history, changes, and variations in structure, form, and meaning. They sought it out, is what we're saying, gravitated towards it, and once they had it, they spent an awful lot of time looking and thinking, then going for more.

One consequence of this expertise is that for many years, there was a widely held belief that the primary job of the designer was to be an arbiter of taste. This was true to roughly the same extent that some humanists were arbiters of taste: they had an axe to grind, or more likely a living to make, in selecting and defending a particular slice, on the one hand of visual culture, and on the other the literary canon. And just as it is slightly distasteful for humanists to remember all the talk about a canon in literature, because we believe we have grown beyond it in both politics and understanding, so it is bruising to the ego of most designers to be reduced to being considered judges of style. You can make a racehorse pull a cart, but you shouldn't.

3.3.5 Prototypes

In principle and in practice, the use of prototypes in design and DH is perhaps surprisingly similar, given the many other differences that exist between the two fields. However, in both cases there are important distinctions to be made between various categories of prototypes. In general, there are three categories of prototype, which are intended for experiment, development, and provocation, respectively. Although it might be argued that the overlap between these three groups renders them useless, if they are construed correctly, it becomes clear that the distinctions are not only meaningful, but can also be suggestive of new methods of working.

The goal of the development prototype is always to reach a product, and it is in this respect that provocative and experimental prototypes differ. The purpose of an experimental prototype is to address a research question, typically by deliberately embodying some aspect of the problem so that it lends itself to closer inspection, understanding, and in some cases, testing. It would seem that testing is essential, but, in fact, it is possible to think of the prototype itself as a kind of direct evidence, as opposed to the evidence produced by seeing how people interact with the prototype.

De la Rosa (2017) argues that we can improve the resolution of our vision of the future through using experimental prototypes as a kind of aggregate lens around the research question (Figure 3.5). Instead of focusing on a single point, the idea is to layer clusters of prototypes that are slightly displaced from the focus of the project.

The goal of a provocative prototype, on the other hand, is to make some kind of a statement that challenges expectations. Sometimes called 'provotypes' (e.g., Boer and Donovan 2012), the purpose of provocative prototypes is distinct from either of the other two categories, in that they do not exist to address a research question or to lead to a product. Instead, their goal is to interrupt people's thinking, to astonish, to disturb – in short to provoke a reaction. In this respect, provotypes align most closely with the fine arts, although they are also a component in what is sometimes called 'critical design', 'speculative design', or even 'design fiction', where the focus is on designing objects that make some social, cultural, or political statement.

Another approach to prototyping is to think in terms of the domains they are setting out to help us understand. Human-centred designer Sharon Helmer Poggenpohl, in her 1999 paper 'Design Moves', describes the application of four kinds of prototypes by designers working at the Illinois Institute of Technology on 'the design of education'. Her prototypes, which are intended to investigate the conceptual, behavioural, procedural, and visual domains of the end user with respect to a given design solution, might all be classified as 'quick and dirty', in the sense that none of them require any substantial degree of technical resources. In fact, some of her prototypes are paper-based representations created in situ by a designer sitting down in conversation with end users, a pad of paper, and a marker.

3.3.6 Metaphors and other figures of speech

There may have been a time when designers, along with practically everyone else, thought of metaphors and other figures of speech primarily as literary tropes, firmly in the domain of the humanists. However, after Lakoff and Johnson (1980) and a few others, it became abundantly clear that among the many figures of speech, metaphors, at least, structure our lives and our thoughts at a pretty fundamental level. See what we did there? Even the idea of thoughts having a fundamental level is a metaphor, with the source being architecture and the target the nature of thought.

For designers, this awareness blossomed into exercises in the undergraduate classroom on the benefits of using metaphors in visual material. Humanists may

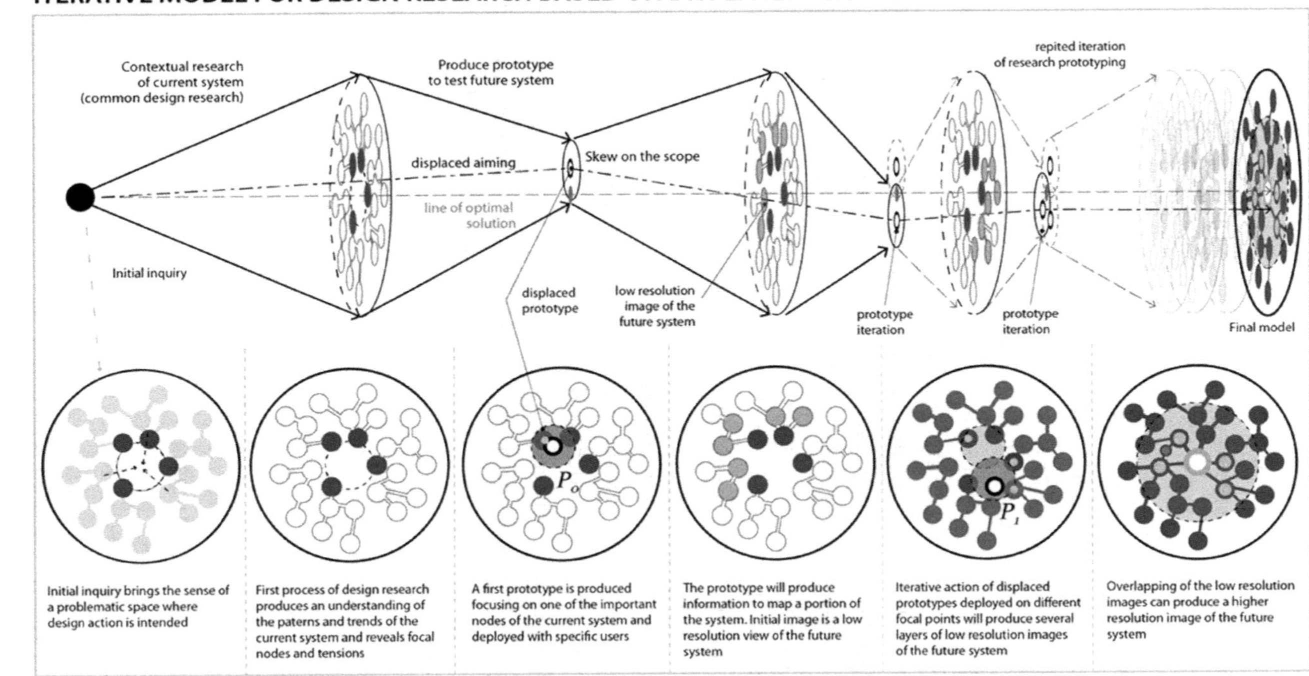

FIGURE 3.5: The conceptual space grows as researchers iterate on experimental prototypes (de la Rosa and Ruecker 2019).

be surprised to hear that for many of them, this was not a straightforward task. The very nature of the visual is that it tends to stand for itself rather than something else, so there had to be clues built in to let people know what aspects of the source were being referenced, and what the intended target was. Not every experiment went well. Go too literal and you just get the visual equivalent of a pun. Too obscure and you risk people not making the connection. Then there is the question of whether you try to convert a metaphor that already exists in words into a visual form, or whether you are better off to start from scratch.

Lakoff and Johnson's book was part of an interdisciplinary intellectual movement that attempted to make the case that metaphor and metonymy are not rarefied literary conventions, but are in fact fundamental structuring mechanisms for human thought. They drew on a wide range of examples to the effect that human language reflects this fundamental metaphoric structuring in many ways. For example, when someone uses an expression like 'I'm in trouble', or 'We're getting out of our current mortgage', there is an underlying idea of containment that has its basis in physical models of the world. It is also possible to understand a variety of descriptions of emotional states as drawing on metaphors that can be quite consistent. For example, the idea of anger as a hot, contained gas that builds pressure finds expression in phrases such as 'he blew his top' or 'she exploded'.

A related discussion occurs in Appleton's 1975 book *The Experience of Landscape*, in which he proposes that there are phylogenically predetermined responses to the environment that can be identified and manipulated symbolically. According to Appleton, three crucial aspects of our awareness of landscape are the degrees to which it affords prospect, refuge, and hazard. His argument is that somewhere in the past of the human species, these aspects of landscape had survival value, and although the necessity for evaluating a given landscape in these ways is not usually a part of contemporary survival, the biological mechanisms still exist. He proposes that these mechanisms are the basis for our affective experience of both painted landscapes and verbal descriptions. If he is correct, then the landscape metaphor may prove to be a particularly useful structuring mechanism for computer interfaces.

Choosing to use a central structural metaphor for an interface design is an activity that has had some discussion in the computer-human interface literature. William Stubblefield, for example, reports on a project where the objective was to create an automated system for identifying potential machinability problems for an industrial parts manufacturer. His team decided to adopt the metaphor of the 'spelling checker' that would review an object and its parts in much the same way that a spelling checker scans a document, looking for errors. Their finding was that the metaphor was a powerful tool in the design process, and was quickly adopted and used by a geographically scattered team. It therefore contributed to coordinating efforts where communication was difficult, and resulted in the rapid development of a working prototype. It also worked as a means of discussing the project with end users, who continued to use the metaphor once the system was in production.

The problems Stubblefield reports are also interesting. The final product was in fact nothing like a spelling checker, since in practical terms the metaphor was too restrictive. A physical device is not like a text document, in that it is not necessarily linear. So, there were decisions that had to be made about the process of traversal, which would not have had to have been made if that condition of linearity had been met. A spelling checker is also not open to query until the document is being checked, which posed a serious limitation on the machinability checker, since the engineers preferred to be able to stop and review particular machining parameters during the early stages of device design, rather than waiting until a completed specification was in place that would then have to be subjected to error detection.

Stubblefield also felt that software design solutions were not introduced in some cases because the mental model of the spelling checker constrained the discourse in such a way that only solutions fitting the metaphor were brought to the table, even when such solutions were not necessarily the best ones. This problem is related to the concepts of failed, positive, negative, and overzealous metaphoric transfer that are discussed in Schwartz et al. (2012).

A similar warning about the use of strong, central design metaphors was issued by Stiemerling et al. (1997) in their discussion of the design of an office automation system. They experienced some strong negative feedback from the early testers of their system when their implementation of the desktop metaphor fell short of the users' expectations. Although the users had been told they should think of the new system as being a virtual representation of their physical desk, the designers had allowed public access to certain documents. One user responded by formulating a stronger metaphor: 'My desk is my castle!'

With respect to the use of a landscape metaphor for interface design, the question immediately arises as to the degree to which such a metaphor should be interpreted literally for the case of an interface designed to represent or investigate text. In general, too-literal an interpretation of any design metaphor is often at least as bad as having no central metaphor at all. Mullet and Sano (1995), for instance, include literal interpretations as one of the pitfalls of GUI designers. Which is not to say that topographical methods of providing prospect on a document collection are necessarily too extreme.

Much of our own work has involved the use of landscape metaphors in virtual environments. A number of principles for this kind of work were suggested by Norman Vinson (1999), in his paper 'Design guidelines for landmarks to support navigation in virtual environments'. Vinson draws on experience in real-world landscapes to formulate advice such as: 'make the landmarks visible', and 'don't make them also represent data', since they would then of necessity need to have the characteristics of data representation rather than the characteristics needed by a good landmark. He also suggests using all five kinds of landmarks found in physical environments, as identified by Kevin Lynch in his 1960 book *The Image of the City*: paths, edges, nodes, districts, and landmarks proper.

Our own thinking about the use of landscape metaphors in designing an interface to text collections is quite modest by the standards of the designers of virtual reality. We think that Appleton is correct in suggesting that symbolic representations are quite sufficient to evoke an awareness of the metaphor. We would therefore suggest that symbolic forms of prospect, refuge, and hazard be used in creating an interface that has the familiarity of a landscape without the literal construction. For example, Appleton points out that the upper portion of a picture is naturally mapped to prospect, while the lower half tends to be associated with refuge.

An implementation of this idea might therefore put the part of the interface intended to give an overview of the collection at the top of the screen. These kinds of decisions can tend to sound somewhat trivial when discussed explicitly, and yet there is also a sense in which the strongest perceptual paradigms are those which seem after identification to be almost mind-numbingly obvious.

And metaphors are not the only challenge. We also have the various forms of metonymy, where the A that stands for B is already a part of B. Conceptually, letting A and B emerge only from their shared aspects is much more liberating than insisting that A represent the B of which it is already a part.

3.3.7 Iteration

The final concept that needs to be unpacked a bit is iteration. For the people in DH, iteration can be synonymous with repetition. We learn to carry out a piece of text encoding, then iterate through all the items in the collection, systematically applying the encoding so that the entire text is infused with it.

In design, on the other hand, while iteration can mean repetition with minor variation, such as when we are building a new product or service, it can also mean discarding the previous concept altogether. In those cases, what is being iterated is the work towards a viable understanding. This approach can be deeply alarming for DH people who were under the impression that a project moves ahead systematically and not by what might be understood as fits and starts.

The goal, however, is not to drive others mad, but rather to make sure that the conceptual space has been sufficiently explored before converging on an outcome. Otherwise, the designers feel that they have run the risk of 'solving a problem', which more often than not means taking the first hare-brained idea that comes to anyone's mind when facing the problem, and trying bootlessly to make it work.

3.3.8 Conclusion

A little caution around vocabulary similarities can go a long way in avoiding the problems that can arise on a project when different people are using the same terms of art to mean or even just to imply very different things. Although we are not necessarily always comfortable with admitting lack of knowledge, on interdisciplinary projects it is one of the times when it is not only expected, but actually required, if things are going to run smoothly.

3.4 Case study 2: What is a book?

To a designer a book is, before all else, a created, manufactured object; an object that has use and function, and that exists for multiple reasons. A book might be a single-use guilty pleasure, or the gateway to personal growth with pencil marks, coffee cup stains, and generational fingerprints. Books are bound memories, status symbols and, when lined up on shelves, good ways to judge your Tinder date. They are more than words on a page; books are colour, rhythm, and texture. While lines, paragraphs, and pages propel us forward, book covers intercept our movement. They call to or repel us. At a glance, we know their fraternity and the quality of their vendor. The primary job of cover design is to create love at first sight; and the job of the book block design (the inner part of the book) is to interpret and communicate the text. Together, the content, style, format, layout, and sequence of the various components form a coherent whole.

A well-designed book must consider certain principles, processes, and practices, and to many designers those are grounded in a history of lead type and manual composition. Books are the colour, thickness, size, and rigidity of their paper. They are the printing process and the colour of ink. They are named designers: Franklin Gothic, well paired with Baskerville. In *Elements of Typographic Style*, Robert Bringhurst calls this the 'grand design':

> In a badly designed book, the letters mill and stand like starving horses in a field. In a book designed by rote, they sit like stale bread and mutton on the page. In a well-made book, where designer, compositor and printer have all done their jobs,

> no matter how many thousands of lines and pages they must occupy, the letters are alive. They dance in their seats. Sometimes they rise and dance in the margins and aisles.
>
> (Bringhurst 1992: 19)

Much of what is used to define a book – its concreteness and embodiment, and the publishing and distribution process – is being called into question by digital distribution, self-publishing, interactivity, and commenting. While some print practices have carried over to the design of electronic books, others (Dr Michura's work, for example) are loosely translated acts of deliberate departure. Individual researchers and scholars, as well as large, multidisciplinary teams – in design and DH – have worked to understand the intersection of the written human record and technology. In an exploratory 2002 study, for example, Ruecker asked the opinions and practices associated with books and readership of a group of English graduate students (Ruecker 2002: 135–46). They divided the discussion into five human factors and found that 'emotional involvement with the many pleasures related to books was central to the experience: for this cohort, books are far from being a simple vehicle for content'. In terms of requirements, this study found that book design should provide all the functional advantages of the electronic medium, but captured in a form that is more like a book and less like a laptop, with 'pages that turn, and a different spine and cover for each book'.

More recently, the Implementing New Knowledge Environments (INKE) project, funded by the Canadian Social Science and Humanities Research Council Major Collaborative Research Initiatives Program between 2009 and 2015, sought to explore the future of reading and the book through a historical perspective. INKE brought together researchers and stakeholders from the humanities, text analysis, information studies, usability, and design, resulting in 15 working tools and prototypes. The work that emerged from INKE is an excellent, multi-year case study of digital humanists and designers working together around a topic of mutual interest and expertise – the book. The tools and prototypes that emerged from said collaboration tackled reading and the book from the perspective of one or more levels of granularity: micro, meso, and macro, an extension of Ruecker's Rich Prospect Browsing theory (RPB).

RPB builds on work by Appleton on prospect and by Gibson on affordances, proposing a new category of interactive displays for visually exploring digital collections. Appleton first introduced the concept of prospect in order to answer the question: 'what is it that we like about landscape, and why do we like it?' (Appleton 1975: 1). His data consisted of responses by critics to landscape paintings, through which he identified two features of landscape that are directly related to survival for people and animals in a natural environment: prospect and refuge. Prospect refers to the human and animal desire to see without obstruction; and refuge refers to the human and animal desire to hide from view (Appleton 1975: 73). The term 'affordance' has been defined by Gibson (1979: 127–140) as possible actions that exist within an environment, and by Norman as the perceived and actual properties of an object, particularly in terms of how it may be most obviously used: for example, 'a chair affords ("is for") support, and, therefore, affords sitting' (Norman 1990). Affordances can be objectively measured; though they exist independently of the individual's ability to recognize them, they are dependent on the individual's ability to act on them. That ability to act is unique to each individual.

RPB aims to challenge one of the fundamental tenets of information retrieval, exemplified by the Google search box: that users are not able to handle large amounts of information; that they need to be protected from it; and guided by various sorting and filtering strategies, devised for them by information-handling specialists (information architects, programmers, usability specialists, etc.). It proposes an alternative model for collections that contain thousands or fewer entries, where people are offered the opportunity to browse the entire contents. In proposing RPB, Ruecker argues that the 'two technologies are not mutually exclusive'; however, combining retrieval and retrieval results within one browsing space provides certain perceptual advantages and new opportunities for action (Ruecker et al. 2011: 28). Thus, in a browsing interface every item in a collection is assigned a visual representation. All items are displayed at once, and users are provided with a set of tools for manipulating – organizing, sorting, filtering – the items in the display. Ruecker posits that RPB interfaces provide affordances – opportunities for action – that are not found in other kinds of interfaces, communicating information about the size of a collection, the kinds of items that make up its contents, how those items are organized, and whether the collection includes any significant features (Ruecker et al. 2011: 153).

In the ten years since its initial proposal, RPB has been applied to a wide range of projects, including, but not limited to, the design of human-computer interfaces for browsing books, conference delegates, pills, research faculty, environmental sustainability projects, medieval woodcuts, heritage buildings, and electron microscope images of wasp wings. These projects have dealt with the design of interfaces for collections that consisted of hundreds, thousands, or sometimes tens of thousands of items, either represented textually, graphically, or both. Most aimed to propose a radical departure from existing browsing models.

The value of the micro and the macro has been considered by numerous, diverse disciplines. In sociological study, macro-level looks at large-scale social processes, for example, social stability, change, law, bureaucracy, and technology; while micro-level considers small-scale interactions between individuals, for example, conversation, patterns of behaviour, and group dynamics (Boundless n.d.). In philosophy of engineering, micro examines the level of individual actors within organizations, meso the intermediate level of organizations, and macro the level of social institutions (Li 2012: 23). In business innovation, problems in decision-making are considered at the micro (individual firm) and macro (aggregate) levels (Bridges, Coughlan, and Kalish: 1991).

In DH, Moretti's call for distant reading (2013: ff.) continues to be hotly debated. While Manovich (2002: n.pag.) calls databases and narratives 'natural enemies' and Whitley (2011: 188) assumes that literary critics 'value close reading [...] over the broad brushstrokes of information visualization', Hoover (2015: n.pag.) criticizes the 'marginalization of textual analysis and other text-centered approaches'. Ross, in her review of *Distant Reading*, on the other hand, writes that surface reading, distant reading, and DH are not inherently in opposition to close reading – it is the potential for the development of bad reading habits that is the concern. Thus, she argues for considering 'new forms of analysis' and suggests that 'moving back and forth between the microscopy of close reading

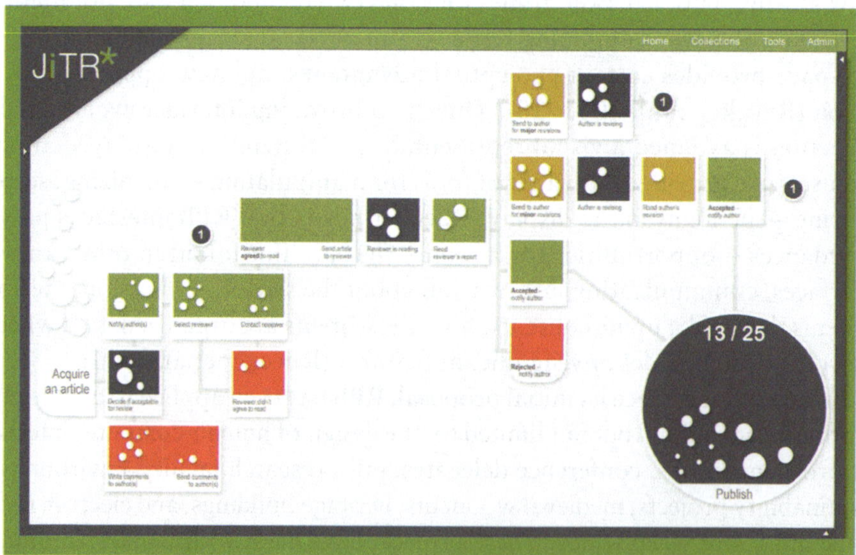

FIGURE 3.6: In the workflow for journal editors project, for example, the team introduced the concept of structured surfaces, extending the metaphor of interactive digital pins on a digital map into interactive digital pins on any data visualization (Radzikowska et al. 2011). The resulting interface is a reimagining of the flowchart of activities that an editor can use to manage the movement of a submitted article or other item of text (such as a book review) through the stages from its initial appearance in the editor's inbox to the final step where it is ready to be sent to the printer. The interface features an abstracted macro view on the entire editorial process.

and the wide-angle lens of distant reading would enrich both methods, creating a dual perspective that boasts both specificity and significance' (Ross 2014: n.pag.).

It may be argued that Rich Prospect Browsing Theory, in some ways, supports macro and micro views through its simultaneous display of every item in a collection and the availability of information on individual items. For example, the Mandala Browser (see Figure 3.7) shows a macro view on the entirety of *Romeo and Juliet*, with each speech in the play displayed as one dot. When a user clicks on a dot, she can read the corresponding speech in a text frame located to the right of the browser, receiving the micro, textual view on the speech. However, the visualization itself – the graphical display – does not offer multiple views. A design that supports macro, meso, and micro views would shift between these views, revealing new, detailed information as it did.

If we accept that the meaningful display of all items in a collection, fundamental to rich prospect browsers, positions the display at the meso layer – that the meso layer is the starting point for the browsing of all RP displays – then we can begin questioning what would be revealed by zooming out to the macro view and zooming in to a micro view of a display. We can also consider whether the change between views would function as a binary switch or a gradation. The MtV (Multitouch Variorum) tool developed by the INKE team attempts to explore the

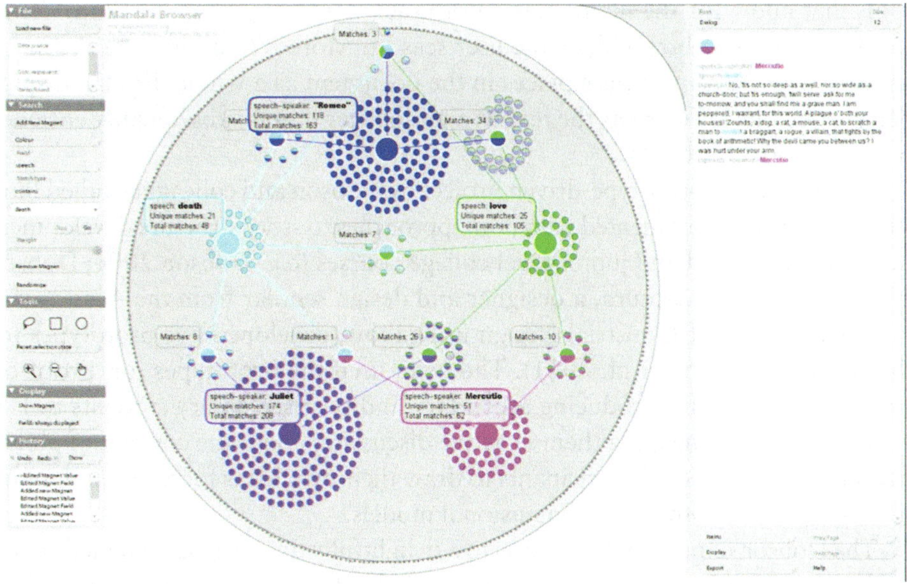

FIGURE 3.7: The Mandala Browser displaying an analysis of 'love' in Shakespeare's *Romeo and Juliet* (Mandala Application).

question of gradation through a multi-touch surface interface for text. The touch screen is meant to enable easy and intuitive operation through familiar gestures, thus lessening the mental workload required to operate it so users can focus on content. Collaborative work is facilitated as multiple people are able to work on the material at the same time. The interface shows a prospect (or macro) view on all the text in the collection, then supports a gestural zooming-in on an individual (or a subset of) document(s). The display is limited, however, in how many documents it can display at the same time and in a way that is still readable (useful) to the user.

Similarly, the Paper Drill interface aims to automate the identification and assemblage of citation chains throughout collections of secondary scholarship (citation chaining is the scholarly activity of finding relevant resources via the reference list of an article and also the articles that refer to that seed article). In the Paper Drill, users see all of the available citations displayed as coloured squares – an abstraction technique that permits the display of thousands of items on a single screen. The 'book' is redefined as one object that exists in a relationship with other objects.

The Dynamic Table of Contexts reflects on new digital allowances for developing digital texts and performing professional reading activities. Instead of porting a conventional table of contents into digital texts wholesale, the Dynamic Table of Contexts provokes readerly explorations and encourages a type of participation with a text that might not be available (or initially obvious) in more traditional, print-based forms. For example, the DTC supplements the table of contents with tools that allow for the manipulation of index items (via XML markup). Items can be added or subtracted, as the user sees fit. Moreover, all lines of the index are linked to the appropriate places in the document as a whole. From a display perspective, the DTC treats the text as a meso layer that is subsequently enriched with micro-levels of data.

In a non-INKE prototype-driven project by Dobson and colleagues called Plot-Vis, researchers experimented with new approaches to story structure development in secondary school and junior-level college courses (e.g. Dobson 2006; Dobson et al. 2011). Piotr Michura, a designer and design scholar from the Academy of Fine Arts School of Industrial Design in Krakow, developed five prototypes for that project (Dobson et al. 2011). The team used the prototypes for 'proof-of-concept feedback in introducing secondary and post-secondary students to DH visualization and engaging them in active discussion about the concept of plot in fiction'. They also asked participants to draw their own ideas for single and multiple timelines, and other two-dimensional models.

The Dobson experiments bring us to a delightfully divergent design method for exploring the book. This approach began with the strategy of removing the conventions of the codex page and starting over again with the rudimentary building blocks of text: words and sequences of words. In considering new interface designs for dealing with electronic text, a perennial difficulty is the prevalence of the metaphor of the page (Stoicheff and Taylor 2004). Although the codex page may be a good design solution for the printed book, it is not necessarily an optimum solution for digital text. In order to consider genuine visual alternatives, it is useful to strip away as many page conventions as possible and start from scratch in the new medium. By starting with a radically reduced representation of the document, we have the opportunity to consider configurations of text that can be developed through two-dimensional and three-dimensional manipulations of the text string.

This project is inspired in part by the 'Object Manipulation Model' conceived and described by John Bradley (2005). His approach, related to the concept of scholarly primitives, is to provide researchers with tools to support existing research processes at their various stages. He takes a look into 'little things' scholars do in their everyday practice and asks whether it is possible to devise ways that computers can 'augment' people's performance by taking advantage of the flexibility of digital text. Bradley uses the process of annotation as an example. Computer-assisted annotation involves the mental organization of information

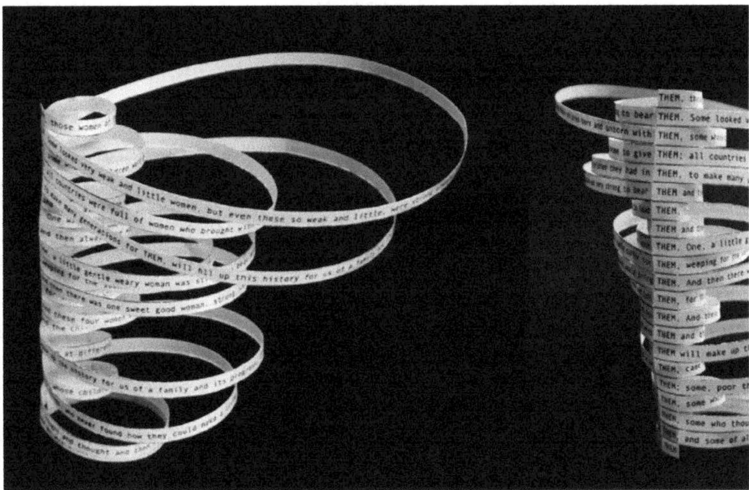

FIGURE 3.8: This paper prototype is a tactile alternative that emphasizes fragility and play. The designer has deconstructed the book into lines of text, cut them apart, then formed sentence loops which are aligned according to the repetition of a particular search term. The length of text between repetitions is indicated by the size of the loops. The advantage of this model as compared to 2D charts is that it is easier to get an overview of the text surrounding the chosen word, and the distance between occurrences is still easily compared (by juxtaposition of ring diameters) when the model is seen from the top or bottom (designed by P. Michura 2007; found in Ruecker et al., 2008).

in notes by directly mapping the relationships between the notes and the primary text into a visual structure – a diagram. The proposed form of the diagram is very flexible, permitting a wide range of interaction and allowing the user to arrange elements of the structure in a freehand way.

More recently, we've become interested in extending Dr Michura's ideas around text sculptures into a larger-scale 'materialization' project. We are interpreting materialization to mean: 'a process of transmutation that has elements of uncertainty and exigency'. The resulting Materializing Bubblelines project is an experiment in creating an alternative physical interface to a comparative search visualization in the voyant.org text analysis tool suite, called Bubblelines. Bubblelines is a text analysis and visualization tool that shows the frequency and repetition of a word's use in a corpus: text is turned into ones and zeros, then turned into lines and dots, actionable via touchpad stroke and key press. In its digital manifestation, Bubblelines is uncluttered in its aesthetic; it is responsive, and reasonably simple to use. We chose it because of its popularity in the DH community, our familiarity with its interface and output, and the good will of its creator Stéfan Sinclair in sharing his knowledge of it and its code.

In Bubblelines, a corpus is depicted using a uniform, horizontal line that is subdivided into segments of equal length. When a user selects or types in their own word, that word is represented as a bubble. The larger the bubble's radius, the more frequently that word occurs in the corresponding segment of a text. A user can select multiple texts and multiple words to visualize. Each text (document or chapter) gets its own line, and each word of interest is assigned its own bubble colour. Our material alternative, called the Milking Machine, consists of a series of vertical transparent tubes, each tube representing the complete document. The tubes are filled with multiple colours of particles (sand) that represent where search terms are located within the document. Thus, the tube is a material version of the line in the interface. At this point, however, the similarity between the digital and the materialized breaks: we've provided an additional level of detail to the analyst's experience through the choice of particles as metaphorical agents for the collection of typographic characters that make up the document. A document doesn't have the sterility of a line; a document is a patterned mess of meaning and emotion. When activated, the tubes begin to fill with plain-coloured sand and then, when the code encounters the term of interest within the document, with sand that has been dyed red. Each tube represents a different search term; from left to right, the terms we chose were: open, free, door, life, and days. In the span of two minutes, the tubes are full of sand, with the red bands illustrating the location of a search term within the text and its frequency. By comparing the tubes, the analyst is able to see how the use of search terms varies across the selected set of documents, or compare different search terms across the same document (see Figure 3.9).

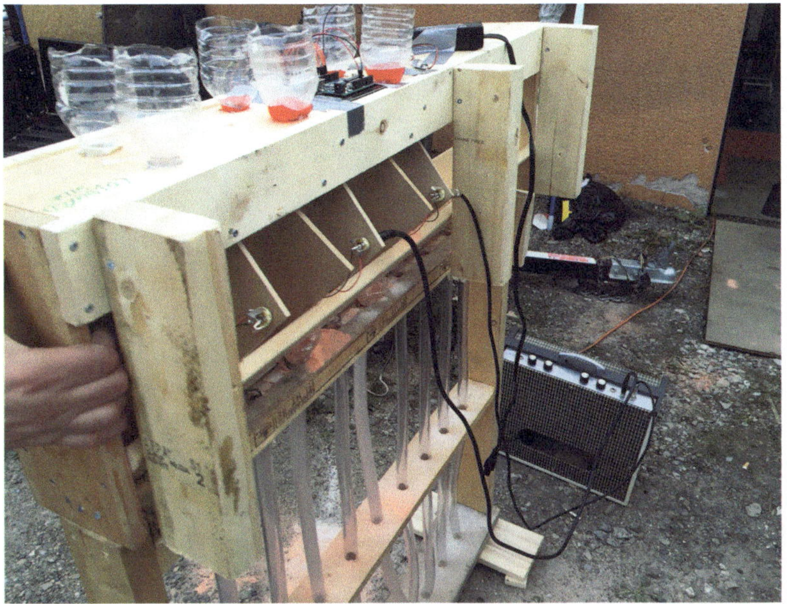

FIGURE 3.9: A material alternative to the digital Bubblelines (Radzikowska et al. 2021).

3.4.1 Conclusion

So, What is a Book? Through design, we are encouraged to consider the totality of the book – physical or digital – and the role and impact it has on individuals, communities, cultures, and environments. Beyond that totality, however, design can encourage us to imagine the book as it hasn't yet been, especially when such interrogation – we argue – takes place with an inclusive, energetic, and collaborative group of scholars.

3.5 Exercises: Collections and territories

Collections, museums, archives, and libraries are places where objects are amassed, examined, and displayed. They depend on some form of a system for the ordering and accessing of their contents. Classifications allow us to follow pre-created pathways, or uncover new connections. Self-directed structuring opportunities may reveal previously unperceived categories of phenomena. Imposing a new order upon things may charge them with new meaning.

The following series of exercises offer opportunities for perception, collection, categorization, and display of the kind often practiced by digital humanists.

3.5.1 Found arrays

What you'll need

- Camera (mobile phone is ok).
- A box to collect your objects.
- Some method for display.

Collect a specific category of objects or images. Choose a category that you have reasonably easy access to, such as erasers, toys, newspaper headlines, keys, or stickers. Develop a system of criteria, rational or otherwise, to classify and analyse your collection. Present your objects according to your system, with annotations if necessary. Your system should allow for others to view the collection through a particular lens (or point of view), focusing attention and provoking thought according to your specific intent.

FIGURE 3.10: Found array by M. Radzikowska.

3.5.2 Tiny museum

What you'll need

- Camera (mobile phone is ok).
- A box.
- Some method for display.

Choose an arbitrary category of items, then collect a set of items that fall under that category. Consider everyday objects, for example, objects of a particular shape or colour, things that fly, skulls, torn leaves, or medical instruments. Present them together in, first, a systemic order (a grid structure where the arrangement of items follows some logical pattern) and, second, incongruous juxtaposition. Display them in a cabinet or box frame. These objects, connected by their proximity to each other and their mutual confinement, take on new meaning – the whole becoming greater than the sum of the individual parts.

FIGURE 3.11: Tiny museum by M. Radzikowska.

3.5.3 Mundane patterns

What you'll need
- Camera (mobile phone is ok).
- Some method for display: digital or printed.

Decide on an unremarkable subject: gas stations, park benches, storm drains, etc. Photograph as many different examples as you can find. Avoid focusing on style – making them look any particular way. Your goal is to capture the ordinariness of the subject. Display them as a grid, column, line, or circle, in an album, printed book, or frame. For this piece, the idea is the most important, not the visual sophistication of the final result – your display becomes a collection of facts, without intentional rhetoric, positionality, or emotional appeal. Wait a week and then review your collection. Do you see any patterns in the choices you've made, or in their sequence? Ask a friend to look at it too; do they notice any themes?

FIGURE 3.12: Mundane patterns by M. Radzikowska.

3.5.4 Lives lived

What you'll need
- Camera (mobile phone is ok).
- A box.
- Some method for display.

Select an abandoned, failed, or forgotten endeavour, then collect its surviving physical evidence through photographs, stills from films, objects, and stories. You're looking for fragments or leave-behinds of lives once lived, adventures undertaken, follies, mistakes, or fantasies, tragedies or moments of triumph. Choose a way to display your collection. This could be through an installation, a presentation, or a scrapbook.

Few things are as striking as the remnants of another time, place, or lived experience. We are drawn to derelict buildings, abandoned towns, half-finished artworks, and broken fragments. Yesterday's people are moving and strange – ghostly and surreal – but traces locked in what's been left behind can lead us to rediscovering what once was, with us becoming part of the results.

3.5.5 Moodboard

What you'll need

- This can be a digital activity with online searching driving the collection gathering.
- Alternatively, you could collect and/or photograph actual objects and bring them into a physical space.

Select one of the following topics: agriculture, motherhood, criminals, disasters, or coal. Collect as much visual material based on that topic as you feel thoroughly covers its diversity and complexity. Feel free to start with a Google image search, but expand to literary references, sensory associations, and historical occurrences. Bring all the items you've collected into one space, then cluster them according to emergent themes. For example, if your topic was 'puppets', you might be looking at such sub-categories as wooden toys, scary clowns, finger puppets, homemade, and 'at the Smithsonian'. Look for patterns and similarities in the items located within one cluster, and what characteristics differentiate one cluster from another.

Moodboards are meant to help designers during the initial phase of a design process, when they're attempting to familiarize themselves with a particular subject area, as well as with a sample landscape of preceding (and in some ways related) design solutions. Looking at and thinking about existing design work is meant to support the extraction of knowledge that might be useful in subsequent phases of the design process. The moodboard helps to establish the context for the upcoming design work and quite often can lead to a shift in the definition of the actual design problem.

FIGURE 3.13: Google image search for Puppets.

3.5.6 Visual repertory grid

What you'll need

- Pencil or pen.
- Paper.
- Glue or tape.
- Scissors or exacto knife.
- Straight edge.
- Several sets of two pairs of colour images of different book covers for the same book.

Exercise type
Group or individual; works well with students.

Psychologist George Kelly was interested in methods to help researchers understand, not just what ideas people share, but what ideas they have on their own, and how they express those ideas to themselves. One result was a tool called the Repertory Grid, which puts a twist on the psychological method called Semantic Differentials.

Semantic Differentials put opposed terms on either end of a line. Participants then place items of interest along the line, between, for example, hot and cold, hard and soft, happy and sad, cheap and expensive.

FIGURE 3.14: An example visual repertory grid made from book covers of *Alice's Adventures in Wonderland*. The numbers indicate how strongly the image snippet represents the concept.

In the Repertory Grid, Kelly proposed that we replace the conventional terms with the specific phrases that people had in mind. So, on a repertory grid, one person might define 'hot' as 'too hot to touch', while another might say 'the surface of the sun' and another 'nice to drink on a cold day'.

In this exercise, folks can work individually or in groups. Pre-select a set of images on a single theme. One possibility is to find a collection of book covers that have been designed for the same book. Group the images into difference poles that they define themselves, by placing an exemplary image at each difference pole and labelling it with a sentence. For example, a pair of cover designs for *The Brothers Karamazov* might have one that is frightening and another that is funny. The poles might be defined as 'the tone of the illustration and the expressions on the faces make this a frightening cover', and 'the bright colours and comical situation here are funny'.

After a sufficient number of pairs has been established, take the other set of images, examine them for details that relate to each difference pole, then cut and paste those pieces of the images on the repertory grid in the proper place (Figure 3.14).

Finally, once the grids are complete, carry out a critique and discussion of the interpretive aspects of the experience: what 'arguments' were made about the covers, and how effective was the visual 'evidence' at substantiating those interpretations?

NOTE

1. A hammer for most of us, for example, is 'ready-to-hand' in that we use it without theorizing.

4

Meeting points

For people who are ready to begin interdisciplinary research collaborations or who want to reflect on those they have already been a part of, this chapter goes into some detail on a number of projects we have experienced, providing insights into what shared research among designers and digital humanists might look like. We conclude with a humanities-style analysis of a somewhat unusual collaboration, where experimental practices from digital humanities (DH) and design were brought to bear on a project in engineering.

4.1 Humanities visualization

When you start thinking about design and DH and some productive ways they might work together, a natural point of intersection is data visualization. For DH researchers, having useful new ways of seeing their object of study supports the core hermeneutic agenda (e.g. Ramsay 2011), by adding a new interpretive lens. Most humanist researchers are not expecting to crunch the numbers and get an answer, but they can crunch the numbers and get some new insights worth examining using their usual process: making cases for a particular way of understanding, using some combination of evidence and argument.

For the design researchers, the challenge of inventing new tools for helping the interpretive process is quite different from inventing new ways of helping people who have crunched the numbers see the answers. Some designers will have experience with one or the other or both, although for many, it may be a new kind of project. Ideally, this will involve more than simply applying the current best practices of design to the data visualization challenges of DH. Instead, the various approaches should result in insights into some larger research question that can be of general use for future designers making decisions.

For example, in our own work, we developed a number of visualizations around the idea that many humanities collections consist of 5,000 items or less, and could therefore all be represented on the screen at the same time (cf. Ruecker et al. 2011). By giving people this prospect on their collection, we argued that they might gain insights that would otherwise be difficult or impossible to attain. In addition, our theory suggests that for each collection, there will be an emergent set of tools that can be used to manipulate the display, and if these are identified and developed, further insights will be possible. Finally, we agree with Brown et al. (2006), Rodgers (2000), and Bederson (2011) on the point that it is always going to be helpful to make it easy for researchers to zoom in and out from the prospect view to the detailed reading view.

Unfortunately, for the most part these experiments were tied to the need, not just to test out new ideas, but to actually produce working tools for the DH audience. As a result, the projects ran longer, required more resources, and did not always produce sufficiently robust experimental evidence. On the other hand, they did contribute to several working systems.

Finally, we can ask whether or not involving both designers and DHers on the same project team is actually worth the time and effort it takes. Certainly, either group working alone can produce their own interfaces without input from the other. However, as in all interdisciplinary research projects, there is domain expertise involved that takes a significant effort to obtain, and beyond that, there is the positive experience of working with other scholars on a matter of shared interest.

4.1.1 Why graphical representation?

The goal of graphical data representation is to aid our understanding of information by leveraging the human visual system's highly tuned ability to see patterns, spot trends, and identify outliers. Well-designed visual representations can replace cognitive calculations with simple perceptual inferences and improve comprehension, memory, and decision-making (Suda 2010: 117). By making data more accessible and appealing, visual representations may also help engage more diverse audiences in exploration and analysis. The challenge is to create effective and engaging visualizations that are appropriate to the data, and that leverage past experience with similar graphical objects. The limited set of visualization examples described below are meant to illustrate the ways graphical data representation can help us filter information according to relevance, and to discover patterns and connections among items. Lima (2011: 123) argues that visualization will soon become indispensable, with technological advancements offering increased opportunity to collect, store, connect, and access data on an ever more massive scale. Not only are we becoming increasingly inundated with information, but we also need a support 'mechanism to the various political, economic, cultural, sociological, and technological advances shaping the coming years' (Lima, 2011: 123). How do we enable the discovery of relevance? How is subsequent, relevant information communicated in ways that are heard above the din? These have become key questions for the future designers of data visualizations.

Graphical representations of data can be, themselves, complex and powerful visual objects. Tufte, for example, describes a map drawn in 1869 by the French engineer, Charles Joseph Minard, as 'War and Peace as told by a visual Tolstoy' (cited in Yaffa, 2015). This infographic, roughly the size of a car window, depicts the fate of Napoleon's Grand Army in the tragic 1812 campaign into Russia (see Figure 4.1). The map is read from left to right, then back to left again. A thick tan bar begins on the banks of the Niemen River, representing the initial invading force of 420,000 French soldiers. As the army marches east, towards Moscow, the tan bar narrows – the soldiers begin to die. The graphic is constructed from geometric shapes and sharp angles. Due to this restraint and a lack of literal depiction of the subject matter, the story of this sprawling, bloody horror takes a moment to sink in. As the French army turns back and the tan (now) line turns to black, we realize we are following the path of whatever French soldiers the Russians haven't killed in battle, as they die from cold and hunger. On November 28, half of the retreating army, 22,000 men, drowns as they attempt to cross the icy waters of the Berezina River – the already thinned, black line is suddenly reduced by half. The entire journey – there and back – takes a mere six months, with only one in forty-two soldiers returning home.

While Minard's map is a rich, multi-layered representation of a fairly constrained time and space, Emma Willard's immensely ambitious Picture of Nations attempts to trace the advent of human civilization across an expansive time and space (see Figure 4.2) (Willard, 2015). Her chart visualizes the progress

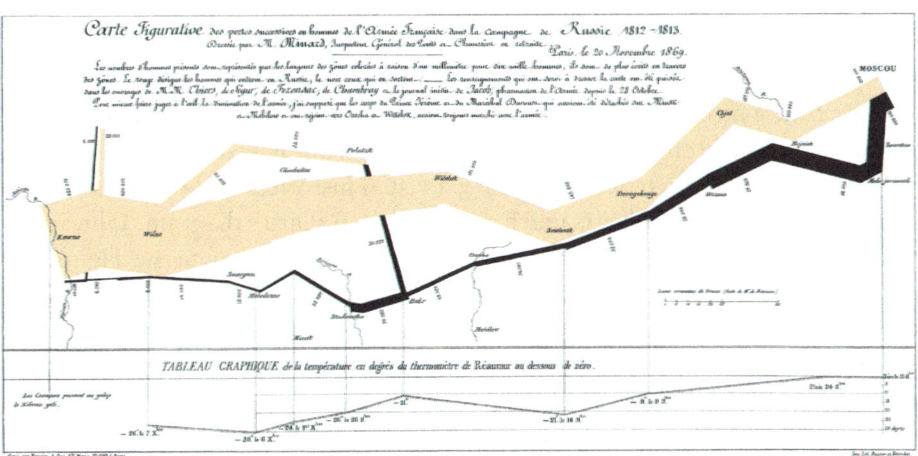

FIGURE 4.1: Charles Minard's map of Napoleon's Russian campaign of 1812 (Minard).

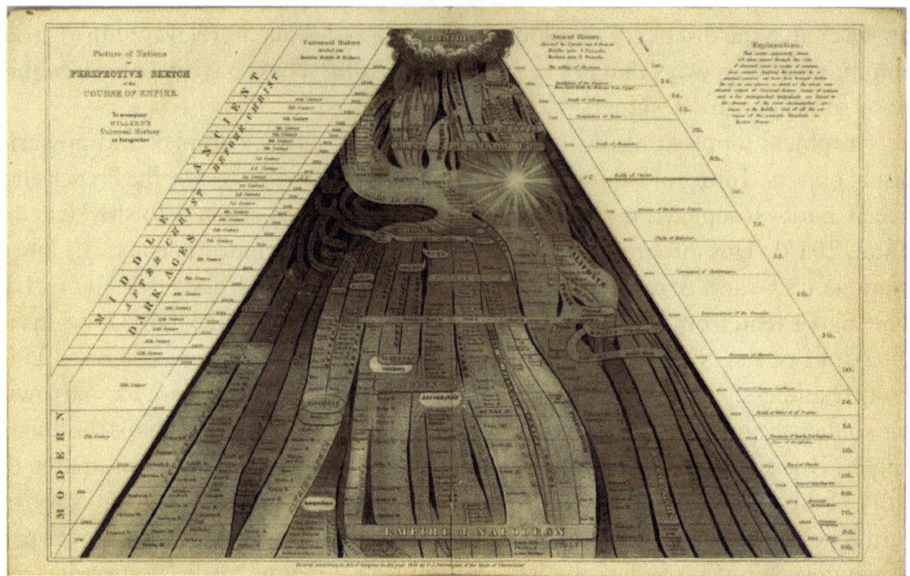

FIGURE 4.2: Emma Willard's Picture of Nations, 1835 (Willard).

of nations and empires from the time of the Christian creation story through to Ancient, Middle, and Modern periods. The purpose of this image was to help students understand a more complex version of history and to, hopefully, understand that history is contextually dependent on both space and time. Willard's map is multivariate in its attempt at showing a universal history through a graphical representation of such variables as cause and effect, connections between nations, connections between events and beginnings of historical eras, and connections between events, nations, and their leaders.

While it may be argued that Minard's diagram is an attempt to build a case against future attempts to invade Russia (a case that has, since the nineteenth century, become both historically reinforced and entrenched in pop culture), the diagram itself was, even during its time, a visual historical record. In its position as a historical account it bears much similarity to Willard's diagram. John Snow's Cholera Map stands in sharp contrast as design for social change (see Figure 4.3). In 1854, a cholera epidemic swept through the city of London, killing thousands. Snow went door-to-door asking local residents about cholera deaths, then marking the location of each death on a map. He used the gathered data to trace the source of contamination to the neighbourhood water pump. He then used his map as an argument and ordered the pump's handle be removed, preventing the further spread of the disease. Snow's map is a combination of two chart methods to form a more complex, early visualization (Pearce 2013).

FIGURE 4.3: 1854 John Snow's Cholera Map of London (Snow and Cheffins 1855: n.pag.).

The polar-area diagram (or Nightingale's Rose diagram) invented by Florence Nightingale is similarly functional in its intent (see Figure 4.4). Illustrating the extent and sources of patient mortality during the Crimean War, Nightingale wanted a way to communicate more effectively with Members of Parliament and civil servants on the conditions of medical care in British military hospitals as a call for sanitary reform and change in medical practices of the time. Small, in his work on Nightingale's legacy, argues that depicting variation of death rates due to hygiene conditions, as can be inferred from her diagrams, was very important to reformers like Nightingale because it suggested a possible way to improve health conditions in the population as a whole (Small 1998).

In the past ten years, our vocabulary for classifying the vast array of graphical objects associated with data representation has become substantially expanded and, currently, there is little consensus regarding the definitions for the categories that have been developed. Determining what type of graphical object falls under the category of chart or graph, information graphic, information visualization, or data visualization is particularly challenging, with little agreement among multi-disciplinary practitioners and academics.

Suda defines a chart or a graph as 'a clean and simple atomic piece', and a visualization as containing 'sometimes complex graphics or several layers of charts and graphs'(2010: 10). Charts and graphs tend to describe a category of graphical

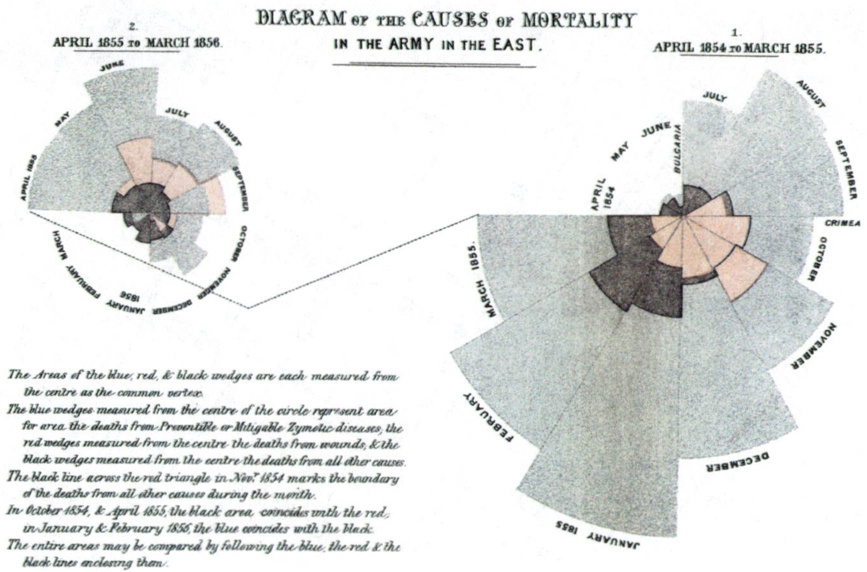

FIGURE 4.4: Diagram of the causes of mortality in the army in the East by Florence Nightingale (1858: n.pag.).

objects that are self-contained and, within the spectrum of graphical data representation, contain a subset that tends to be more often taught as part of a K-12 curriculum, thus more easily read and understood by the general public. Line and area graphs, bar and pie charts, scatter plots, geographic maps, and rudimentary timelines tend to fall into this category; while radar plots, multi-scalar plots, and polar area diagrams (to name just a few) have, thus far, gained marginal popularity (Suda 2010: 171). Few describes tables and graphs as the 'two primary means to structure and communicate quantitative information', and argues that we 'now thoroughly understand which works best for what type of information and why' (Few 2004: 4).

A chart organizes and represents a set of numerical or qualitative values. Charts are often used to help communicate large quantities of data and the relationships between parts of the data. A chart can take a large variety of forms; however, there are common features that provide the chart with its ability to extract meaning from data. Typically, a chart will have a title (often placed at the top of the main graphic). A horizontal (x-axis) and a vertical (y-axis) axis may be used to communicate dimensions. Each axis will have a scale, denoted by periodic graduations and usually accompanied by numerical or categorical indications, as well as a label placed outside, but close to, the body of the chart, describing the dimension represented. A grid of lines, placed either in regular intervals or at significant graduations, may be used to visually align the data. Chart data may be rendered using dots, shapes, and/or lines, in a wide variety of colours and patterns. A chart may include a legend containing a list of the variables appearing in the chart and an example of their appearance.

Information graphics or infographics are most often defined as graphic visual representations of information, data, or knowledge – a definition that could easily be applied to charts and graphs. However, while charts and graphs tend to be fairly simple graphical translations of quantitative information, information graphics are either (1) innovations or modifications on pre-existing models; or (2) collections of tables, graphs, and textual content into one, pre-defined space. Both categories of objects are meant to enable the telling of more complex stories through data, and support the filtering of information, establishing of relationships, discerning patterns, and representing them in ways that support the construction of meaningful knowledge (Rajamanickam, 2010). They may include complex diagrams, timelines, maps, or schematics. Qualitative or textual data may also be visualized either via a graphical metaphor or through a more direct representation, by using the data itself as the visualization. In its innovative combination of timeline, line graph, and geographical map, Minard's March to Russia could be defined as an early example of a category one infographic, innovating on pre-existing data representation models. However, some may categorize it as a data visualization for the same reason. Figure 4.5 is an example of a second category infographic, exploring healthcare spending in the United States; Jones uses a collection of numerical values, area graphs, bar charts, and tables to display costs associated with hospitalization, procedures, and medications, contextualizing the display within a theory on healthcare reform proposed by businessman, Steven Brill (Jones, 2015).

Data visualizations most often tend to be comprised of one, very complex graphical representation of data, sometimes displayed with smaller supporting statistics in the form of charts or graphs. Figure 4.6 is an example of a data visualization exploring the story of Nobel winners between 1901 and 2012. Within the primary graphic (the award timeline) are displayed the six prize categories (colour coded according to discipline), the average age of the recipients, recipient's gender, grade level, and university affiliation. Each dot placed on the timeline stands for one prize recipient, positioned according to the year the prize was awarded and the age of the person at the time of the award (Lupi et al. 2003). A legend and a support graphic have been included, but the bulk of the display is made up of the one, multi-layered visualization.

Circos stands at the far end of static data visualization. In one graphic it shows the entirety of the human genome: 22 pairs of chromosomes 1-22 and the pair of sex chromosomes X,Y (see Figure 4.7) (Krzywinski et al., 2015). Chromosomes

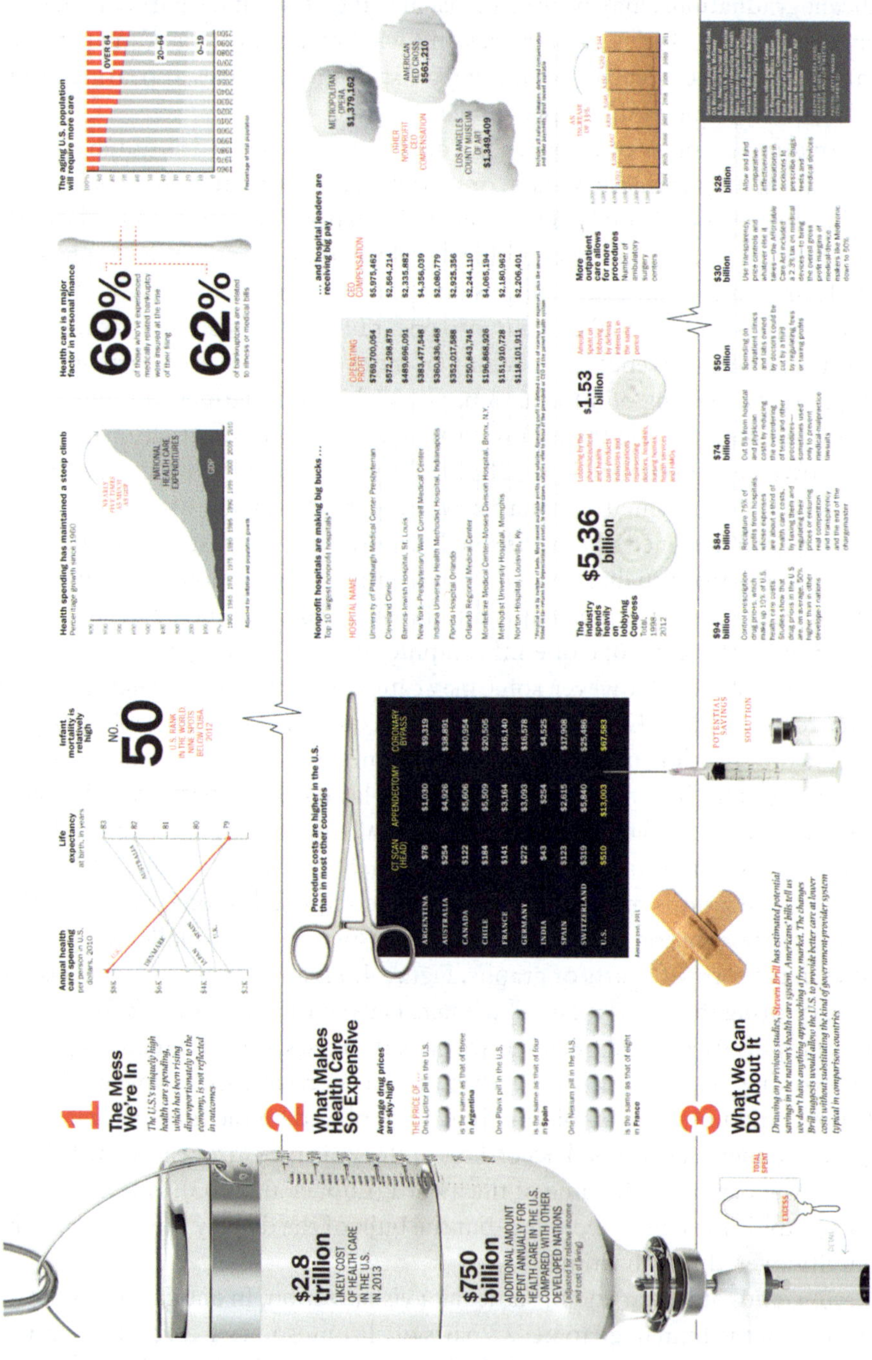

FIGURE 4.5: Why healthcare is so expensive by Heather Jones (Jones, 2013).

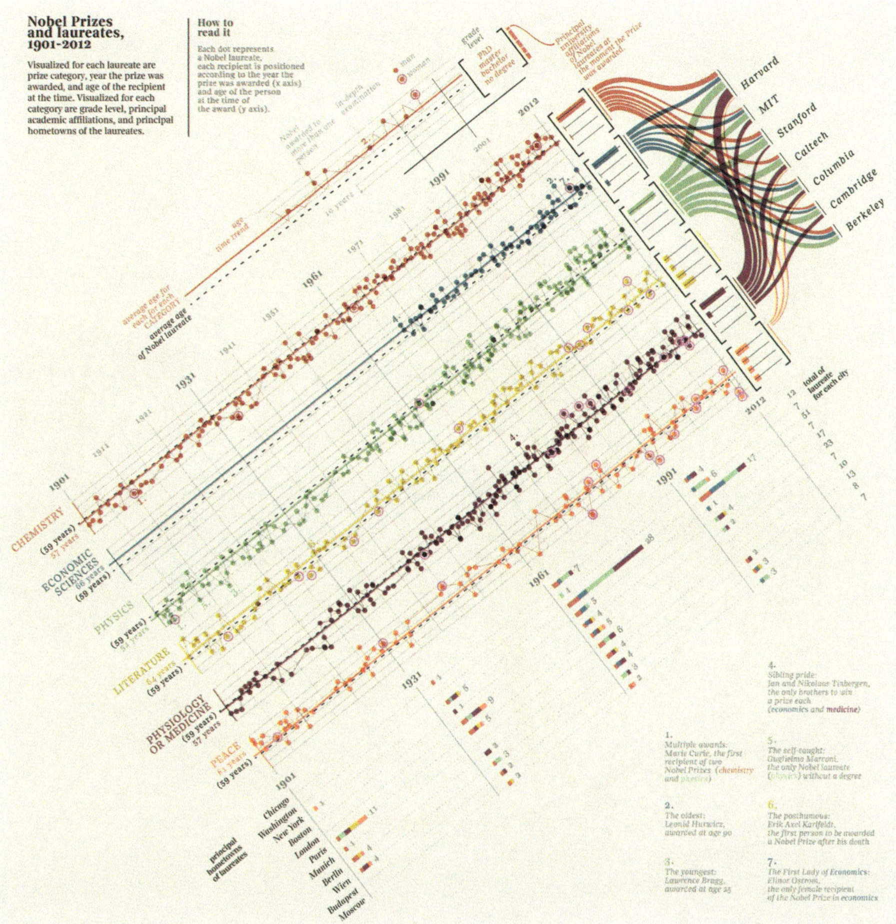

FIGURE 4.6: Exploring Nobel Prize recipients (Lupi et al. 2013).

are shown as wedges and arranged in a circular orientation. Their length is marked with a scale. This data is supplemented on the outer ring with tracks representing genomic variation between individuals and populations. Data within the grey ring highlights positions of genes implicated in cancer, diabetes, and glaucoma. Grey links inside the circle illustrate disease-related genes found in the same biochemical pathway; whole coloured links connect those genomic region pairs that are highly similar, illustrating the deep level of similarity between genomic regions (Circos). This is an incredibly complex visual display, requiring not only a high degree of familiarity and comfort with the act of reading graphical objects that are of similar complexity, but also discipline-specific knowledge in genetics. At the same time,

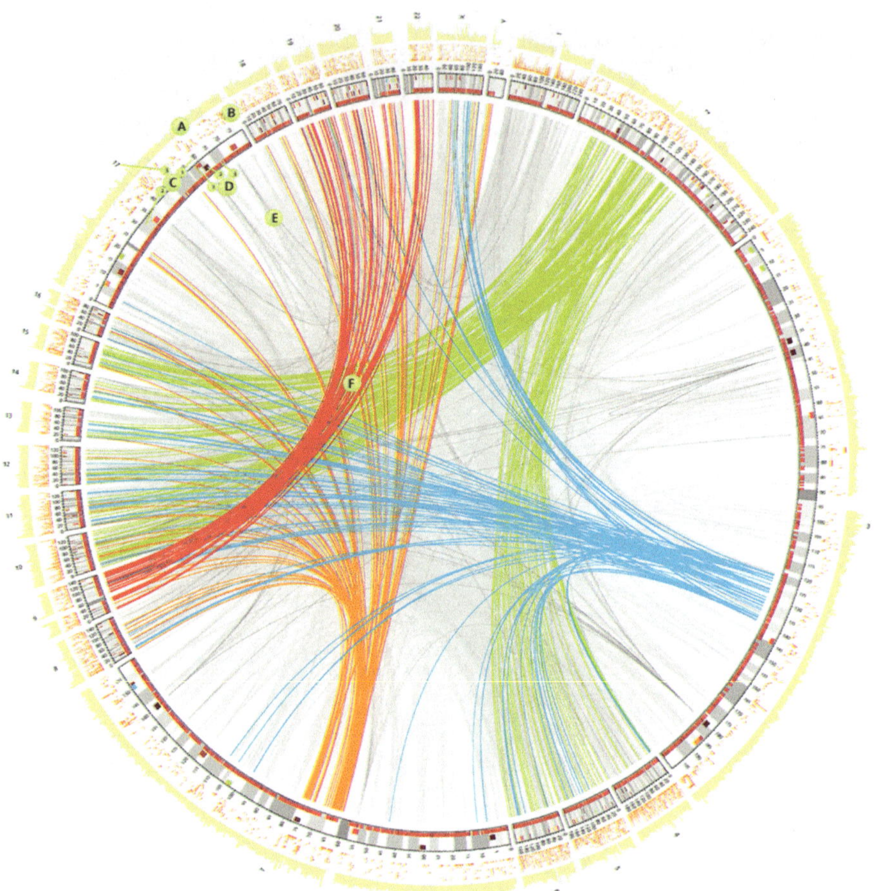

FIGURE 4.7: A static data visualization of the human genome (Krzywinski 2015).

however, it is, perhaps accidentally, aesthetically compelling – suggesting the vastness and beautiful complexity that is the human existence.

Information graphics can appear in either static or kinetic form. Minard's diagram, Nightingale's Rose, and Willard's Picture of Nations are all examples of static displays. Static displays produce no sound, show no movement, and offer no opportunity for change through interaction: they are, essentially, for-print posters, even if displayed on an electronic screen. In contrast, kinetic displays (motion graphics) show movement in the form of video or animation. Sound is sometimes added to kinetic displays. Figure 4.8 is an example of a motion graphic that takes the viewer through a one hour, one day, and one year period, at the end of which New York City adds 54 million metric tons of carbon dioxide to the atmosphere. Neiman argues that this terrific number for atmospheric pollution is meaningless

FIGURE 4.8: Still from a motion graphic (Nieman and Dickinson 2013).

to most people since few of us have a sense of scale when it comes to such large values. Using 3-D modelling, Nieman gives the collective New York emissions physicality, by turning them into giant, blue balls. By the end of the short movie (and the end of one year), most of New York is buried under a mountain of these carbon balls. Specific numbers are less important in this graphic; what is important is the emotional impact provided through the contrast of emissions to the cityscape (Nieman and Dickinson 2013).

More recently, some data visualizations are intended not just as reference or argumentation objects, but as tools for analysis, discovery, or research. In literary studies, data visualization tools have been used for exploring single or multiple texts, as well as text and image collections. In the field of digital humanities (DH), researchers have built, modified, and used tools for the analysis of large text collections in order to gain relevant insights or propose new arguments regarding narrative structure, style, or associations within and across texts. TextArc, for example (see Figure 4.9), is a 'combination of an index, concordance, and summary', mapping word frequency and associations in Lewis Carroll's *Alice's Adventures in Wonderland* (Paley 2008). Upon launch, the tool first draws the entire text of the novel, sentence by sentence, in the shape of an ellipse. Every word is then repeated according to its sequence within the book, and positioned next to the sentence in which it appears. Words that are in proximity to one another in the book are brighter and share a similar colour. Users can select any word and view where it occurs in the book (Lima 2011: 123).

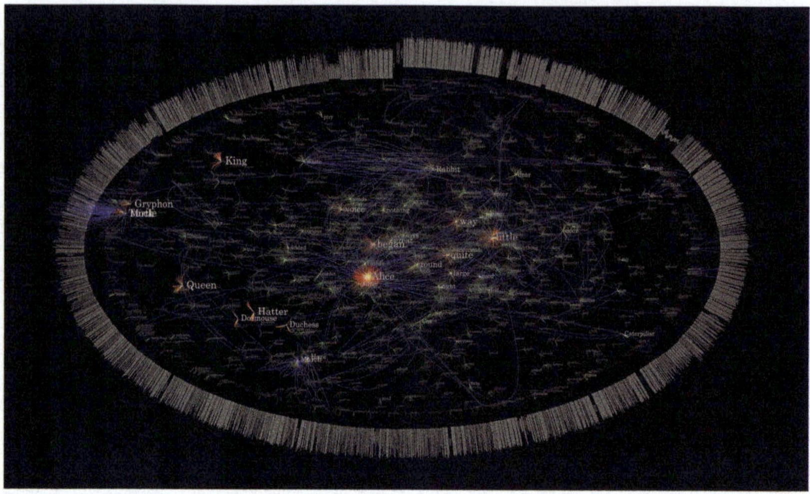

FIGURE 4.9: TextArc, illustrating relationships between words found in *Alice in Wonderland* (Paley 2008).

The TAPoR 2.0 gateway provides a good snapshot of the kinds of tools (and their sheer volume) that are currently available for humanities-emergent scholarship. It lists 463 tools for text manipulation, analysis, and visualization, and describes itself as 'a place for Humanities scholars, students and others interested in applying digital tools to their textual research to find the tools they need, contribute their experience and share new tools they have developed or used with others' (Rockwell et al. 2009).

In its 2.0 iteration, users can discover historic tools, read tool reviews and recommendations, learn about papers, articles, and other sources referencing specific tools, and collaboratively tag, comment, rate, and review tools.

Numerous such gateways or collections of data visualization tools currently exist, outside of those specific to the DH community. The website datavisualization.ch, for example, short lists 55 tools: libraries for plotting data on maps, frameworks for creating charts, graphs, and diagrams and tools to simplify the handling of data. Visual Complexity is a multi-disciplinary resource for anyone interested in the visualization of complex networks, providing an access point to 777 data visualization projects with 'one trait in common: the whole is always more than the sum of its parts' (visualcomplexity.com). Similar to TAPoR, Visual Complexity offers encyclopaedic-like entries for every tool, with a title, screenshots of the interface, author attribution, date of creation, URL, and a short description. Users can add their own experiences or observations in the form of comments, to

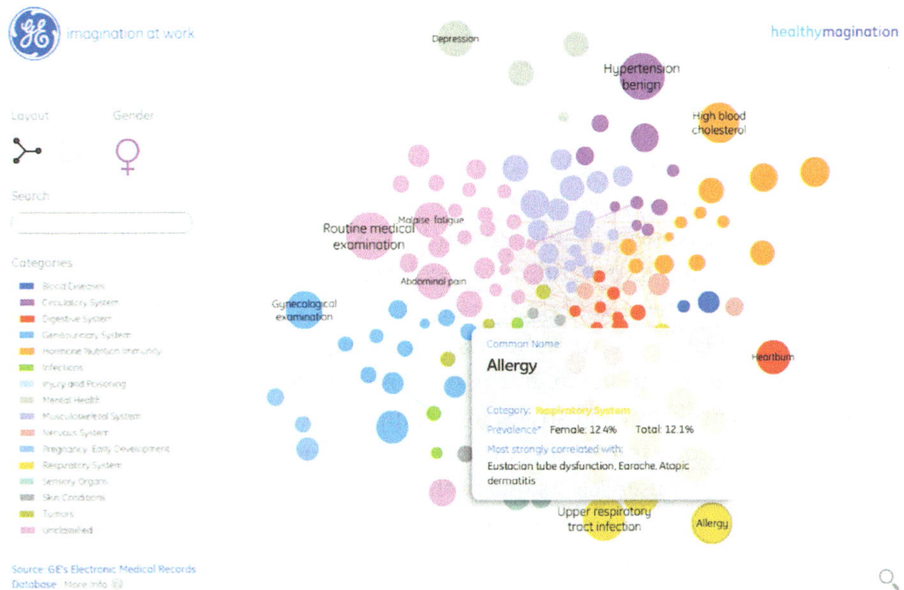

FIGURE 4.10: The Health InfoScape project (MIT SENSEable City Lab).

any tool. Visual Complexity, unlike TAPoR, provides access primarily to interactive data visualizations that aid in data exploration, not tools for research or work-task completion. For example, the Health InfoScape project, designed by the team at MIT SENSEable City Lab, visualizes 7.2 million patient records from General Electric's proprietary database. It aims to foster an exploration of the connections between health conditions found in American patients in order to answer such questions as, for example, 'When you have heartburn, do you also feel nauseous? Or if you're experiencing insomnia, do you tend to put on a few pounds, or more?' (MIT SENSEable City Lab). Users can select conditions from 16 ailment categories. Conditions are then associated with gender prevalence and correlated with other, relevant, conditions (see Figure 4.10). It may be argued that interfaces such as Health InfoScape help users in preliminary research towards self-diagnosis or subsequent discussions with their healthcare provider; they are primarily intended as, what we would term, education-light, similar to WebMD.

Notable about Health InfoScape is its visualization-navigational model. The interface consists of one visualization space. Within this space is located the navigation system (through which users can explore the data) as a side category menu, and the data visualization itself, which is also interactive. There are, in fact, two visualization layouts made available to us, and switching between does not change the data, just its display. All exploration is contained within this one space.

While both the Health InfoScape and the TextArc projects are highly graphical and display substantial data sets, they are limited in terms of user interaction and contribution. In contrast, the Johnny Cash Project supports user engagement through navigation, and contribution of content into the collection, both on a micro and a macro level (Milk n.d.). Working within the original music video for the song 'Ain't No Grave', users are invited to draw their own versions of a frame from the video. That frame is then combined with frames by other users from around the world, and integrated into a collective reconstruction of the video. This interface provides a prospect view on all the user-created frames, with the added functionality of switching the view between frames that received the highest user rating, those that were selected by the site's curator, or those that were defined by a particular artistic style (pointillism vs. abstract, for example). Each representation of an item in the collection (video frame) becomes the means of accessing further information on that item. When a user selects one of the frames, an information panel appears to the right of the frame listing such details as the frame number, artist's name and location, drawing time, and number of brush strokes (see Figure 4.11). Users can easily navigate between frames using the prospect view below the video playback or, when in the detailed frame view, by using the previous and next frame buttons.

The Health InfoScape project relies on a pre-existing dataset that is made available for exploration to its users. The Building Hopes Project relies on user-generated sculptures as their data set. Thus, the dataset grows as the community of user-contributors grows. Building Hopes is an 'immersive data-art experience that invites people to materialize their hopes as permanent augmented reality

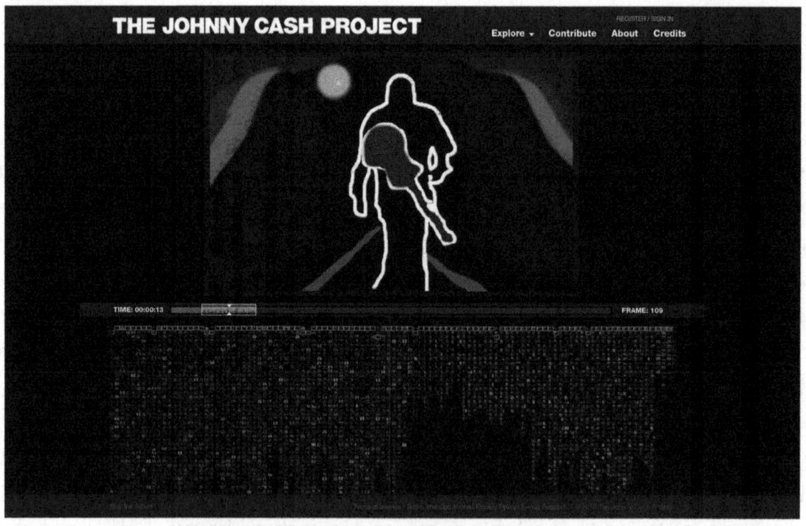

FIGURE 4.11: The Johnny Cash Project (Milk n.d.).

FIGURE 4.12: Building Hopes (Accurat 2018).

sculptures and to use them as a lens to explore and understand Google Trends data' (https://www.accurat.it/works/buildinghopes/).

In contrast, the We Feel Fine project is based primarily on user created content from numerous, continuously and independently generated datasets (see Figure 4.13) (Kamvar and Harris 2011: n.pag.). Its search engine continuously crawls blogs, microblogs, and social networking sites looking for sentences that include the words I feel or I am feeling. It extracts these statements, as well as the gender, age, and location of the people authoring them, and displays them within an ever-changing and interactive art installation. The We Feel Fine interface allows users to search, browse, or ask specific questions such as 'How did young people in Ohio feel when Obama was elected?' It is an interface for qualitative exploration of emotional data, and its flexible data collection system enables the continual growth of the dataset. The result is a database of over 14 million expressions of emotion, increasing by 15,000–20,000 new feelings per day. Notable about the We Feel Fine interface is the complexity of its interaction model. It enables users to perform sentence-level analysis: sentences are the canonical documents in the dataset. Each sentence is combined with, and can be searched and sorted by, contextual information: time of the emotion, and location, age and gender of the speaker. We Feel Fine uses the sentiments themselves as the primary organizing principle – they are the underpinning of its interaction model – and, based on the principle that feelings are never wrong, there is no statement ranking in the interface. Instead, the interface emphasizes browsing and summarization, thus

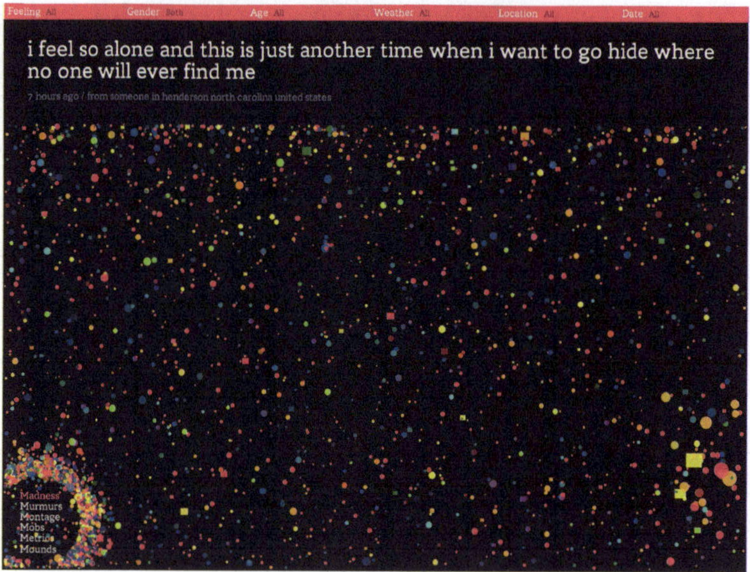

FIGURE 4.13: The We Feel Fine interface (Kamvar and Harris 2011).

enabling users to shift between macro and micro views of the data. The visual form of the interface is meant to reflect their human origin as well as the diversity inherent to emotional states, while providing functional and direct access to the data.

Treemaps stand in sharp contrast to the delicate and organic display of We Feel Fine. Invented by Ben Shneiderman in 1992, treemaps are a way to visualize tree structures within a contained space (Shneiderman, 1998). Each branch of a tree is given a rectangle, then tiled with smaller rectangles that represent the sub-branches of the tree. The size of the rectangle is proportional to the size of the others: think of cutting up a rectangular pan of brownies amongst a room-full of relatives, each one with a differently sized appetite. Colour is often used to separate dimension or to create categories. Newsmap (http://newsmap.jp) is one of many examples of treemaps currently in use. It is a news aggregator that displays stories, organized by popularity and volume of reporting. World, National, Business, Technology, Sports, Entertainment, and Health categories help users subset the data. Users can also toggle their view based on the country from which the feed has originated. Figure 4.14, for example, shows news stories coming out of New Zealand, related to technology. Mousing over a square reveals a small pop-up summary of the story, and clicking on the square directs you to the story's origin, where you can read the entire text. What stories are displayed and how often the display updates with new content depends on the type and level of news activity that is occurring at any given moment.

FIGURE 4.14: Newsmap (http://newsmap.jp).

While We Feel Fine continuously grows its dataset through its emotional search engine and Newsmap updates according to changes in news feeds, the Bubblelines tool provides users with two options for the origins of their dataset: using a set that has been preloaded into the tool, or uploading their own set (see Figure 4.15). Bubblelines visualizes the frequency and repetition of words in a corpus (created by Rockwell and Sinclair, https://voyant-tools.org/?view=Bubblelines). Documents are represented as horizontal lines, divided into equal segments. Users can search for words in the documents; words are presented as bubbles with their size indicating the word's frequency within a particular text segment. The larger the bubble, the more frequently that word occurs in a segment. Users can view all words on the same line, with overlapping bubbles, or on separate lines. The tool is significant to this discussion in the way it enables users to upload their own corpus, however large, containing any number of documents. These documents can then be displayed in parallel to one another, enabling comparison and juxtaposition.

4.1.2 Conclusion

Not every data visualization was created by people who self-identified as designers, but every visualization has been designed, and as a set they help us to understand the territory of what is possible in data visualization. One future development that we believe holds promise was suggested by Ichikawa (2016), who explored the idea that every visualization should be designed, not as a digital artefact per se, but instead as a form of experience.

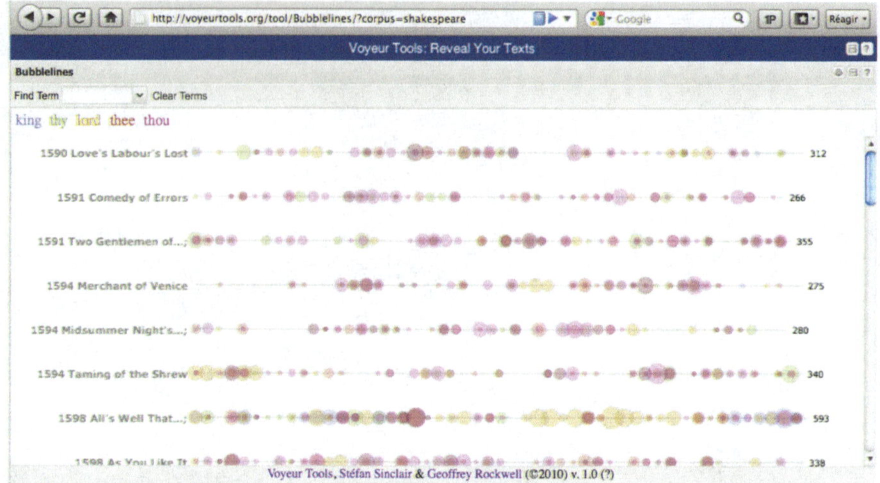

FIGURE 4.15: The Bubblelines tool with a preloaded corpus (https://voyant-tools.org/?view =Bubblelines).

4.2 Rich prospect browsing

> In the case of rich-prospect interfaces, the benefits are that the combination of meaningful representation of items with emergent tools for manipulating the display potentially results in an intuitive way for users to understand an entire collection and how its designers conceived of it. People are also able to see information that can remind them of things they've forgotten, or suggest to them things that they never knew. They can be reassured about what is included in a collection and what is not there.
>
> (Ruecker et al. 2011: 171)

In our first book, *Visual Interface Design for Digital Cultural Heritage: A Guide to Rich-Prospect Browsing* (2011), we introduced, then argued the benefits of rich-prospect interfaces as intuitive and highly flexible alternatives to the Search box. In order to be considered a rich prospect browser, an interface must meet five criteria. First, the primary screen of an RPB will show a meaningful representation of every item in a collection. Such representation may, in some instances, be closely evocative of the collection item's original form, or the form may be arbitrarily assigned. For example, in the Slot Machine interface (see Figure 4.16) the first column features the entirety of Gertrude Stein's *The Making of Americans* in micro text, with subsequent columns generated based on a user's search of a repeated phrase (Stein 1995; Radzikowska et al. 2007). All columns are aligned along a reading slot that magnifies the repeated phrase and its immediate context. The Slot Machine is a good

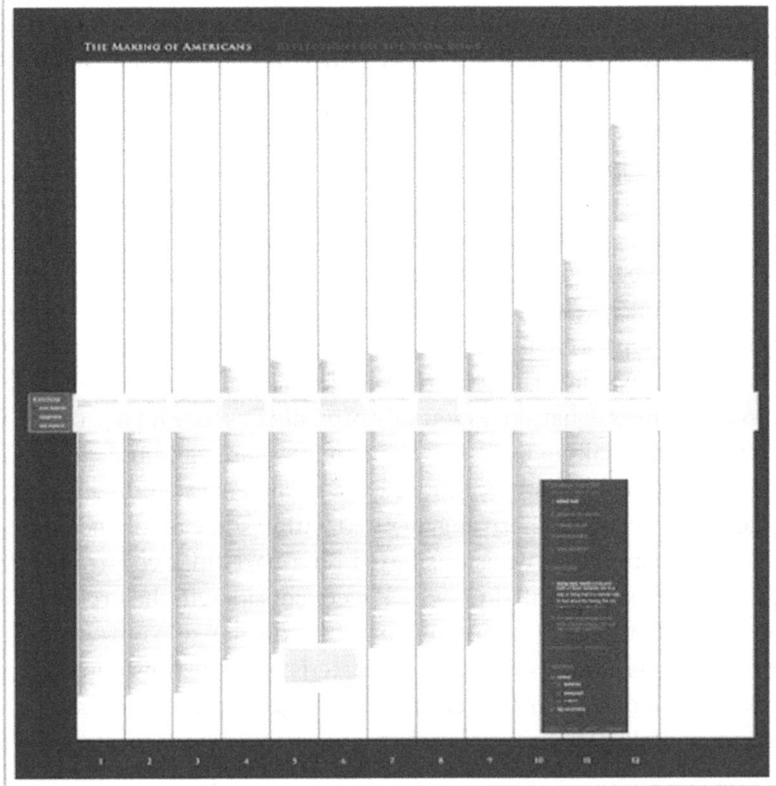

FIGURE 4.16: The Slot Machine (Radzikowska et al. 2007).

example of an interface where there is a close connection between the item in the collection (the novel) and its graphical representation (a column made of a micro text version of the novel). Using Peirce's terms (Chandler, n.pag.), the micro text is an icon: the signifier (column of micro text) is perceived as resembling or imitating the signified (the novel). In the case of the Slot Machine this close connection in representation facilitates an exploration of the text across and within multiple contexts. At the same time, a micro text representation of a novel (even one that is not 1000 pages in its original form) requires the use of specialized technology, such as a wall-size display, making such representation possible but impractical.

In contrast, the Paper Drill interface displays an article's citations (items in that collection) using a gridded series of coloured squares, with each square representing one citation source and the colour the distance of that source from the citing article (Ruecker and INKE Research Group 2011). Using Peirce's terms (Chandler 2007: n.pag.), these squares are symbols, arbitrarily (though carefully) assigned to represent not only the citation, but also the original text. This connection – between a square, its colour, and the text – must be made explicit in the interface, and learned by its users. In the case of the Paper Drill, symbolic representation allows for a prospect view on all the items in a very large collection (Figure 4.17 shows 1666 citations by 36 authors).

For some collections, an iconic item representation may be not only possible, but preferable given the nature (and size) of the collection and the types of tasks that are likely to be performed with it; while for other collections a more abstract (or symbolic) item representation may be required. In the context of designing an RPB for decision support in manufacturing, we must first consider what constitutes a collection of items. The primary screen could show a meaningful representation of all parts of a linear equation, essentially providing users with a prospect view on the entire decision-making process. Or, in an alternate view, users could explore multiple solution scenarios, once those have been generated. In such a case, the display could show all alternatives generated within some predefined time period, or enable the clustering of decisions based on a particular constraint, or which alternatives were implemented vs. which were considered, then rejected. We can also consider extending the notion of a prospect display to controls or processes.

The following is a list of collection characteristics to be considered when determining whether a particular collection would make a good candidate for an RPB (Ruecker et al. 2011: 101):

- possible uses of the collection;
- number of items;

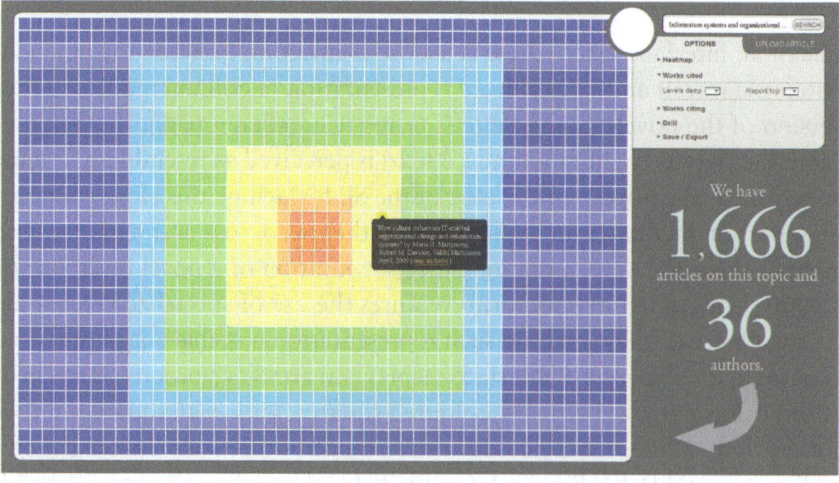

FIGURE 4.17: Sample sketch from the Paper Drill (designed by Radzikowska, 2009).

- characteristics of the items;
- degree of homogeneity among items;
- possibility of providing some logical, consistent, and meaningful representation of each item; and
- extent of the markup of the collection.

Many of these collection characteristics also determine what kind of meaningful representation (iconic, indexical, or symbolic) may be possible for a given collection. For example, a collection of 1,000 pills that in their original form have a simple graphical composition (limited set of geometric shapes, little detail, limited colour palette) may be comfortably displayed in their original (iconic) form, using the one-screen RPB model. Even at a relatively small size, individual pills can be reasonably distinguished from one another and from their contextual space. Faces, on the other hand, require greater size to be effectively differentiated from each other. Thus, the digital versions of the photographs could be used for smaller collections. For collections with items numbering in the thousands, a graphically simpler symbolic form would need to be created.

Out of Sight, Out of Mind (Pitch Interactive), an interactive project on the use of drone technology in Pakistan, based on a dataset maintained by the Bureau of Investigative Journalism, hopes to inform us about the number of drone strikes, and the number and type of casualties that they have caused (see Figure 4.18). The visualization's creators at Pitch Interactive aim to emphasize the low success rate for the strikes and their impact on civilian populations: since 2004, there have

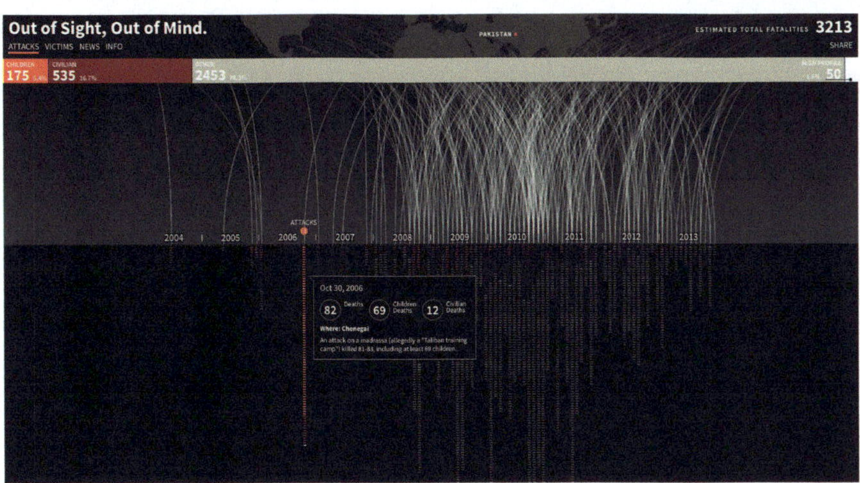

FIGURE 4.18: Out of Sight, Out of Mind (Pitch Interactive).

been 3,213 casualties attributed to drone strikes, with only 2% of those identified as high-profile targets. While graphically abstracting both the drones, in the form of curved, moving lines, and the casualties, in the form of rectangular boxes, the visualization provides a prospect, multi-year view on the strikes. At the same time, the design includes a meso view on the human component in the form of group statistics that appear when you roll-over the collection of rectangles – all casualties from a single strike. The strikes are also contextualized through the display of key political events, such as the beginning of the Obama presidency.

This design strikes a beautiful balance between the meso and the prospect, or macro view, personalizing each event, while overwhelming us with the number of strikes and nature of the casualties. They place emphasis on the comparison of impact on the four human categories: children, civilian, other, and high profile. The shape and movement of the curved lines used to represent the drones creates a pattern that suggests the relentlessness of a rainstorm.

The U.S. Gun Deaths (Kirk et al. 2013) project goes a step further, by giving us the micro view on not only the name and age of every person killed, but projecting the length of years they may have lived (see Figure 4.19). Some of their data comes from the FBI's Uniform Crime Reports, combined with a projection of alternate stories for those who have been killed using data from the World Health Organization, while some comes from a collection gathered by an anonymous Twitter user, @GunDeaths, gathering and tweeting gun-related deaths in the United States.

In both the drone and the gun death project, graphical representation takes the form of simple, curved lines that have vastly different meanings. The lines in Out of Sight, Out of Mind are a visual metaphor for the path to earth taken by the dropped aerial bombs. In U.S. Gun Deaths each line represents a length of time – one person's lifespan. The orange segment is the actual life, and the grey segment

FIGURE 4.19: U.S. Gun Deaths (Kirk et al. 2013).

is the remaining years if they had not been killed. In both cases the collection of lines overwhelms us with its dense pattern.

The second RPB criteria (Ruecker et al. 2011: 3) states that the user will be provided with a set of controls for the manipulation of the display and the re-organization of the items found in the collection, for example by grouping or subsetting the meaningful representations.

Controls for such manipulation emerge out of the type of items found within the collection (the third RPB criterion). Additionally, for most (if not all) RPBs, controls are proximally located to the area of the display that is housing collection items. Thus, when users manipulate the display, they can immediately see the effects of their choices. Complex collection sets will tend to have more and more complex tools than simpler sets. In the Paper Drill, for example, all controls for manipulating the display sit to the right of the collection display. These controls include a search function specific to searching either cited or citing articles, and options for how the results will be displayed.

Requiring a set of emergent controls for the manipulation of the display stands in direct contrast to displays where users must navigate multiple, hidden menu systems or screens to see results. One example of a multi-screen display is ManyEyes (IBM Cognos and IBM Research Group), where users are provided a three-step process to complete their visualization task, with every step located on a separate screen (see Figure 4.20).

The fourth RPB criteria asks that, where possible, more than one meaningful representation of collection items be provided. For example, in a collection that supports browsing prescription pills, the display would support the viewing of either side of a pill, or both sides simultaneously, and changing the display between these three representations would be under the user's control. The Johnny Cash Project (introduced previously) is a good example of a browser that supports nine different views. This interface provides a prospect view on all the user-created frames, with the added functionality of switching the view between frames that received the highest user rating, those that were selected by the site's curator, or

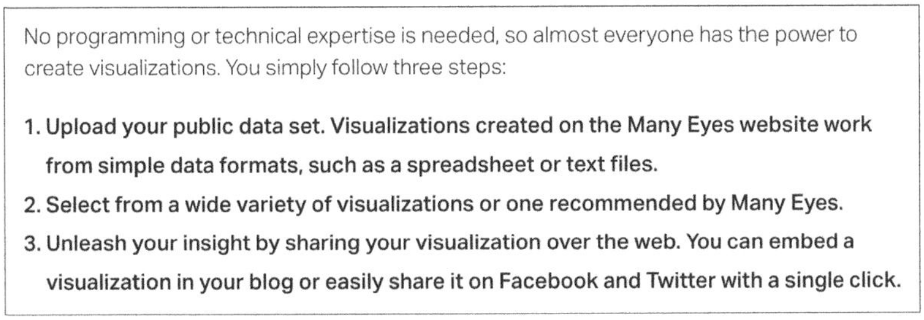

No programming or technical expertise is needed, so almost everyone has the power to create visualizations. You simply follow three steps:

1. **Upload your public data set. Visualizations created on the Many Eyes website work from simple data formats, such as a spreadsheet or text files.**
2. **Select from a wide variety of visualizations or one recommended by Many Eyes.**
3. **Unleash your insight by sharing your visualization over the web. You can embed a visualization in your blog or easily share it on Facebook and Twitter with a single click.**

FIGURE 4.20: The ManyEyes interface (IBM Cognos and IBM Research Group).

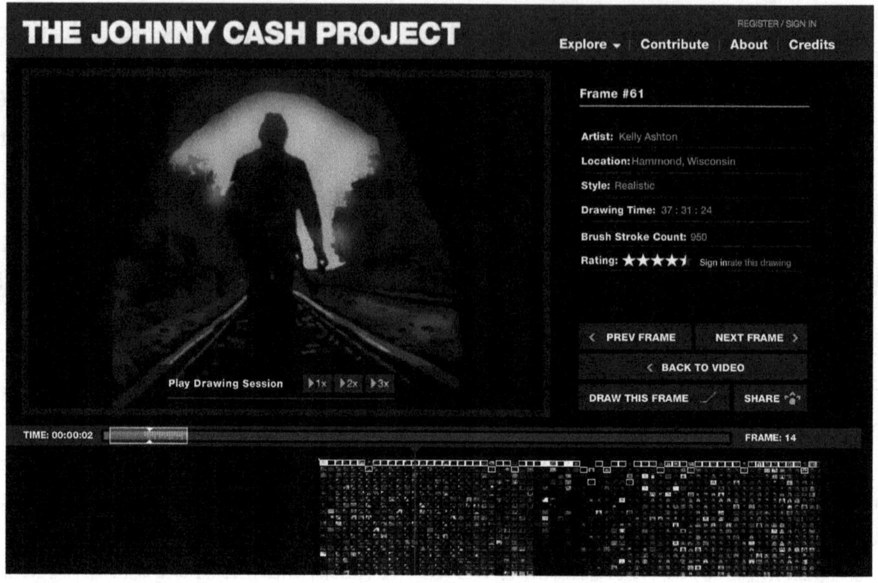

FIGURE 4.21: Detailed view of one frame found in the Johnny Cash Project (Milk n.d.).

those that were defined by a particular artistic style (pointillism vs. abstract, for example).

The Johnny Cash Project is also an excellent example of the fifth RPB criteria: each representation of an item in the collection becomes the means of accessing further information on that item (Ruecker et al. 2011: 3). When a user selects one of the frames, an information panel appears to the right of the frame listing such details as the frame number, artist's name and location, drawing time, and number of brush strokes (see Figure 4.21). Users can easily navigate between frames using the prospect view below the video playback or, when in the detailed frame view, by using the previous and next frame buttons.

Subsequent work by Giacometti proposed that users should be provided with the ability to mark collection items in some way, and that the items should start out with an appropriate, initial organization (106). These are both valuable contributions to RPB theory when you consider a display such as the one found in Figure 4.22 where the user is faced with an initial display of 1,000 pills (Ruecker et al. 2005).

There are certain challenges with any rich-prospect interface. The primary problem is that showing so much information on a single screen can be an overwhelming experience to users (Ruecker et al. 2011: 135). Two strategies that help deal with so much visual data are (1) represent collection items in a way that is meaningful and (2) provide users with tools for manipulating and organizing these

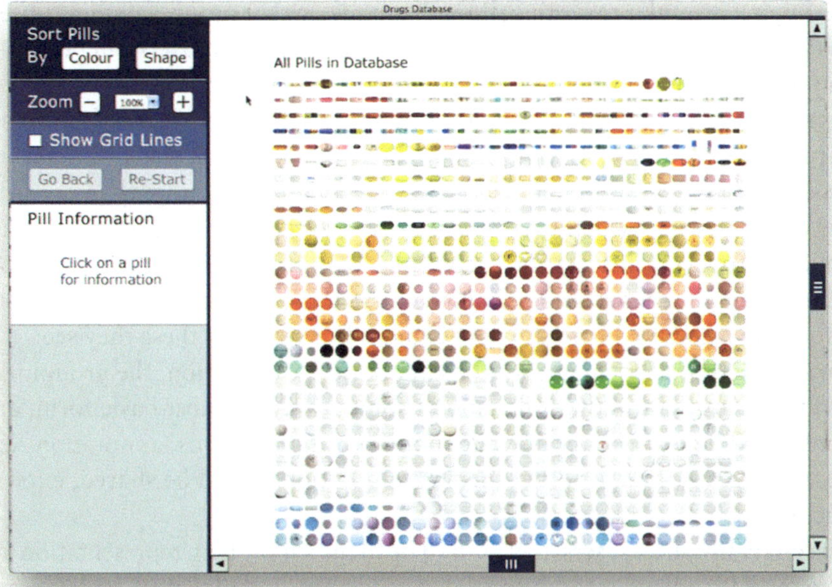

FIGURE 4.22: An RPB of pills (Ruecker et al. 2005).

items. In addition to these primary strategies, designers can add any of the following nine interface tools to an RPB: zooming, panning, sorting, selecting, grouping, renaming, annotating, opening, and structuring.

While zooming and panning changes the user's relationship to the data found within a display while not actually modifying the data's display, sorting tools affect the data's organization. Numerous sorting strategies exist that allow for the arrangement of items in a display. Of particular importance are those that support the creation of meaningful relationships between the data. Most commonly, items are sorted according to one of the LATCH strategies proposed by Wurman: location, alphabet, time (chronology), category, or hierarchy (1989: 40). For example, articles could be sorted according to their citation frequency, or solution alternatives could be sorted according to their date of implementation or number of consequences.

Users need the ability to work with individual items or a subset of items within a collection. Many standard selection mechanisms exist, from menus to shift-clicking on an item (for an extensive list see Ruecker et al. 2011, or visit usability.gov for a short list). Applications such as Adobe Illustrator use toolbars containing a wide range of selection tools and tool-specific palettes. Other applications use the right mouse click action to bring up item-specific options that may include a detail view, reserving the single or left mouse click to selection and a repeated mouse click to de-selection. There is an opportunity for further innovation in this area.

Grouping is similar to sorting, though unique, in that groups contain subsets of items while a sorted list only contains the items themselves. Users can be provided with pre-established groupings, as well as with the ability to customize their own sub-groups. Groups can be compared against one another according to some criteria. There is an opportunity for further innovation in the visualization of cross-belonging: where an item belongs simultaneously to more than one group. Users can also be provided with the option of selecting the representation most meaningful to their particular task from a list of options. For each item in a collection, for example, there could be some text, an image, a diagram, or a mathematical formula associated with it. Users could select which of these they see.

In some cases, users might want to annotate the collection, the groupings, or individual items within the collection in some way. In a most basic form, annotations could be text or labels, while in more complex forms, annotations could be text, images, sound, or other media. Annotations could be shared, exported, or hidden.

In certain instances, users may wish to open the simple item representation available in the RPB, revealing additional data or a more complex item representation. For example, the simple item representation may be in the form of a cropped-in image thumbnail, while the more complex representation could be the entire image at a large scale, combined with relevant metadata. The simple representation could be in the form of a bar graph, while the more complex representation could be a larger version of the bar graph with detailed numerical values, the formula, and annotation.

4.2.1 Proposing new RPB principles and tools

Since its publication in 2011, we've had the opportunity to experiment with RPB and, eventually, consider opportunities for its extension. The following are four new principles of Rich Prospect Browsing, inspired by Bardzell and colleagues in the area of Feminist HCI:

- principle of participation;
- principle of association;
- principle of contextuality; and
- principle of pluralism.

Principle of participation

Most rich-prospect browsers utilize pre-existing collections (Ruecker et al. 2011: ff.). For example, the Pill Browser uses an existing image and metadata collection of pills (Ruecker et al. 2005). In certain RPBs users have the ability to load their own collection, though even in those cases the collections are not user-generated, but user uploaded (speeches in Shakespeare's *Coriolanus*, for example). However, users could start off working with items from a pre-established collection then, once they generate their own items, a new collection would be created. The collection could consist of items generated by single users, or by communities, and within one browsing session, or across multiple instances. Finally, users could be provided with a combined view from multiple data sources. Participation in the co-creation of collections already takes place. Consider Behance.net, for example, where you can showcase and discover a wide range of creative work – its value is in its existence as an amalgam of work from an ever-growing, diverse community of makers. Certain communities, however, have yet to embrace interface design that actively seeks out and foregrounds individuals who are conventionally silenced (Muller 2011: 447–49). In the case of interfaces for decision support, for example (discussed at length in this chapter's subsequent section), participants could become co-creators of collections, and provided with advanced annotation functionality. Such collection items would gain a connection to their originators – real people with experience in considering and implementing decisions within a particular manufacturing context. Alternatively, a system could be designed that considers all combinations of available decision constraints, then pre-calculates all the possible solution alternatives that could be generated through their manipulation and stores them in a database. Then the starting point for the decision support system would not be its controls, rather the entire collection with appropriate tools for its manipulation – a fundamental shift in the power dynamics between system/technology and person.

Principle of association

This principle is similar to the existing RPB Grouping tool, but calls for a permanent graphical representation of relationships between items. Relationships could take several forms. For example, a relationship could mean the visualization of connection between an item that's become the cause of change or that has made some impact on another. Or, relationships could mean some kind of visual grouping of like items. This principle could appear similar to the second, original RPB principle of providing users with tools to manipulate the display. However, this principle differs from a tool in that, in the examples described above, certain items in the collection can't be manipulated by a tool independent from one another. When this is the case, the relationships between these collection items need to be made explicit at the start of the browsing. For instance, if A causes B or A opposes B or B can't exist without A.

Related Tool: Connection-Making – In order to recognize the users of an RPB as creators, we must also empower them to construct relationships between items in the collection.

Principle of contextuality

Contextuality asks that collection items still exist independently but, when appropriate, become automatically connected to a contextual surface space. This notion is particularly powerful in manufacturing scenarios where decisions are connected to a limited set of constraints (cost of materials, labour, and waste disposal, transportation, and production time), but are viewed independently to individual, social, or ecological impacts. Current displays for alternative solutions fragment the reading experience. Contextuality suggests that certain collections require a situated reading to be fully understood. Thus, decisions never stand on their own – as independent collection items – but become situated within a surface that is made up of information about their decision-maker, related key performance indicators, consequences of implementation, related factors, etc.

Related Tool: Structuring – In addition to tools for sorting or grouping, the RPB could allow users to arrange items (or subsets of items) within some other more complex, meaningful structure in order to make the display easier to browse and the items more meaningful to explore. For example, items could be arranged in columns or according to a grid system, or browsed according to a visual timeline. More complex structures are also possible. One example of a complex structure applied as an organizational system for data is provided by the Structuring Surfaces project (Radzikowska et al. 2011: 19–21) described later on in this chapter. It enables users to generate visual diagrams from their data, and then introduce an additional cognitive layer underneath the data display in order to help the user mentally structure the information. The surface also helps to extend the diagrams' meaning.

Principle of pluralism

Pluralist design resists any single or universal point of view (Muller 2011: 448). Pluralism could mean opening space for that which occurs on the margins, or nudging users to select a different starting point than the one they are most familiar with or use most often. This principle may lead us to consider interface solutions that challenge the growing problem of browsing echo-chambers. Increasingly, web platforms, particularly social media services, serve up content by using algorithms to calculate what you're most likely to consider engaging and eliminating what you won't. These algorithms look backwards at your past actions, and edit (or personalize) your future content encounters – past behaviour determines future behaviour. Hence, you're more likely to find the type of content you've seen in the past, and less likely to encounter new (foreign) ideas. The downside of this type of algorithmic treatment of data is confirmation bias. Pluralism attempts to challenge singular viewpoints.

> **Related Tool: Inverting** – This tool would enable users to make the invisible, visible. It would flip the display and give graphical form to that which is opposite of what is currently being viewed, or that which sits on the outskirts. This tool is different from the sorting or grouping tools in that it looks at what is a part of the collection and assesses that which is not, then makes it browsable.

4.2.2 A critical challenge to the power embedded in prospect and refuge

We close this chapter by reflecting on refuge as discussed through Rich Prospect Browsing Theory. Appleton argued that two features of landscape are directly related to the survival of people and animals in their habitats: prospect and refuge: 'Where he has an unimpeded opportunity to see we can call it a prospect. Where he has an opportunity to hide, a refuge' (1975: 73). Appleton based his theory on natural selection, where survival was the result of, in part, the ability of the individuals of a species to identify and capitalize on opportunities for prospect and for refuge. Such individuals had, theoretically, more opportunities for hunting, shelter, and concealment, as well as for the establishment and maintenance of territory, with the emotional results of ease and satisfaction (Appleton 1975: 41). If we support the natural selection argument we will, undoubtedly, consider the use of prospect and refuge to be a positive, survival-enabling skill. Fair enough. Those who can seek shelter are more likely to survive. Those who can hide in ambush are more likely to surprise their opponent. Those who can utilize a prospect view, observing their prey or predators at a large distance, are more likely to go unnoticed or circle around for an attack. Distancing acts that result in anonymity, concealment, and secrecy become rewarded with survival, creating a power hierarchy between those who have and do not have the ability to take advantage of said skills. In fact, the concepts of prospect and refuge are both positions of power: prospect gives power through increased perception, while refuge gives power through concealment. Thus, it raises the following questions: who gets to see and who doesn't? Who gets to conceal and who doesn't? The DS interfaces designed as part of the Oil Sands Project were meant to be used by managers to aid in decision-making around production and distribution. Most corporations are heavily hierarchical. While the span of control (the employee-to-manager ratio) varies across industry types and individual corporations, a ratio of supervising 6 to 10 employees per manager is common, with some literature suggesting 15 to 20. In situations where employees are performing repetitive work and the management team is fairly experienced, a larger span of control is possible (Davison 2003: 23). It is important to recognize that there are many layers of management in organizations, each one with a different type of decision-making, with consequences to a varying number of individuals. BP Oil, for example, has an executive team of eleven that makes decisions affecting over 84,000 international employees. In a manufacturing scenario, the higher up the managerial hierarchy, the more of both prospect and refuge is gained by a manager.

It is not within the scope of this text (nor our desire) to construct an argument against corporate secrecy or for government transparency. Much valuable work exists on both fronts. However, given our own positionality and desire to critically engage with design and designed objects, it would be unethical to not question the privilege that appears embedded in the concept of prospect and refuge. For example, arguments for fiscal government transparency through 'ready access to reliable, comprehensive, timely, understandable, and internationally comparable information on government activities [...] so that the electorate and financial markets can accurately assess the government's financial position and the true costs and benefits of government activities, including their present and future economic and social implications' have been made by the International Monetary Fund, World Bank, and several independent research institutions (Kopits and Craig 1998: 1). Counter arguments have also been made that 'transparency results in government indecision, poor performance, and stalemate' (Bass et al. 2014: 1). However, from a Critical Theory perspective, the economic and political dominance gained by the bourgeoisie through the use of capitalism and industrial mass production continues to be problematic. Lack of transparency, control over the availability of information, and silencing of diverse voices prevents users from being able to fully engage in questioning and examining our worlds.

Refuge, in particular, if it supports already-established positions of power, lies in direct opposition to several principles of the Critical Action Design Framework proposed above: challenging existing practices; looking for what has been made invisible or under-represented; considering the micro, meso, and macro; privileging transparency and accountability; and welcoming rigorous critique could be interpreted as direct challenges to the idea of a power hierarchy created through the use of refuge. However, refuge can act in service to those who need it most: workers and communities that are impacted by managerial decisions.

4.3 Case study 3: Experiments in DH data visualizations

In Fall 2008, the Faculty of Communication Studies at Mount Royal University (MRU) launched a four-year Bachelor Degree in Information Design. The degree combines work experience with core and general education courses in writing, visual design, typography, design history, computer programming, usability, research methods, rhetoric, and ethics, in order to ensure that graduates have both the knowledge necessary for the information design profession and sufficient academic background to apply for graduate studies (Ruhl 2008). As part of the third-year core curriculum, we introduced a pair of courses titled Visual Communication for Information Designers I and II. VC I occurs in the Fall and VC II takes place in the following Winter semester. While both courses deal with advanced topics in information design, in VC I we focus on information design for print, and in VC II on information design for interactive media. In VC II, students are asked to solve complex information design problems, through interactive media, while carefully considering user needs, usability, technology constraints, context of use, and aesthetics. Students explore how the features and functions of an interface get translated into something humans find usable, useful, and desirable. In addition, students continue to challenge software dependency and self-expression, in favour of a user-centred, reflective, and iterative approach to interface design (Radzikowska et al. 2009).

In 2011, we challenged our students with a new type of design task, meant to provide them with the experience of working as part of an experimental interface design research team. They had a choice to work on one of two research projects in collaboration with researchers from MRU and the University of Alberta: the BigSee project (http://tada.mcmaster.ca/view/Main/BigSee), or the Structured Surfaces project. We pitched this brief as, primarily, a thinking design task. Yes, the deliverables had to exhibit excellent aesthetic judgement, in addition to a careful consideration of the potential users and context of use. However, the students' main focus was on creating interesting solutions to intriguing problems. Our objective was to give students ample room to be innovative, challenging, challenged, and pushed into previously unexplored territory. They were asked to contribute intellectually and practically on a task that did not have a fixed or pre-imagined end result. Their expertise was in terms of design thinking, and the tangible imagining of visual solutions that had little to no precedent.

We somewhat complicated the situation by asking these students to work on projects that are inherently interdisciplinary in nature, dealing with content domains that have been, in some respects, chosen serendipitously. In fact, the content domain was, for us, inconsequential; a design research project in systems design can be carried out with practically any system that has the right combination of complexity and the particular features of interest to the researcher. Whether that system is in the content area, for example, of health, manufacturing, retail, banking, government, or the not-for-profit sector, is a central consideration to what shape the project will take, but the system design focus will tend to render the researcher agnostic with respect to the choice. The same holds true for research projects in areas such as optimization, decision support, communication, interaction, and so on. This is despite the fact that academic fields are largely arranged according to content area, and that even research funding[1] is divided at the federal level into medicine, science, the social sciences and the humanities, and the fine arts.

In order to have students accept a brief of the kind that deals with a cross-disciplinary area, we gave them the control to choose a content domain that interested them, while extending one of two ongoing research projects for information visualization in DH (Rockwell et al. 2009; Radzikowska et al. 2011). Students were asked to meet a set of criteria independent of the project they choose to work on – BigSee or Structured Surfaces – with the final deliverable presented in the form of polished proof-of-concept sketches:

- *attempts to provide opportunities for a positive user experience (useful, usable, memorable, delightful)*: Aims at long-term and/or repeated use, and privileges the exploration of and experimentation with textual content;
- *pushes away from conservative interface solutions and towards the experimental*: Not based on commonly used or pre-established models for website design. Instead, looking for design that adds variety to the 'gene pool of existing ideas' (Ruecker et al. 2008);
- *re-interprets and builds on the work of others*: Students were exposed to Rich Prospect Browsing theory (RPB) (Ruecker et al. 2011) as part of the preparatory phase of the brief. Interfaces based on RPB theory are composed of well-designed visual representations of all items in a particular collection, and a set of tools for manipulating the display; and
- *integrates the structural/aesthetic*: This course is, fundamentally, about solving problems using visual methods. Designs were expected to demonstrate advanced-level aesthetic judgement and typographic elegance and appropriateness.

In addition, students followed an iterative design process while pursuing a wide variety of distinct initial scenarios of use. For example, one designer wanted to 'explore the challenges and insights that would arise if people could compare sections of written material based on rhythm and repetitions of tempos, sounds, and terms' (Radzikowska et al., 2015: 40). Another designer determined that there were five functions to the handling of text – opening/browsing, reading/comprehending, analysing/interpreting, editing/constructing, and publishing/sharing – and aimed to create an interface that enabled all functions in a collaborative setting (Radzikowska et al., 2015: 39).

4.3.1 BigSee

Display size and resolution have been increasing at a steady pace with the economies of scale of personal computing. Wall-sized displays, previously only seen in control centres like NASA, are now affordable and being used for information visualization. But what do we know about the constraints and opportunities for the design of information interaction for such large-scale information displays (LSIDs)? The objective of the BigSee project is to explore the visual representation, exploration, and analysis of a text, using high-resolution displays (data walls), 3D displays, and animated displays. The team located at the University of Alberta is investigating how LSIDs affect visualizations of text. Some of the questions they have been exploring are: is it possible that using a large display will enable us to gain new insights into written works; what can we do visually (with text) on a large display that we cannot on a regular one; and, are large format displays used in a different manner than regular displays?

Students who chose to work on the BigSee project were asked; first, to propose a scenario of use for an LSID that included the display and exploration of large amounts of text; second, to create a set of polished proof-of-concept sketches that showed an experimental interface that enabled text exploration.

4.3.2 Structured surfaces

The Structured Surfaces research option is part of the larger Implementing New Knowledge Environments (INKE) project (http://www.inke.ca), and aims to extend conventional diagrams – such as timelines, radar plots, and targets – by introducing an additional cognitive layer on top of a given data display. The principle is much the same as placing pins on a map, except in this case the map is replaced by a data visualization of some kind, and the pins represent an additional phenomenon being discussed, or better yet, evidence for an argument being made.

Structured surfaces are therefore a natural extension of the way people have handled data and made arguments for centuries. A Cartesian coordinate system, for instance, is a kind of structured surface, except the X and Y axes only provide a very limited kind of data, consisting of the position of pins (or, more conventionally, plotted points) within a space representing whatever variables the X and Y axes have been defined to be. Timelines and calendars can be slightly more sophisticated, with the surface being comprised of points in time or rectangles for dates, with the 'pins' in this case representing events corresponding to those dates and times.

A more useful approach, however, may be to consider the completed Cartesian graph, timeline, or calendar as comprising the underlying information visualization, with the 'pins' for the additional layer being superimposed on the other data.

The display may show either correlated data or it may show data that is causally related. It should be noted that the default expectation of people viewing a structured surface is that there is a correlation, but that more work would need to be done to suggest causation.

4.3.3 Results

Some students encountered logistical and conceptual challenges while working through their projects. In the logistical category, the students who chose to work on the BigSee were somewhat hampered by the lack of a data wall to display and iteratively refine their work. Designing for a large scale is different than designing for the laptop screen, and many of the weaknesses from this group of students arose from the difficulty of imagining how what they were seeing on the small screen would work as an interactive visualization on a much larger scale. One strategy for addressing this equipment deficit was to encourage the students to project their work onto a large screen, so that at least it would be possible to get a sense of what the elements looked like at the proper size. Unfortunately, not all of the students attempted this approach, and the results suffered accordingly. On the conceptual side, the problem faced by many of the students was in distinguishing between an underlying information visualization and the additional layer of information being superimposed on it. In the case of a map with pins, the cultural convention, at least in the western world, is quite well established – so much so, in fact, that one of the students ended up producing a map with pins. For some of the others, however, there were questions about what would constitute a sufficiently useful layer of underlying information. In some cases, they took the stance that a structure of any kind – such as a Cartesian coordinate system – would be sufficient. While strictly speaking this is true, in practice it is more interesting and useful to have as rich a layer of underlying information as possible before the additional 'argumentative' or 'evidential' layer is superimposed. A common problem faced by all students was the extent to which their visualization ideas were derivative – in some cases directly reproducing the examples they were given in the brief for the assignment, and in other cases mashing up a set of visualizations from previous researchers. It is too much to expect genuine invention to take place in a class assignment at this level, but what we were hoping to find were interesting and novel variations on existing visualization approaches, and some of these did occur.

More students worked on the Structured Surface project than on the BigSee project. In terms of the choice of topic, students ranged widely. In fact, although most of the visualizations were to some extent data agnostic, and the data used was not from real sources, the selection of use cases proved to be one of the more interesting outcomes of the project. Here are some examples:

BigSee:

- Tweet*istics: Tracking trends on Twitter;
- Textwave: Finding the literary DNA of texts for *The Shining;*
- TAAVS: Text analysis and visualization system for Cubist Art; and
- a collaborative secondary research and authoring environment on psychology.

Structured Surfaces:

- days of the week, months, national holidays, daylight savings time, and suicides for men and women;
- coffee intake, country, year, and homicides;
- world religions, numbers of believers, geographic dispersal, and wars;
- countries and endangered species;
- search engines, time, and numbers of search terms;
- NHL player statistics, home games, and away games;
- US population by state and year, and obesity;
- internet activities, year, and age of user;
- newspaper sales by month, and subject area of cover story;
- US expenditure per student by state, and teenage mothers;
- types of advertising and website hits per day;
- # of Mount Royal degrees awarded, field, year, and # of exchange students; and
- new Facebook accounts, new MySpace accounts, month, and year.

In some cases, students were suggesting a causal relation that would have required much more work to establish. However, the Structured Surface is primarily intended as a research tool where people are able to look for interesting correlations that are then subjected to further scrutiny, so in that sense, the choices the students made were appropriate.

As an undergraduate classroom experience in participating at the level of experimental design research, the results were of a strictly limited scope, but within that scope they were surprisingly positive. Our previous results from including individual undergraduate design students on research teams have not been promising, with the students needing an unusually lengthy period of acclimatization, during which they are alternately helpless and patronizing, before they can finally settle on the possible contribution that they are actually capable of making in relation to the other members of the research team.

In the case of the classroom assignment, the other students in the class helped to create an environment – perhaps we might say a temporary community of practice – that was initiated, informed, and supported by the assignment, the instructor, the critique process, and guest lecturers.

4.3.4 What we'd change

There are several strategies that could be used to improve future iterations of this brief. Access to a data wall would make the BigSee choice more straightforward to design and test. Further emphasis on the usefulness of a meaningful lower layer in the data visualization would improve the Structured Surfaces choice. This assignment focused on the visual representation of information, to the exclusion of many other salient concerns for researchers. For example, requiring the students to use actual data would make the results vastly more interesting, although it would necessitate more commitment to the project. This could perhaps be alleviated by having the students work in teams, or by running the course over two semesters. It should also be reiterated that in some cases the students were not sufficiently careful in distinguishing between correlation and causation. An implied causation where none is proven is a weakness that needs to be handled carefully, both by the instructor and the students, and one where learning needs to happen over the length of multiple semesters, with repeated opportunities for practice. Finally, the BigSee and Structured Surfaces projects followed a much simpler brief that was assigned earlier in the semester: to re-design an existing website for a not-for-profit agency. This was a deliberate choice made by the instructor, in order to provide students with a broader, more complete perspective on interface design, and the kinds of contributions that can be made by information designers when collaborating on cutting-edge design research. It is worthy to note, however, that previous to this project none of the students had any familiarity with DH, yet their previous training made it possible for them to not only engage with DH, but to make modest contributions to the field.

4.4 Case study 4: Design as inquiry

Thus far we've attempted to make a value case for research partnerships between design and DH. What follows is a case study of a project that brought together design, DH, computing science, and chemical and materials engineering. While working on this interdisciplinary team, we designed interfaces that facilitate human decision-making within a manufacturing context. Our goal was to extend the territory of acceptable design alternatives by looking into the space defined by an intersection of design and DH.

We treated our designs for decision support as cultural objects, or in Derrida's terms 'texts' that could be read and analysed from the perspective of comparative literary studies. This way of dealing with the topic, even though it was funded through Engineering, clearly put us in the realm of DH. If something is being read, and even more so read both at a distance, as a cultural phenomenon, and up close, in its details as revealed through a close reading, then it is a DH-style project. This perspective was brought home with startling clarity when the technical side of the team, particularly the computer scientists, wholeheartedly rejected the attempt as a waste of time, a misguided kind of scholarship, and, well, let it be said: blasphemy.

From our perspective, this kind of reading and re-reading provided us with valuable insights into how these graphical interfaces could, subsequently, be read and understood by their users – a critical concern to the design of effective user interfaces. This approach to interfaces is also somewhat similar to the practice of critique, which is fairly common to design. Arguments can and have been made, however, that human-computer interface design (HCI) can benefit from a more rigorous engagement with design criticism (Cockton et al. 2010: ff.). Criticism, or critique, in design most often takes place within the process of creation, partnered with the practice of design iteration. In iteration, designers cycle through making-thinking-remaking until either they become reasonably satisfied with the emergent result or they, simply, run out of the time that has been allocated for the project (hopefully the former). Too often, however, critique and iteration are used to make incremental adjustments to existing artefacts, too narrowly focused on the functionality or the aesthetics of the object, rather than to enable substantial challenges to or shifts away from the status quo.

Further, this was for us a DH project because it was an attempt to interrogate the theory of rich-prospect browsing from a new perspective. We had primarily dealt with data in the form of text and images, and although both were involved here, too, the main objective was to use numerical data and calculations around it to produce an environment for decision support.

In the place of design critique, we therefore proposed the use of critical design theory, which provokes designers to reflect on and critique existing cultural values, mores, and practices. Critical design emerges out of constructive design research, positioning design activity as a form of research (Bardzell et al. 2012: 289). Popularized by Dunne and Raby, critical design looks beyond issues of usability and functionality, beyond 'how users interact with the designed product on a day-to-day basis'(Kannabiran and Petersen 2010: n.pag.), instead using 'speculative design proposals' (Dunne and Raby 2014: n.pag.) to challenge our assumptions about design, asking us to reconsider the positive and negative roles it plays in our daily lives. Design is seen as opportunity for provocation rather than an exercise in 'rearranging surface features according to the latest fashion while obfuscating the norms and conventions inscribed in the designs and their use' (Bardzell et al. 2012: 289), a particularly important, weakly addressed, point in HCI. In constructive design research, or research through design, 'design experience in the form of designers' judgements is equally important to the analysis and reasoning activities that are common to all kinds of research' (Bardzell et al. 2012: 288). A design research activity 'can start with just imagining future states, and in HCI, how technology can improve the current state of human existence' (Bardzell et al. 2012: 288).

In his 1973 edition of *Design for the Real World,* Papanek calls out industrial design as being one of the most harmful professions, and advertising for its lack of authenticity. He states that, while advertising designers persuade 'people to buy things they don't need, with money they don't have', industrial designers create unsafe, unnecessary, 'tawdry idiocies' to be 'hawked by advertisers' (Papanek 1973: 14). Papanek's judgement on these areas of design goes even further. He calls design in the age of mass production 'the most powerful tool with which man shapes his tools and environment (and by extension, society and himself), then accuses it of putting 'murder on the level of mass production' (Papanek 1973: 14). As evidence he points to the industrial process and product-use that create exorbitant waste material, pollute our air and water, and are capable of causing injury and harm to a cross-global population. HCI-emergent artefacts straddle both categories: some have the tangibility of industrial design, while others have the promotional qualities of advertising. And some, we would argue, embody the negative aspects of both, as described by Papanek. Though most websites are not the outcome or the mass producer of industrial design, many enable mass production, distribution, purchasing, and obsolescence on a scale that does not have its equal in a physical counterpart.

Take Amazon as an example. In 2014, they reported almost 89 billion in net sales (Clement, 2015), with almost 114,000 total office and warehouse units, 181.12 million unique monthly visitors, and 305,258,547 unique products (Clement, 2015). While Amazon is not responsible for manufacturing all these products, the company and its website do provide unprecedented access to them in terms of availability and lower cost, with little substantial information regarding the products' origin or value. If we wanted to know which specific sheep helped to make my sweater, we would be out of luck.

Thus, we looked to theories emergent from the humanities to inform our design work for decision support – critical theory, feminist HCI, and Rich-Prospect Browsing Theory. In our most cliché terms – we looked through the unexpected to see beyond the conventional solutions.

The Decision Support for Multi-Mode Oil Sands Operations project,[2] briefly described in Chapter 1, extended Rich Prospect Browsing in order to propose novel approaches to interface design for manufacturing decision support. More precisely, we aimed to diversify the existing discourse about what design strategies help to make an effective human-computer interface for use in manufacturing decision support, while including not just the quantitative, but also the qualitative experiences of the decision-makers within the design. Rather than following the usual path of making technical tools from the sciences available to humanists, we were, in effect, borrowing ideas and processes from DH and design, and importing them into engineering.

The existing discourse for decision support in manufacturing is defined, in large part, by linear programming (LP) – the standard tool for many businesses and organizations for determining optimal solutions (MacDonald 2009). Most recently, several standard business packages (Microsoft Excel, for example) included an LP solver (see Figure 4.23).

Plug-ins such as the one for Excel shown in Figure 4.23 and applications such as LP Solve are limited to computing the minimum or maximum of a linear objective function within user-defined linear constraints. New solutions require the adjustment of numerical values and re-solving (re-calculating) the formula. Thus, unlike Rich-Prospect Browsers, Solver, LP Solve, and others are limited in their

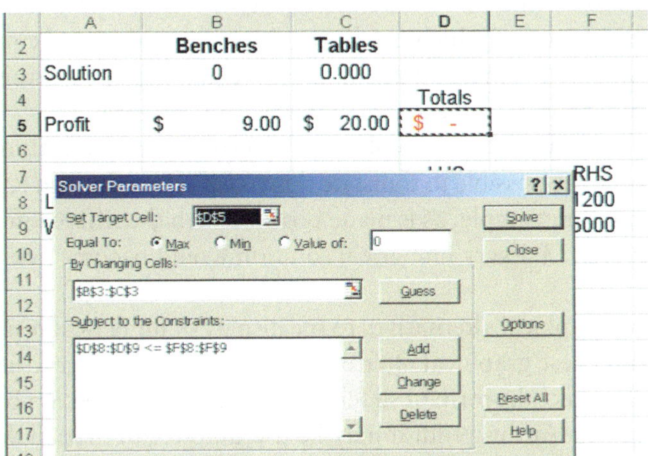

FIGURE 4.23: An example of the Microsoft Excel Solver (Microsoft).

$$\begin{array}{ll} \texttt{maximize} & C^{T}\ x \\ \texttt{subject to} & A\ x <= B \\ & x >= 0 \end{array}$$

FIGURE 4.24: Sample linear programming problem, written in the standard form (Free Software Foundation).

ability to support data exploration, knowledge discovery, and hypothesis formulation, leaving ample room for critical innovation within this domain.

Several properties make interfaces for decision support good candidates for RPB. Decision support is essentially made up of a series of subsystems, each with an interconnected set of processes. Imagine that the starting point for a user is the question ‘should I allocate 20 four-ton trucks or 50 two-ton trucks to transport this month’s raw product?’ She will manipulate the constraints (a subcategory of variables), then generate and review the optimal solution. Viewing every part of the formula all at once may be beneficial since it makes visible the specific factors being considered by the system in generating the solution. If the generated solution is displayed on the same screen as the controls, the user can go back and forth between controls and solutions, adjusting then reviewing the results. There is a potential for immediacy to this kind of display that is not available on multi-screen alternatives.

A linear programming problem of the type that underpinned the design task defined by the Oil Sands Project is mathematically formulated as shown in Figure 4.24 (called the Standard Form) (Free Software Foundation). Thus, the model we used to calculate potential optimization solution alternatives consisted of one objective function which is a linear equation that must be maximized or minimized, combined with a number of linear inequalities or constraints. This was our starting point for the design of DS interface alternatives.

Once the formula has been calculated, the result is a numerical solution to the problem. It would be possible to translate this visual system into an RPB, presented in tabular form, for example, as is made possible with the Microsoft Excel Solver shown in Figure 4.23. Every numerical solution would become one item in a cell of the table.

Other, more graphical alternatives to the display of numerical results are possible. In Design Z these graphical alternatives take the form of gear-like shapes. In Design A+1 they take the form of sliders and bar graphs. In Design B, they appear as lines and circles. At this point it may be useful to recall that all designs generated for the Oil Sands Project are based on an ice cream manufacturing scenario, as dictated by our industry partner.

As there are different methods to understanding and writing about text, there are different methods to understanding and writing about a piece of design:

1. *descriptive*: Articulates what we see, how it's made or how it works, what happens, or how it sounds, tastes, or smells;
2. *analytical*: Takes what's been described and groups it into emergent categories;
3. *systematic*: A walkthrough of the process of how a design has been done (how it became what it is);
4. *persuasive*: Expresses a position or opinion in order to sway others regarding the value or worth of design;
5. *critical*: Brings into focus by analysing for strengths or weaknesses, either through one or several lenses or points of view (other than your own); and
6. *expository*: Requires extensive research on the ideas or issues that are contextual to the design, then aims to bring a new perspective on the design activity.

Below is a descriptive reflection of the three design alternatives – Z, A+1, and B – at the leaf, or micro, level, followed by a critical reflection on the design choices made regarding the designs' visual form, and the consequences of these decisions.

4.4.1 Descriptive reflections

Design Z (gears)

The visual system for Design Z assigned meaning to differences in a gear's internal structure, use or lack of a border, border shape, and gear colour. Manipulating the size and the number of gears, the complexity of their shape, their colour, and level of transparency allowed us to develop a set of rules governing a gear's visual appearance:

- a gear's border would have meaning;
- the colour of a gear would relate, cognitively, to the type of item it is representing;
- colour use would remain consistent;
- a colour that attracts a high-degree of visual attention will signal importance or alert (more than one colour may be needed here, depending on the level of alert); and
- a relationship between gears will be visually represented, as will a lack of a relationship.

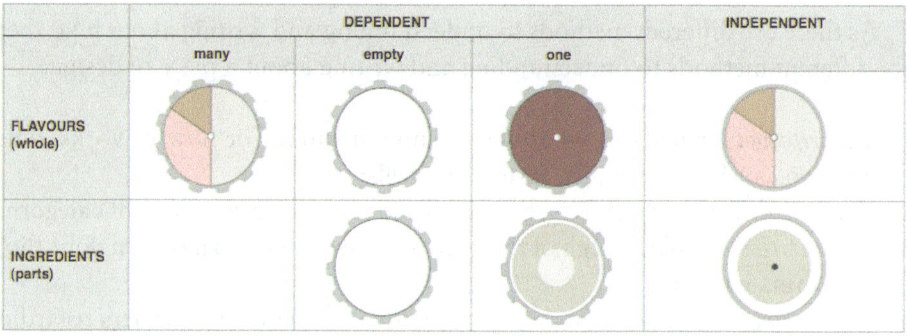

	DEPENDENT			INDEPENDENT
	many	empty	one	
FLAVOURS (whole)				
INGREDIENTS (parts)				

FIGURE 4.25: Two gear designs: one for flavours and one for ingredients.

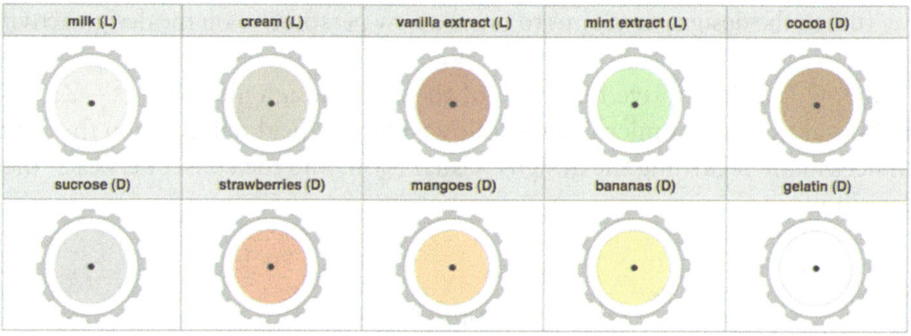

milk (L)	cream (L)	vanilla extract (L)	mint extract (L)	cocoa (D)
sucrose (D)	strawberries (D)	mangoes (D)	bananas (D)	gelatin (D)

FIGURE 4.26: Colour as applied to the ingredient gears.

We designed two gear structures: gears for parts (ingredients) and gears for wholes, containing parts (ice cream flavours) (see Figure 4.25). The flavour gear design can accommodate situations when a flavour is made up of multiple ingredients and situations when a flavour is made up of only one ingredient. A toothed-border, common to a gear, signifies that a gear has a dependent relationship to other gears. A lack of a toothed border means that the gear is independent of other gears.

Each ingredient has its own colour and/or texture (see Figure 4.26). Coloured gears signify liquid ingredients, while coloured and textured gears signify dry ingredients. This distinction provides an additional layer of information and a greater range of options for colour coding.

Flavours are made up of a combination of those colours and/or textures that have been assigned to their ingredients. The recipe for every flavour is viewable at a glance: every gear is a pie chart displaying the ratios of each ingredient to the

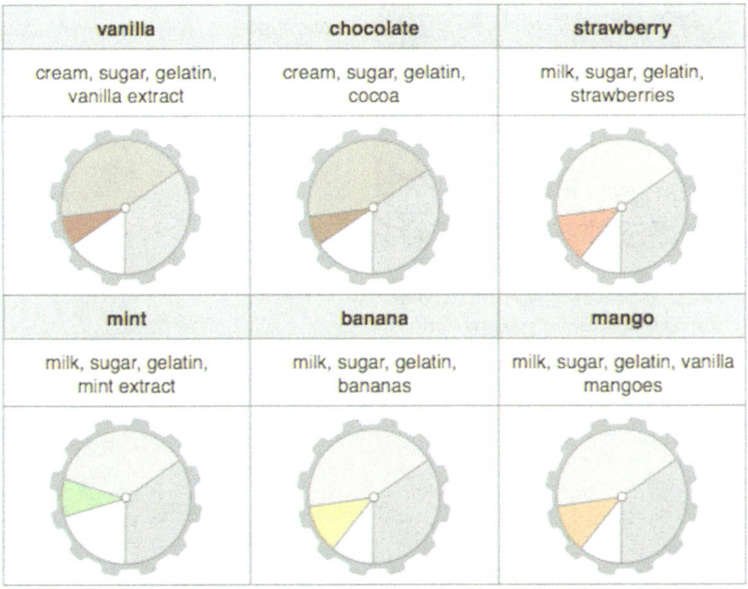

vanilla	chocolate	strawberry
cream, sugar, gelatin, vanilla extract	cream, sugar, gelatin, cocoa	milk, sugar, gelatin, strawberries

mint	banana	mango
milk, sugar, gelatin, mint extract	milk, sugar, gelatin, bananas	milk, sugar, gelatin, vanilla mangoes

FIGURE 4.27: Flavour gears.

whole recipe (see Figure 4.27). For example, the recipe for vanilla-flavoured ice cream is made up of almost equal parts cream and sugar, with some gelatine and a bit of vanilla extract.

Design A+1 (bars & sliders)

After a thorough exploration of alternatives to the visual representation of the solution portion of Design A+1 (located at the bottom portion of the display), we emerged with 24 unique designs, sub-divided into 7 categories:

1. visualizing current vs. solution vs. total capacity values;
2. visualizing the increase or decrease of production values;
3. exploring options for numerical value treatments;
4. exploring horizontal instead of vertical bar graphs;
5. exploring regular instead of stacked bar graphs;
6. exploring pie charts instead of bar graphs; and
7. exploring an experimental solution.

The 24 alternatives included bar graphs, stacked bar graphs, and pie charts, with varying amounts of labelling and numerical support. Each design alternative had

2e

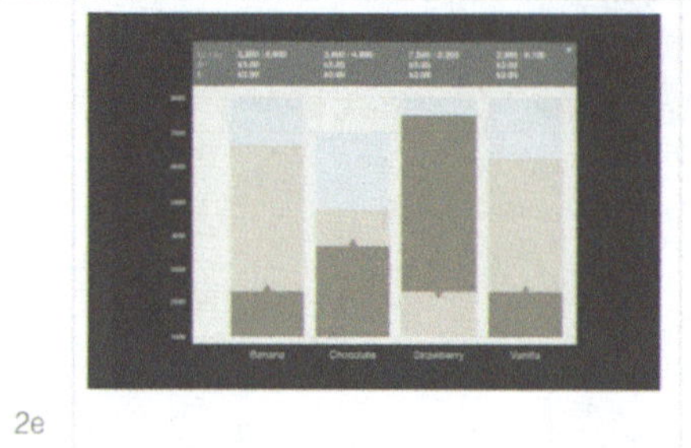

Small, triangular arrows (without stems), placed on top of the "current level" portion of each bar.

Advantages:

- The arrows' proximity to the current level portions of the stacks may provide a clearer reading than in 2d.

Disadvantages:

- In a situation where the increase or decrease of a value is very small, the space won't be able to accommodate the height of the arrow.
- This alternative has the potential to be confusing – should the current level be read to the height of the bar, or the height of the arrow?
- Due to the small size of the arrows, the above-mentioned disadvantages have a lesser degree of impact than alternatives 2a–2c.

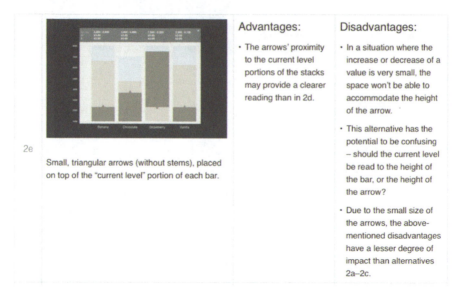

FIGURE 4.28: One of the 24 unique designs explored for Design A+1.

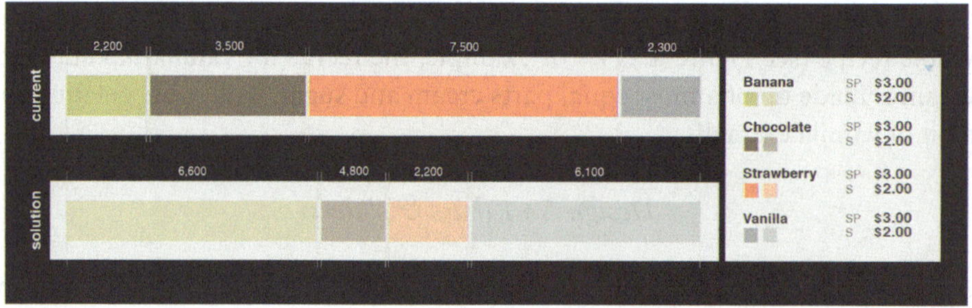

FIGURE 4.29: The final, experimental solution alternative, from Design A+1.

its own functional advantages and disadvantages (see Figure 4.28 for one alternative and its functional overview).

The experimental solution alternative (see Figure 4.29) emerged as particularly unique and compact. Although, still a stacked bar graph, it combines all four flavours into one graphic, making comparison of the flavours against one another easier, for both the current and solution levels. The addition of vertical lines also supports comparison of current values with solution values. In this design, numerical values are proximal to the graphical representations, while still using less space than the other solution alternatives we proposed.

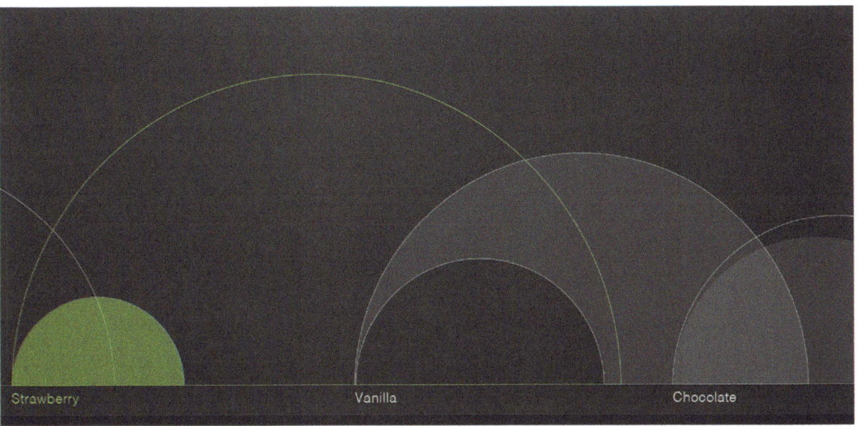

FIGURE 4.30: Partial solution visualization, from Design B.

Design B (lines & dots)

Design B emerged as the graphically simplified version of Design A+1. Solution alternatives are presented as half circles, with the outline representing the current state of production and the solid fill representing the suggested level (recommended solution). For example, in Figure 4.30, the system recommends a substantial decrease in the production of strawberry ice cream and an increase in the production of vanilla.

Each design – A+1, Z, and B – consists of two parts: the controls and the solutions. In the gear design, the controls and the solutions are intentionally combined into the same set of graphical objects. Users would drag the appropriate gears into the central screen space, then manipulate them: increasing a gear's size, for example, to signify an increase in production. Constraints that are dependent on one another remain spatially connected and change together as needed. For example, if an increase in the production of strawberry ice cream affects the number of trucks required for distribution, the gear representing trucks connects to the gear representing strawberry ice cream, and their sizes change accordingly. In contrast, both Designs A+1 and B contain a spatial separation of controls and solutions. Controls are located at the top of the screen, and solutions appear at the bottom, once the appropriate set of user actions (setting up the constraints and selecting 'Solve') have been completed. At the same time, controls and solution alternatives remain visually connected through the use of a unified colour palette, typographic structure, and graphical system.

4.4.2 Analytical reflection of Designs A+1, B, and Z

Above is, more or less, a visual and functional description of the three designs, derived primarily out of discussions with the academic team and our industry partner. Next, we will carry out a reading of these designs as text, to determine not only what has been graphically constructed, but also how the choices around the details of that construction may be interpreted.

This is, of course, only one form of analysis. We might alternatively have taken the more conventional approach of carrying out some kind of user study, where people who were not involved in the creation of the system use it. Often we ask them to think aloud about what they are doing and why, sometimes sitting with them and prompting them when they forget to describe their actions. This is referred to as following a 'think-aloud protocol with sideshadowing'.

Often, the people and the use are somewhat contrived, consisting of a set of participants who are not part of the actual intended user group, but were chosen because they were easy to reach. Many studies, for example, draw on university students who might be familiar with the field but do not necessarily have relevant work experience. The tasks may also reflect a set of research questions rather than the typical conditions of use, which might not touch on all the design features of interest.

An alternative, and arguably better, approach to user study would be to embed the system in a working environment where it can be adopted by participants who are using it for its intended purpose. This approach has the advantage of getting more 'authentic' feedback, especially if the system has been equipped with a means of recording interactions over time. However, this strategy requires that the system be robust enough for actual implementation with real data, that there is sufficient use to see how participants repeatedly interact with all the features, and that the potentially massive amounts of data are somehow useful in interpretation. It also requires that participants and their organization have sufficient patience and commitment and training to include this new system for a limited trial in their regular work pattern. That's quite a lot of commitment.

The approach we take, of treating the interfaces as a kind of text, echoes the approaches to analysis described in Muratovski (2016) in his discussion of hermeneutics in design research. In particular, he identifies three specific methods: compositional interpretation, content analysis, and semiotics. These focus, respectively, on the formal properties, the subject matter, and the interpretive aspects, particularly in the sociocultural domain.

In terms of the formal properties of the designs, we will begin with the geometry. Designs A+1, B and Z range from the simple to the complex. Design Z constitutes a layering of circular shapes that suggest gear-like structures, reminiscent of the inner working of clocks, car parts, and machines. In this way, Design Z can be read as iconic, indexical, and symbolic. As an index, these gears represent factory production or industry. Symbolically, they are meant to represent connectivity and interdependence, since a gear's teeth make it possible for it to connect with other gears in order to form a more complex system. Thus, the fact that the manipulation of one gear affects or changes another constitutes a rather short metaphorical leap – a reasonable mapping to the physical world. Furthermore, in the specific instance of the case study presented by our industry partner – decision-making in manufacturing – gears are part of a familiar, if rather dated, visual language. This design leverages what has been recently termed skeuomorphism: where an artefact retains ornamental design cues from structures that were necessary in the original (Basalla 1989: 107). An e-mail application using the iconic graphic of a paper envelope to suggest the sending of written communication is one example of skeuomorphism in HCI.

Adding the soft colour palette to the gears – pinks, yellows, blues, and tans – is meant to suggest a particular type of machine-based production: ice cream flavours. This particular colour choice moves the design away from the harsh contrasts typically associated with metal gears and industrial machinery: greys, blacks, and dark browns. The pastel colour palette has a potential downside, anchoring the design in ice cream production, making it less transferable into other types of manufacturing.

Direct gear manipulation provides users with the perception of unmediated control over outcomes – for example, as a user changes a gear's size to suggest an increase in the production of a flavour, that increase initiates the calculation, generating an appropriate set of codependent outcomes.

Design A+1 borrows from a visual language of bar charts, familiar to those who use Excel spreadsheets or read financial reports. The colour structure in this design consists of greys, white, and black, with a simulated-metallic background pattern. Thickness of bars represents lesser or greater amounts. Lack of direct manipulation, the visual separation of controls from outcomes (solutions), and the addition of the 'Solve' button place the system (the algorithm) in the authority role – the user asks, waits, and receives the 'optimal' answer.

Design B is, in many ways, very similar to Design A+1, with two major differences. While Design A+1 is rigid with its use of vertical and horizontal lines and rectangular shapes, Design B appears much more delicate and organic. Numerical detailing has been intentionally omitted. This, combined with swooping arcs, a green tone, and an overall lack of mass, gives Design B an almost ephemeral quality. The potential result may be an increased willingness to consider the interaction as decision experimentation rather than decision implementation. Though the colour structure – green on black – may suggest a 1980s computer terminal, the overall look and feel invokes the more technological science fiction (see Figure 4.31).

While each of the three designs uses a different look-and-feel (some more literal, some more metaphorical) in an attempt to connect with its users and the subject matter, each one is also in some way allied with the visual language of industry or

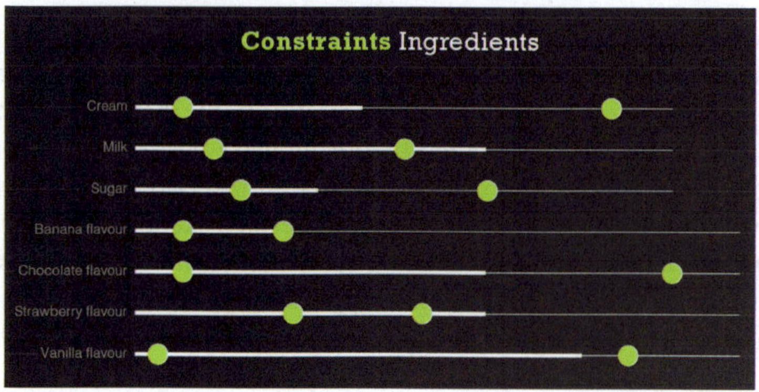

FIGURE 4.31: Controls for setting the ingredients bounds, from Design B.

technology and its emergent social and cultural traditions. Design Z appears the most connected to its industrial legacy while, at the same time, suggesting the most recent use of interaction technology (through its application of direct manipulation). In design, there is now widespread recognition of the need for user involvement throughout the design process, and various methods to achieve this have either been developed or imported from the social sciences. In the case of the Oil Sands Project, our team had contact with three people in upper-management positions, all male with backgrounds in industrial engineering. We were unable, due to understandable constraints, to engage a wider and more diverse user group. Thus, it is reasonable to question the appropriateness of a visual language connected to an industrial past or a futuristic, technological future. Aside from concerns over look-and-feel, there is an aura of hierarchy and authority that is suggested by the functionality expressed through Designs A+1 and B: selection of constraints, request of formula, and review of generated solution. It removes the user from a place of ownership and accountability that may or may not be appropriate within manufacturing decision support.

4.4.3 Feminist RPB in manufacturing DSS

Woodrow W. Winchester III, in his paper on culturally responsive design tools (2010: 14), reflects on Elizabeth Churchill's exploration of gender in design as she asserts that designers 'are not passive bystanders (of the process) […] we design products with implicit or explicit assumptions about how products will be used and by whom' (Churchill 2010: n.pag.). Both Churchill and Winchester challenge the notion of the universal user as, somehow, representative of the diverse populations that typically engage with technology. Most product and technology designers are male, white, and most likely of a higher socioeconomic status (plus, further provoked by Winchester, tend to identify as heterosexual) (Winchester 2010: 15). As a result, that 'universal user' becomes an unexamined and unquestioned self-reflection of the dominant group. The manufacturing domain appears particularly problematic in this respect. In the United States, for example, while manufacturing companies face a 'widely acknowledged talent shortfall', women remain underrepresented at all levels of the workforce (Manufacturing Institute 2013: 3). The literature in decision support design, with its recommendations regarding standards and best practices, is also predominantly written by men.

At the start of this project we challenged ourselves with these questions – what falls outside the typical discourse that surrounds both decision support and manufacturing; what will offer us unique perspectives on this particular wicked problem? For us, the answer became critical design, Rich Prospect Browsing (with its feminist origins), and feminist HCI and, as is common in complex design problems, we ended up with even more questions:

- What decision factors are made part of the decision-making process, and which are made obscure or invisible?
- How are different types of decision factors currently represented and, through such representation, given a hierarchy of priority or importance?
- Are we considering the situated (contextual) nature of decision-making?
- Are current systems obscuring the role, characteristics, and responsibility of the decision-maker, and how is such lack of self-disclosure impacting those imbedded within the decision-making process?

Critical reflection using feminist HCI

In an effort to answer these questions, we undertook a critical reading of Designs A+1, B, and Z through the lens provided by the six feminist HCI qualities proposed by Bardzell: pluralism, participation, advocacy, ecology, embodiment, and self-disclosure, once again focusing on the graphical representation of solutions (items in the collection) (Bardzell 2010: 1305).

Pluralist design challenges the notion of the 'Universal User' by recognizing that its default is white, middle class, heterosexual, and, most likely, male. In contrast, pluralism aims to be sensitive to marginal or marginalized users, thus becoming more inclusive, more diverse, and more representative of particular, specific user communities (Burnett et al. 2011: 450).

Current iterations of Designs A+1, B, and Z resist pluralism in several ways. They do not consider the diversity with which different types of users may want to engage with the interface. According to the formula used to underpin the decision calculations, users must select and manipulate some set of constraints in order to generate a solution. Thus, all users must follow the same process in order to engage with and/or construct their solution collection. On the other hand, since users are generating their own collection and, according to RPB Theory, can subsequently browse and manipulate that collection, there is promise that different types of users could generate different types of collections (based on their own interests and agendas). When considering what kinds of items act as constraints, it would be important to require those that represent marginalized interests, not only those that are most often considered in terms of manufacturing decision-making (cost of materials, production levels, distribution, etc.). Then the question becomes whether all types of constraints should be given the same type of graphical form. In Design Z, all constraints are circles or gears, though differently coloured. In Design A+1, all constraints are squares or rectangles. In Design B, they are the same line and green dot pattern. If we expanded what we considered as a constraint into, for example, hours worked by the employees of the plant, should we then consider a different graphical representation for, in this case, human versus mechanical constraints?

The qualities of participation and embodiment contribute to this argument, warning us against speaking for others (Muller 2011: 447–49) and emphasizing that our understanding of ourselves and our world 'derives crucially from our location in a physical and social world as embodied actors' (Harrison, Tatar, and Sengers 2007: 6). It encourages us to actively seek out and listen to the voices we are describing or discussing. Thus, if we support the user in manipulating constraints that have human consequences, should we not give those human constraints a voice, some form of agency in the manipulation? Of course, it would be irresponsible not to, at this point, underscore the reality that certain groups will hold more privilege than others within the decision-making process. Privilege, in this context, refers to the position that some groups hold unearned advantages (and power) relative to those of others, thereby perpetuating social inequality – some are more likely to be the decision-makers while others are the human agents, affected by the decisions (Twine 2013: 8–10).

As described above, both Design A+1 and B have the potential of disempowering users by suggesting that the formula is the agent of knowledge – the one who will determine the best solution to the human-proposed problem. Reinforcing the browsing model – where users generate numerous potential solutions, then are encouraged to browse them in order to determine 'best fit' – has the potential of remediating the disempowerment. Additionally, browsing supports advocacy (the third of Bardzell's Feminist HCI qualities [Bardzell 2010: 1306]), in enabling users to take a position or course of action. In the end, it is the users who determine the best decision to implement, not the formula. In order to make the connection between person and action more transparent, each decision that has been selected for implementation should be connectable back to the person who generated it, thus providing the potential for future retrospection.

Assigning different graphical forms to solutions that privilege different types of outcomes (production optimization vs. labour hours, for example) can also support a questioning of the point of view (lens) and the position(s) that individual decision-makers aim to assert in their communities. A design that considers the quality of self-disclosure renders visible the ways that it affects its users. It calls to attention what the design is trying to make of its user, introduces a critical distance between itself and the user, and creates opportunities for users to define themselves.

The quality of design ecology considers the ways that an artefact exists in relationships with other artefacts, how they affect one another, and how these relationships determine meaning. Most recently, designers are particularly focused on environmental, gender, race, social class, and international consequences (Bardzell 2010: 1307). Thus, should all solution alternatives be given the same graphical form, even if they carry with them negative consequences? Currently all three designs equalize decision alternatives, independent of their outcomes.

4.4.4 Reflection using a critical design framework

The relationship between a paying, industry partner or client and the designer is, acknowledgedly, complicated. On the Oil Sands Project, our industry partner made the decision for our team to use an ice cream instead of oil production scenario. They argued that ice cream manufacturing was the same as oil in terms of the formula that would drive the decision support system, with similar number and type of constraints. However, the ice cream scenario hides the context of the real problem: in Alberta and beyond, the oil sands are controversial in terms of their environmental and community impacts (Gosselin et al. 2010: ff.). The same level of controversy is not attached to ice cream manufacturing. Similarly, when issues of gender, diversity, or inequality are either not perceived, or are perceived with hostility, transparent negotiation about including their consideration as an important aspect of the project becomes challenging if not outright counter-productive. Hence, such questions as who works at an oil extraction and processing facility, what kinds of positions they hold, who is impacted by whose decisions and in what ways, are there differences in decision-making styles or approaches, where the inequality lies and how it manifests, and others can never be explored. Acting as though potential differences in status and authority do not exist isolates the design process from critical engagement, reinforcing the status quo and entrenching the resulting artefact in a fundamentally patriarchal understandings of its users. Finally, positioning the scenario in ice cream instead of oil adds a level of insignificance to the DSS that, once again, does not match real-world application.

If we are to make a difference in the form of implementable design, must we accept the reality of most (if not all) design practice: those who pay the bills, make the rules? In certain situations it may be enough that we are open and transparent about the limitations placed on us and our design efforts, acknowledging the narrow view addressed by an artefact. Designers do this already, and the design discipline, in fact, celebrates the successful focusing of a problem and addressing of specific, well-defined client and user needs. If we add to that a transparency around what has been excluded and why, and a visibility around the designer's positionality, there will be no shame in meeting the project brief. However, we are still accountable (should be held accountable) for not questioning if there were options other than ice cream for our scenario. Could we have successfully pushed back against that decision, or proposed a scenario not grounded in oil that has a similar potential for human and environmental consequences? In the Oil Sands Project the significant, unspoken power hierarchy that placed design research as in service to other disciplines made such a challenge highly problematic (impossible). In collaborations between design and DH, where we may not necessarily have the ethical dilemmas associated with hazardous materials, there are likely to still exist issues of power, race, representation, appropriation, gender, ableism, etc. that call for transparency and positionality.

If we fail to challenge the agendas established by industry, what happens to Z or Z+1? Under client-driven constraints, how can design move beyond incremental improvements and into design innovation? On past projects in DH, we have argued the following: for interdisciplinary research to be a worthwhile endeavour for all the disciplines involved in the project, we must agree to respect and work towards accomplishing every discipline's research agenda and meet its publishing requirements (Ruecker and Radzikowska 2008: 288). One discipline cannot become in service to another. Such a hierarchy is easily the default in design, since its research practice is newer than most others, while its industry practice is one of the most visible. However, in academic projects, design researchers must strive for equal representation by seeking funding and establishing and promoting their own research agendas.

In light of our concerns around accountability and our desire for movement beyond the status quo, we developed a six-part conceptual framework for the interrogation, construction, and reflection on artefacts created as part of a critical design practice:

1. *challenges existing practices*: intentionally diversifies the pool of existing design ideas, with a focus on extreme departures;
2. *aims towards an actionable ideal future*: creates actionable design that is meant to enact positive change on its world;

3. *looks for what has been made invisible or under-represented*: searches for what exists outside the bounds of typical discourse;
4. *considers the micro, meso, and macro*: designs to support micro, meso, and macro views on the collection, offering tools for changing between these views, revealing new or more detailed information;
5. *privileges transparency and accountability*: self discloses about the design's position on and perception of its users, and the positionality of its designers; and
6. *expects and welcomes being subjected to rigorous critique*: considers every instance of critical design as an iteration, thus subject to interpretation and questioning. Invites and engages in such critique.

The first three principles in concert – challenging existing practices while striving for an actionable ideal future and considering that which has been made invisible or under-represented – are where we encountered the wicked problem of interface design for decision support in manufacturing. Seeking an actionable, ideal future begs the question: ideal for whom? While A+1, B, and Z differ in their likelihood of implementation (and the amount of resources they would require to be implemented well) each of them is, in fact, implementable. If we consider the perspective of the industry partner, two of these designs would be considered ideal: A+1 and B are successful in visually representing the linear programming formula and in guiding users towards generating an optimized solution. The fact that these designs ignore human and environmental constraints may also be considered a positive. If we shift perspectives and attempt to challenge existing beliefs and practices, such a narrow definition of manufacturing decision-making comes under question – we can't accomplish one without discarding the other, or shifting who we consider as the ruling authority over our design. Thus, who is our master? Is it the client, with his requirements, constraints, context of use (as well as the monetary and logistical support for the project)? Is it those who will affect and be affected by the decision-making? Or is it the designer, with her moral code and design research agenda?

4.5 Exercises: Data visualization and interface design

A map reduces three-dimensional topography to a two-dimensional diagram. Maps are representations of a particular place in time that have been intentionally reduced in size, their contents selected and distilled to some purpose and according to some particular point of view. Given enough time and changes to the place they are meant to represent, maps lose their reflective capacity, becoming more abstractions than representations. According to John Pickles, a geographer with interests in social power and maps, a map is text: maps have words associated with them, function as a form of writing, and use a system of symbols within their own syntax. Maps are designed social, cultural, and historical objects that can be read and interpreted from multiple points of view.

Through the act of map creation, we get to ask ourselves:

- What is revealed by what was forgotten?
- Are we remembering/reconstructing a place as it was in one specific moment in time, or is our map a collage of multiple instances, compressed and overlapped in our memory?
- Is scale objective, or does it change based on what we considered and consider to be of most importance?

4.5.1 Altered map

What you'll need

- Photocopied map.
- Mark-making materials, various colours.

Photocopy a topographic map in black and white. Using watercolours, crayons, or markers colour in alternate spaces between its contour lines. Select colours to maximize effect – consider contrasting colours such as blue and yellow, green and red, orange and purple. The bands of colour will reveal and sharpen how the map is configured. In purely pictorial terms the result will be dynamic and multidimensional. Consider adding a layer of meaning – data – to what parts of the map you choose to colour and how, moving the activity beyond abstraction.

4.5.2 Memory map

What you'll need

- Various materials: paint, markers, cut paper or fabric.
- Surface material (large piece of cardboard or foam core should work well).
- Adhesive.

Think of a place that holds some meaning to you but that you haven't visited in quite some time. Create a memory map using drawing or paint, or with fragments of cut paper, pottery, or fabric. You can add words or texts. Though likely to be faulty, your map will be oddly recognizable, but transformed through the fallibility of memory, lack of knowledge of certain parts of the landscape, or through the limitations introduced by hand-making. Your map will be a creative reinvention – a visualization of your unique perspective. In creating this map you are subverting and transforming the rules of objective cartography. Consider gathering a group of friends who had a shared experience and asking each one to create their own map based on their memory of it. Compare the finished maps; they will reveal differences in perception, memory, and emphasis.

4.5.3 Walking map

What you'll need

- Camera (for record keeping as you walk).
- Mark-making materials.
- Surface material.

Exercise type
Individual; can work with a group.

Take your camera for a walk, tracing a simple line or a circular route. Look for repetitions: lines in the sidewalk, sequence of light poles, shapes of green spaces. You're paying attention to the sequence of occurrence (objects being) and the breaks (not being) that will create a pattern. Using any medium, create a colour-abstract equivalent of your walk – develop a code of colours and shapes then translate the walk into that visual code.

The experience of your walk will become both an evocative image and a piece of data display.

Group modification: Folks can pair up, then attempt to follow the path described by their partner's walking map.

4.5.4 Stretch quests: Digital life edition

What you'll need

- Camera.

Exercise type
Group or individual.

Complete one quest in each of the following categories. The quests should be, in some way, related to interface or interaction design or digital life:

1. mental – this could include reading, listening, or watching;
2. physical;
3. social;
4. professional; and
5. curiosity conversation.

Complete a reflection after every Stretch Quest. Post each one on your blog and include an image (authored by you) with your post that is related to the quest in some way. Each reflection should be 75 words long, and focus on connecting the quest and the insights gained to the subject matter. For each quest, record your level of comfort on a scale of 1 to 5 where 1 is comfortable and 5 is way out of your comfort zone. Rate each quest on the comfort scale, first, before you engage in it and, second, after you've completed the quest.

The objective of this exercise is to push against your comfort zone; to try new experiences or talk to people who you consider remarkable or unlike yourself; to grow as a person and, through that growth, grow as an interface designer. Therefore, your quests must fall beyond 3 on your comfort scale (i.e., be very uncomfortable). You are permitted to complete a quest with a buddy, but you must take some time, by yourself, to reflect on and write about the experience (while the experience can be shared, the reflection is your own).

4.5.5 Interface sketches

What you'll need

- Sketchbook; graphic pens, and ruler (optional).

Exercise type
Individual.

The intent is to get you drawing and sketching, improving your understanding of design for the interactive space.

Step 1: Create at least 20, separate sketch sequences. Each sketch must be located within a visible, 3.5-inch-wide rectangle (many websites are constrained in terms of width but not length, so draw your sketches as long as required to complete the design).

Step 2: Do this work in your sketchbook, then consider taking a snapshot of your favourite sketch sequence each week and posting it to your blog. Describe what you created in a 50-word post. Why does this design work (focus on design, not on function). Include an image of the sketch, and a screen shot and URL of the original.

Topics

1. *Good brochureware sites*: Find brochureware sites that you think are well designed. Sketch the first page with enough detail that it would be recognizable to another person.
2. *Bad brochureware sites*: Find brochureware sites that you think are terribly designed. Sketch the re-design of the first page with enough detail that it would be understandable to another person.
3. *Good task-ware sites*: Find task-ware sites that you think are well designed. Sketch screens that show one task from start to finish, with enough detail that it would be recognizable to another person.
4. *Bad task-ware sites*: Find task-ware sites that you think are terribly designed. Sketch the re-design of one task from start to finish, with enough detail that it would be understandable to another person.
5. *Re-design a Google results screen*: Sketch the re-design with enough detail that it would be understandable to another person.
6. *Re-design your alma mater's website*: Sketch the re-design with enough detail that it would be understandable to another person.
7. *Good interactive visualization*: Find interactive visualizations that you think are well designed. Sketch a meaningful, high-data page with enough detail that it would be recognizable to another person.
8. *Bad interactive visualization*: Find interactive visualizations that you think are terribly designed. Sketch the re-design of a meaningful, high-data page with enough detail that it would be understandable to another person.

4.5.6 Website design

What you'll need

- Access to resource material (likely digital) and ways to construct new material.
- Sketchbook; graphic pens, and ruler (optional).

Exercise type
Individual.

Select an existing website for a not-for-profit or cause-based agency. It must be a 'terrible' design and supporting, discussing, or engaging in a subject matter or issue that you can be excited about exploring. Conduct a visual review of the site by selecting three good quality online plus two analog resources on the subject addressed by your website choice. Your goal is to familiarize yourself with the existing visual landscape of this subject. Dive deep. Think critically.

Determine the characteristics of the groups who are expected to make use of the website you selected. These groups may be emergent from the website itself, or out of your research. Generate as many of these as you feel is necessary. Challenge assumptions and stereotypes.

Develop a new, concept-based proposal look-and-feel for the website. Your concept and design must be emergent out of (and reflect) the research you conducted in Parts 1 and 2. Your choices must be justified, and capable of withstanding scrutiny. Maintain the organization's existing logo.

Part 1: Produce the following

- Unique concept statement, in one sentence and up to three additional sentences explaining/elaborating on your concept.
- Colour palette.
- Typographic hierarchy palette.
- Graphical elements and/or image samples.
- Very brief discussions on how the colour palette, and typographic and graphic choices reflect your concept.

Part 2: Site structure and content

- Create a new site structure and present in the form of a site map.
  - You may reorganize the current information and how it is accessed, but you must include the majority of the existing site content.
  - Indicate levels of site hierarchy.
- Re-write content for all navigation plus three pages of the website (one being the home page).
- Write a rationale for (reasoning behind) choices made around site structure and content re-writes.

Part 3: Home page re-design

- Propose three new home page design alternatives, based on an appropriate and unique concept: Include one concept statement and a brief discussion of how each design reflects the concept.
- Work to a width of a minimum of 1,024 pixels.

- Include page background.
- Use real content and high-quality images.

Part 4: Site re-design

- Choose one of the design alternatives from Part 3 and design two additional site pages:
  - Work to a width of a minimum of 1,024 pixels.
  - Include page background.
  - Use real content and high-quality images.
  - Use a grid (submit an additional view of all three pages with the grid overlay).

4.5.7 Experimental interface

What you'll need

- Access to resource material (likely digital) and ways to construct new material.
- Sketchbook; graphic pens, and ruler (optional).

Exercise type
Individual.

In this exercise, we will shift away from our specific organization (and its website re-design), and experiment within the broader topic defined by your agency's subject area.

Your job is to propose an experimental interface design, through which users can explore an emotionally compelling, engaging, and immersive story that is, in some way, related to a topic inspired by your organization.

Requirements

- The interface is meant to be an experience, not just a resource.
- The interface must attempt to contribute innovation, not be a copy of existing design solutions.
- The user interaction must accommodate (and privilege) prolonged engagement (not in and out) within one session and across multiple sessions.
- Technology used to display and interact with the interface must be commercially available.
- The interface cannot be a stand-alone entity; it must leverage and contribute back to some form of 'external' data source.

Part 1: Storyboard
Map out one user's experience in exploring the interface. May be done in pen or pencil. Include sketches and short descriptions of what the user is doing, how the interface reacts, and the results from the user's actions (both tangible and experiential).

Part 2: Design
Create a minimum of five screens that show the function and user experience proposed by your interface. These do not need to be programmed, but do need to have enough design detail within them to clearly demonstrate how the interface will work if implemented.

4.5.8 BigSee or structured surface

What you'll need
- Access to resource material (likely digital) and ways to construct new material.
- Sketchbook; graphic pens, and ruler (optional).

Exercise type
Individual or group.

This is, predominantly, a thinking design task. Yes, the end result has to exhibit excellent aesthetic judgement. Primarily, however, this exercise is about creating interesting solutions to interesting problems. Develop a set of polished sketches (with explanatory text if needed) that clearly illustrate your concept. I fully acknowledge that these requirements may appear vague at first. However, my objective is to give you the most room possible to be innovative, challenging, challenged, and pushed into previously unexplored territory.

BigSee

Large displays are becoming more and more popular. Currently, however, researchers have not fully investigated how a big display affects the design of visualizations. Research has used large screens as simply a place to display things for many people to see, or concentrated on the interface and control aspects. The questions we are asking are slightly different. We will be investigating the following: How do LSIDs affect visualizations of text? For example, is it possible that using a large display will enable us to gain new insights into written works? Also, what can we do visually on a large display that we cannot on a regular one? And finally, are large format displays used in a different manner than regular displays?

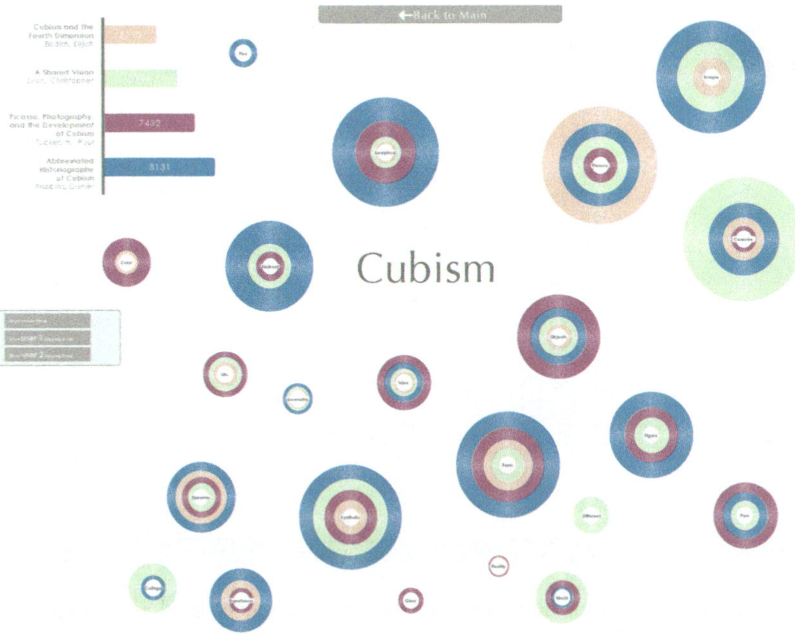

FIGURE 4.32: Exploring Art Movements, a BigSee project by Siobhan Rottger (2011).

There are several possible ways to explore the ideas presented through the BigSee project (Figure 4.32). For example, we could explore what answering and sorting our e-mail would look like when working with an LSID. If we had a whole wall, how would you use that screen real estate to handle all of your e-mail? Or, we could look at a novel such as Frankenstein. How can the big screen help us understand the whole novel quickly? Since we have a whole wall, how can we use it to allow multiple people to interpret one piece? The specific way you choose to tackle this project, is up to you.

Structured surfaces

Our goal in the Structured Surfaces project is to extend conventional diagrams – such as maps, timelines, radar plots, and targets – by introducing an additional cognitive layer underneath a given data display (Figure 4.33).

We provide the user with a graphical surface. The user can then integrate this surface with textual data – from one or more sources. In addition to the surface itself – the graphical area plus data representation(s) – we also provide several tools for interactivity and, in certain cases, dynamic content. We want to help the

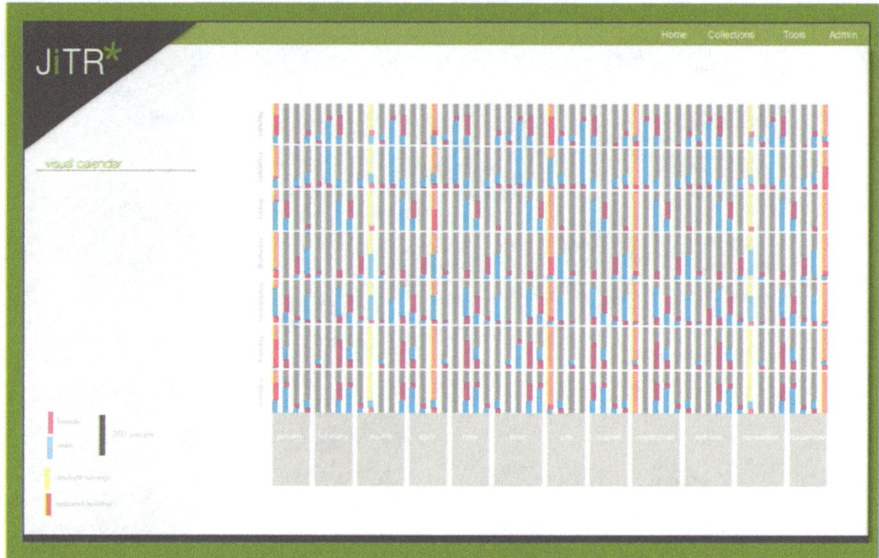

FIGURE 4.33: Exploring national holidays and suicide rates, a Structured Surfaces project by Amanda Howard (2011).

user to mentally structure the information. And, perhaps, help discover new relationships between data from diverse textual sources.

4.5.9 Prototyping for hermeneutic inquiry

Interpretive or hermeneutic inquiry is the primary mode of activity in the arts and humanities, as well as in much of the social sciences. It is also the approach most commonly used by readers in all professions. Interpretive inquiry involves iteratively identifying and analysing patterns in whatever materials are being examined. The goal of each analysis is not to find a single best answer or one right interpretation, but instead to enrich the object of study. By identifying and applying a new perspective or approach, the researcher acquires a new theoretical 'lens' that reveals new insights.

In DH, researchers attempt to create new tools for assisting other scholars with various forms of hermeneutic inquiry. Typically, when we think of visualization in the service of research, we expect to see forms that provide the researcher with a visual representation of statistical data, often near the final stage of the activity. However, in developing interactive prototypes for use in the hermeneutic process, we often aim instead to create visual models that support the iterative investigation of data like texts and images.

This exercise consists of the design of an interactive system for the exploration of patterns in collections of texts or images or other digital cultural heritage materials. Topics to be covered that may also serve as projects include but are not limited to:

- patterns of repetition in documents;
- phenomenological timelines;
- structured surfaces for collection browsing;
- rich-prospect browsing for concept maps;
- improved entity-relationship (network) diagrams;
- interfaces for cultural analytics; and
- visualization for document comparison.

Work individually or in pairs to produce a set of design sketches or a working prototype that communicates the interaction model for someone using the system for hermeneutic inquiry.

NOTES

1. It is perhaps worth noting in this context that neither Canada nor the United States has federal research funding designated specifically for design per se, although funding programs do exist that take proposals from design researchers, and some fields (e.g. engineering) include a specific subset of design research within them.
2. The Oil Sands Project benefited from a collaboration with several engineering departments and the Computing Science Department at the University of Alberta, and a partnership with a local oil company. The engineers and computing scientists on our team pursued interests rooted within their particular domains, while we considered HCI design through the lens of humanities theories and reflected on the applicability (and potential extendibility) of these theories to a problem outside the humanities.

5

Working better together

For researchers planning to do interdisciplinary research, this chapter outlines some of the obstacles that are introduced by the university, as well as some techniques for overcoming those obstacles.

5.1 Developing interdisciplinary researchers

It might seem a natural assumption that the goal of the academy is to find and nurture interdisciplinary researchers. We live, after all, in a culture that appreciates interdisciplinarity, and if the academy is where we suggest that smart people should congregate to learn not only their disciplinary knowledge, but also how to work together, then after gathering the smartest of the smart, we will end up with some interdisciplinary researchers.

Certainly, this is true. Unfortunately, however, from the perspective of interdisciplinary researchers, the academy does all kinds of things, and nurturing interdisciplinary researchers is actually not all that high on the list. One thing the academy does is put a stamp of approval, an imprimatur, on intelligence. 'This', we say as professors, 'is the kind of intellectual person that we can recognize as a good potential contributor to the larger enterprise of building knowledge in our society. This is the kind of person you can hire and trust to do some thinking for you'.

We therefore spend a lot of time grooming people into the kinds of thinkers that will fit into the 'disciplinary' academic way of doing things. Our students need to be able to write and present material that is, as we say 'contestable, defensible, and substantive'. That is, they must find topics where not everyone agrees on what is right (contestable). They must be able to ask questions where it is possible to produce evidence that would help to convince a reasonable person to accept the position they are defending (defensible). They need to know what is worth the time and energy it takes to do the research, write it, and for other people to read it (substantive).

Having learned how to identify questions that can be usefully pursued, the students must also learn how to communicate. They need to write papers and give presentations. They need to engage in discussions with their peers and the faculty members. Many universities, recognizing that propinquity is essential to enculturation, insist on a 'residency requirement' so that the students will spend time with other people in the same discipline.

Saying 'the academic way of doing things' may also be somewhat misleading. A university is a complex environment, and what is a perfectly orthodox way of proceeding in one research discipline may seem like madness to colleagues just down the hall, and vice versa. At a fundamental level, we often do not even agree on what we are trying to do, or what is the best means of doing it.

Scholars from different disciplines are introduced to the conventions and approaches of their own fields, and do not always have experience with approaches used by other fields. For research projects that involve only one academic or a research team from within a single discipline, not knowing about other approaches may limit their choices, but will not necessarily cause problems. For collaborative interdisciplinary projects, on the other hand, it is useful to try to get a sense of what other researchers consider to be either normal, acceptable but unusual, or downright strange.

For cultural and historical reasons, some of the research approaches have been more heavily adopted by some disciplines than by others. A subject domain has in these cases been somewhat gratuitously associated with an approach to research. There is always a danger in adopting an approach not normally seen by peer reviewers, which can potentially reduce the success of publication, promotion, and scholarly influence. The advantage, however, is that a new approach can also open previously unseen opportunities for scholarly activity.

Here is an inventory of some of the approaches to research. Note that these are distinct from research methods, which are recipes for obtaining the evidence to be used in a scholarly argument. All of the approaches to research outlined in this inventory require evidence; how that evidence is derived or developed is in many cases up to the choice of the researcher.

1. Choose a single cultural phenomenon and explicate it (e.g. Foucault's story in Renaissance France of a Trojan origin).
2. Identify an unexplained but repeated pattern and suggest an explanation (e.g. urban myths of organ theft).
3. Take two opposed hypotheses. Decide what evidence would allow a reasonable person to choose one or the other, then invent an experiment to produce that evidence (dichotomous exclusion).

4. Take two opposed hypotheses and develop a new position that incorporates both of them (Hegelian synthesis).
5. Choose a theory with insufficient evidence to support it and produce the evidence to make the case convincing (e.g. phosphates in water will feed algae).
6. Extend and promote a non-dominant discourse (e.g. rich-prospect browsing).
7. Use someone else's theory as a lens on a document (e.g. performative utterance in *Pamela*).
8. Observe and report on something previously not observed and reported on (e.g. archival work; Chris Fletcher's report of the signing of an Arctic peace treaty).
9. Ask a lot of people about a topic, and discuss what they tell you. Their responses might be in a variety of forms including statistical data (surveys), text or transcriptions (interviews, questionnaires, ethnography), photos (photovoice), video (video ethnography).
10. Collect a body of pre-existing data around a topic and analyse it (e.g. web scraping or log analysis).
11. Provide participants with a limited means of expression, then analyse the patterns that emerge (e.g. cartoon sequence test).
12. Develop a computer simulation of a phenomenon that is difficult to observe directly.
13. Conceptually structure some phenomenon previously not systematized, whether by taxonomy, classification, or enumeration; assemble or reassemble data in some meaningful order (e.g. Linnaeus; chronology).
14. Identify a process or device that is awkward or inefficient and make it less awkward or more efficient (e.g. functional MRIs; digital collections; visualization).

The approach to research that a given set of students learns will depend to a great extent on the field where they end up focusing their attention and who they have worked with in the past. However, since subject matter and approach to research are intertwined, it does sometimes happen that a student who would be an interdisciplinary researcher interested in a particular way of working has to work another way because the subject matter has accidentally become associated with one approach to research rather than another.

It is also the case that there is one subclass of interdisciplinary researcher that is typically unwelcome at the academy, and that is the person with the skill of getting other people to work. We start early in weeding out this particularly useful personality type: when students show a talent for having other people write their essays, we do our best to get rid of them. They then leave the academy, at worst ignominiously and at best without formal training, and go on to become successful as rich and powerful leaders.

5.1.1 Undergraduate interdisciplinary researchers

It is undoubtedly true that we lose some potentially excellent interdisciplinary researchers before they get to the university. High school is a fairly regimented environment, since one of its primary purposes is to prepare people for a workforce that is fairly regimented. Not everyone takes well to the indoctrination. One question that arises is whether regimentation is helpful for interdisciplinary researchers. That is, do they work more effectively if they are able to accommodate a 9-5 schedule or is that training bad for them, or is it irrelevant?

In any case, the institution's goal for the ones who make it through to an undergraduate program is to continue the process of providing them with a relatively scheduled environment where they can internalize the conventional received wisdom in a particular field, and contextualize that knowledge by being exposed to a range of other fields. At the same time, there is the complementary goal of encouraging some of the students to continue to graduate studies, where the focus shifts from understanding the knowledge in a field to expanding the field.

The connection between these activities and the interdisciplinary researcher is somewhat puzzling. On the one hand, the conservative tendencies of a culture and the institutions that support it are going to attempt to channel the influence of the interdisciplinary researcher so that it is in the best interests of the persistence of what already exists. On the other hand, one possible interest of an interdisciplinary researcher is in improving on what already exists. Since we would generally agree that this is not yet the best of all possible worlds, in the particular case of interdisciplinary researchers, it might be useful to allow scope for the introduction of new and better ideas into the culture.

The standard resolution of this dilemma is to say that new ideas are built on old ideas, that innovators, even interdisciplinary researchers, stand on the shoulders of giants of the past, and it is necessary before making any genuine contribution to first learn the current state of the field. In many fields, this learning takes the form of a respect for the history of the discipline. In the arts, operating in the hermeneutic tradition, it is important to know what has been already observed and reported, so that there won't be an unreasonably high degree of redundancy in the literature. In the sciences, the tendency is to ignore the full record and concentrate instead on the most recent developments, so that material tends to be considered stale at a much faster rate. Even in cases where a trajectory has been drawn from the past to the present, there is a process of selection at work, so that Kepler's work on planetary motion, for instance, is described in every undergraduate survey textbook in physics, while his work on the music the spheres create is only known to specialists in the history of science. We have sifted the wheat from the chaff, and the undergraduate students are expected to be able to understand the wheat and describe it using their own words.

What is missing from this approach is the complexity of attempting to move knowledge forward. It is seldom if ever the case that the future is readily predictable to the people who are producing knowledge, and the complex terrain of trial, error, hunches, funding, politics, fashions of ideas, and the strength or weakness of previously accepted theories all contribute to the life of the interdisciplinary researcher just as it does for the researcher in a single discipline. But the undergraduate student is sheltered from much of this complexity, and undergraduate interdisciplinary researchers may find the results at least puzzling and at worst absolutely confounding. One of our colleagues, who has spent her career as a librarian and education scholar, echoes our experience adding that this problem is often compounded by assignment criteria – psychology students, for example, not allowed to reference sociology journals and vice versa.

The difference between the research record as it is described for undergraduates and the daily experience of taking an interest in something, what it means to form a question and produce evidence around it, can suggest that there is no satisfactory existing trajectory that the interdisciplinary researcher can follow, that it is necessary not only to take an interest, but also to invent from scratch how to go about taking an interest. Nothing could be further from the truth, but unless the interdisciplinary researcher should happen to chance across educational theorists like Paulo Freire, it is unlikely that there will be much evidence to go on.

The other difficulty faced by undergraduate interdisciplinary researchers is that the university is often not universal enough. Although some interdisciplinary researchers may focus their contributions through expertise in a single specialized field, we haven't personally met them. All the interdisciplinary researchers we know have been interested at different times in different things, and many interdisciplinary researchers are interested in several things at once. This is not the same, however, as becoming famous for a particular contribution to knowledge. It does happen that someone who has been interested in many things is somehow identified in the public mind for one of the subjects of interest. It also occasionally happens that someone famous for one interest becomes well known for having other interests. Richard Feynman, for instance, was well known as a physicist who suggested a new visual form to describe a specific kind of knowledge. Through his biographical writing, however, people came to understand that Feynman was also interested in lock-picking and drumming, and that he had spent some time as a painter. Some people suggested that this combination of interests was unusual – that it marked Feynman not just as a brilliant physicist, but in fact as an interdisciplinary researcher. We would tend to agree.

Taking an interest, however, is somewhat distinct from developing an interest, and that is where the university actually does have something to offer. By exposing young interdisciplinary researchers to an environment that is rich in information and where other people thinking about things are thick on the ground, it is possible to stimulate and encourage some persistence in following an area of interest for some extended period. Malcolm Gladwell points out that it takes at least 10,000 hours for a person to become good at something – to reach a minimum bar of competence. Ten thousand hours is perhaps not coincidentally about the same amount of time it takes to earn an honours undergraduate degree, which is the form of the degree intended to lead to graduate school.

5.1.2 Master's-level interdisciplinary researchers

At the graduate level, there is a marked transition. Whereas the undergraduate students are expected to be learning enough to describe the state of the art in their own words, the student in a master's program is expected to take that level of knowledge as a starting point, and begin to learn how to make a contribution, to extend the state of the art into new territory. In institutional terms, it is the beginning of a new phase of intellectual effort.

For interdisciplinary researchers, however, it is often the first stage in the reduction of frustration. For people who have all along been taking an interest in the world around them and in the previous results of the human archive, it hasn't been possible to accept years of internalizing the results of the work of others and accepting them as the state of the art. Every impulse towards understanding also includes an impulse of questioning the basis for that understanding. For example, we once knew an interdisciplinary undergraduate student who had given some serious thought to the validity of Einstein's famous equation, $e = mc^2$. If there is a time dilation effect as we approach the speed of light, the student argued (and there is) then it may be that the energy only appears to be increasing because the speed of light has a time component, and we have been looking at the result from the wrong frame of reference. This student went on to complete a degree in political science.

Some teachers and professors would endorse the opinion that this questioning is as central to an undergraduate education as is the internalization of knowledge, and would propose further that both components are essential parts of the larger agenda of internalizing the cultural values around the production of knowledge.

There is an extent to which this more sophisticated understanding is true, but in practice it is not all that large an extent. Paulo Freire spent decades encouraging educators to involve students in the active formation of understanding, in the belief that transmitted knowledge is soon lost, but constructed understanding endures, and more importantly, has the capacity to influence behaviour. However,

Freire's influence has not been as widespread as some would wish, and it is often not until the master's program that a student is really introduced in a practical way to the possibility of making a contribution to knowledge that can be recognized by the academy. Undergraduate institutions, such as Mount Royal University in Calgary, Canada, are attempting to change this landscape and, over the past five years, much more attention, funding, program development and publishing have been focused on undergraduate research.

The consequence is often that the student, and particularly the interdisciplinary student, slips the reins entirely, and begins to conceive of projects that are far beyond the scope of what can be executed in a year or two, which is the typical duration of a master's program. It is not uncommon, in fact, to see early drafts of MA thesis proposals that could only be reasonably addressed by consuming the efforts of an entire career. This is a sensitive time, because the student – if left to pursue too ambitious a project – will experience either the failure of not completing it or, worse, of believing it has been completed when in fact it was never tenable. On the other hand, if constrained too tightly, the result can be just another phase of frustration, as the student feels held back or unnecessarily limited in ambition and scope.

Since one of the characteristics of interdisciplinary researchers is interest in a wide range of phenomena, it is also necessary for the supervisor to help guide the student into ways of thinking through a multiplicity of possible pursuits, in order to begin developing decision criteria for what to pursue when. One useful approach is to point out that only one project is required for a master's degree, but there is no limit to the number of projects that can be conceived, recorded briefly somewhere, and left to wait for a future moment when they can be activated and pursued. There is something reassuring in knowing that good ideas don't have to be abandoned altogether, but that they can be kept on the back burner for a moment when more time or resources become available.

For example, in one of our master's seminars on interdisciplinary research project management, the students were asked to assemble a research team from people not in the class, then lead the team in carrying out a research project and producing an extended abstract and conference presentation, suitable for submission to an appropriate conference. It is not uncommon for students to spend some weeks trying to formulate a possible collaborative research project, considering the various factors such as who might be candidate members of the research team, what area they should work in, and so on. However, students with an interdisciplinary trajectory will often arrive in the first few weeks of the course with half a dozen or more possible research projects, including some that have already been initiated.

The instructor's job is significantly different in dealing with these two kinds of students. In the first case, what is required is a series of guiding questions around experience and interest, intended to move the student towards taking a sufficient interest in something to be able to flesh out the project and pursue it. In the second case, the instructor needs to enter the whirlwind of ideas, and help to sort through them, knowing that the logistical factors will in the end come to bear a deciding role in the choice of project, while the student will often have the habit of being guided most strongly by the constellation of interests, typically selecting from the various options the one that currently appears to be most interesting, independent of its possible scale or duration.

The introduction of practical factors into the project planning of a graduate student learning about interdisciplinary research is one of the most useful and difficult contributions that an instructor or advisor or supervisor can make. Little or nothing in the undergraduate studies of the student will have prepared them for using practical considerations as the basis for making selections among which ideas to pursue, and the unnatural, almost arbitrary quality of the constraint often poses an immediate obstacle to its acceptance. Having for the first time been encouraged to make a contribution, the concept of limiting that contribution because work requires time and planning seems almost an insult to the young interdisciplinary researcher.

5.1.3 Ph.D.-level interdisciplinary researchers

In academic programs in North America, it is normal for a student entering a Ph.D. program to have already completed a master's degree. In some cases, the basis of the master's program is just more coursework, albeit in graduate seminars instead of undergraduate lectures, but in most cases the master's will have involved a thesis. What this means is that the Ph.D. student will have had some experience with framing an appropriate research question, collecting evidence to support some contention, and writing up the results. A master's thesis does not necessarily need to make an original contribution to the field, although many of them do, and for design in particular, the master's was for several decades the terminal degree.

What is normally required is that the thesis show that the student has some familiarity with the relevant literature, has considered some research methods and chosen among them, perhaps even trying out more than one at a small scale, and is capable of writing half a book.

At the Ph.D. level, the bar is somewhat higher. Typically, there will be two or three different categories of previous literature to become familiar with, and all of them should be understood at a deeper level, involving more items, than would be expected from the master's student. There is an additional candidacy exam introduced in the process to test that this has happened. There is a larger examining committee, including faculty members who weren't involved in the student's work. Finally, the dissertation at the Ph.D. level is essentially a book, although it is a particular genre of book designed to convince the committee, rather than a more general readership, of the student's expertise in the area.

The Ph.D. is therefore the first real opportunity at the university for the interdisciplinary researcher to begin to feel at home. The scope is larger. The expectation from the institution is that the student will be at least partly motivated by taking an actual interest in the subject matter. There is also somewhat more pressure to present the research at colloquia or conferences, and to publish some or all of it in journals or as a revised monograph. Thirty years ago it was possible to publish a Ph.D. dissertation more or less unedited, but contemporary practice is to archive the dissertation and select only a small percentage for subsequent re-writing for publication.

The supervisor of an interdisciplinary researcher who is working on a Ph.D. is faced with a new challenge. Given the larger scale of the work and the tendency of the interdisciplinary researcher to pursue an interest that spans multiple fields, it can happen that the pursuit becomes somewhat more exhaustive than it needs to be. Many Ph.D. programs are officially four years long, but in the Arts it is not uncommon to have students take nearly twice that long to complete a Ph.D., and many students don't complete at all. Given the trajectory in their previous degrees through all the various kinds of constraint, the reduction in constraint for the Ph.D. student can result in a kind of meltdown.

One strategy is therefore to help create an environment for the Ph.D. interdisciplinary researcher that includes other interdisciplinary researchers working at the Ph.D. level or above. One approach is to make use of a shared physical space, such as a graduate studio or lab. Regular weekly meetings or work sessions with several people present can also help.

Another ongoing responsibility of the supervisor is to help the student choose an appropriate reading list, and encourage sticking with it rather than hurrying off on too many tangents. Since opinions will vary somewhat on which readings are appropriate for which kind of project, there is always a tendency to want to read just one more book or just a few more articles before sitting down to start on the project, and this tendency needs to be kept in check. That said, an interdisciplinary project will usually involve a reading list that can best be expressed as a Venn diagram of overlapping fields.

Time management is often a difficulty for interdisciplinary researchers, since the need to accomplish something can seem secondary to the pleasure of pursuing an interest, but the proper environment combined with enlightened mentorship can help the interdisciplinary researcher to begin to think in terms of producing deliverables in addition to engaging with the material. A simple timeline or Gantt chart can help to frame the Ph.D. project, and in many cases the construction of a visual of this kind will be a new experience for interdisciplinary researchers, unless they have happened to take an interest at some point in project management.

Spreadsheets are also useful, of the kind where the student breaks the task down into small sections, then provides estimates of time to completion for each of the sections. Ideally, if it is subsequently possible to keep track of actual time spent on each section, the resulting spreadsheet becomes invaluable in encouraging the interdisciplinary researcher to overcome the natural tendency to believe that research tasks can't be accurately estimated, since it is impossible to know in advance what will be involved. Although it is true that research can lead in unexpected directions, it is equally true that there are only so many working hours in a year (about 2,000), that people tend to read and write at a fairly consistent pace, and that carrying out various kinds of research activities takes an amount of time that can be predicted with reasonable accuracy. Running a user study with six participants, for instance, will take somewhat less time than running the same study with 20 participants. Transcribing interview notes will proceed at roughly five pages per hour. And so on.

As at the master's level, the increasing awareness of the logistics of academic life is a healthy area of professional development for interdisciplinary researchers during their Ph.D. programs, and every effort should be made to help them begin to think in terms of how long it takes to do things. Having this kind of knowledge will contribute to success in writing grant proposals for research funding, which can be a significant part of the professional life of the interdisciplinary researcher who holds a professorship.

5.2 What is respectable?

For academic researchers in any field, publishing research results is crucial. But, once again, there are significant variations in the details of the implementation of the idea. DH and design, as academic disciplines, are at an approximately same stage of development, with national and international organizations, conferences, and journals. However, DH conferences have, in large part, adopted the humanities approach of peer-reviewing conference presentations based on either short or long abstracts, on the assumption that complete papers will, subsequently, be published by a journal or as part of a book. Design, on the other hand, has followed the pattern of the sciences and the social sciences, so that conference proposals are invariably judged based on the full paper, which then appears in the conference proceedings. For a designer and a DH researcher working together on a research project, it is important to have a publication of each kind.

Portfolios and design competitions are also a form of publication, but one that DH simply does not possess. For designers, high-quality images of the work they helped produce are critical in demonstrating their expertise. That work will be judged, to a varied degree, on both its intellectual and formal (or aesthetic) merits. Lack of typographic quality, for example, may make even a brilliant interface unworthy of attention. Design also tends to place a higher value on completed artefacts, rather than on prototypes. Design competitions in particular prefer to recognize launched campaigns and objects that have reached the hands of the intended consumer. In critical and speculative design, emphasis shifts to installation in a museum or gallery space.

Portfolios are the primary way that non-academic designers demonstrate their skills and expertise. Jorge Frascara (who was one of Milena's MDes supervisors and Stan's Ph.D. supervisor) always said: 'the design of a design project is, in itself, a design project'. In other words, the quality of how a design is presented to others is as important as the quality of the design.

When designers from industry evaluate each other's work, they're interested in the following:

1. What was the design intended to accomplish and who was its audience?
2. What problem was the design trying to solve?
3. How was the problem identified?
4. How was the problem validated?
5. What role did you play in solving the problem and who else did you work with? How much of the design is yours alone?
6. How did you solve the problem?
7. Has the design shipped/become public and, if so, where and how?
8. What was the design's impact and how was it measured?

Though what we state above is technically true, it is also the case that we judge design at its most surface:

1. Are you using a style or visual treatment that was popular 2, 5, or 10 years ago?
2. Are you using a style or visual treatment that's very popular now, thus likely indigestible in six months?
3. Did you use Arial, Comic Sans, or Papyrus?
4. Have you used discount stock imagery?
5. Is anything bevelled, embossed, or sporting a dramatic shadow?
6. Are there boxes or borders around every grouping of items?
7. Why didn't you use Helvetica?

Designers know that these two groupings of expectations exist though, individually, their attention to one or the other may differ. Some designers are eager to demonstrate their own, carefully developed stylistic skew, while others are more flexible as to style, but more rigid in their process (how they get there). And before we reject industry expectations in favour of academic benchmarks, note that there are circumstances where academic designers may desire to gain acceptance by their industry. National and international design societies are one such arena. In Canada, graphic (and, increasingly, digital) designers have the option to belong to the GDC (Graphic Designers of Canada); in North America, AIGA (The Professional Association for Design). Though both are not, technically, accreditation bodies the way that is common to architecture, they host competitions, conferences, and occasionally offer incentives attractive to designers that require an industry-aligned portfolio.

Open-access publication and online self-publication are emerging trends in both fields. While open-access publication aligns well with some researchers' ethical landscape, self-publication offers the benefits of engaging with your audience faster, more efficiently and, depending on the method, with fewer expenditures than traditional publishing routes. Neither method, however, has become fully embraced by our disciplines.

5.2.1 Resource needs

If you're planning out grant money, consider allocating some of the resources towards design-friendly production equipment. Most designers still use pencil and paper to explore ideas and develop rough sketches, but will be absolutely thrilled if you can support their work via a new laptop and a layout, illustration, and photo-editing software package (ask them what they need, then get that – everyone works harder and faster if they don't have to share their toys with others). Add a typeface (font) budget, since a good typeface will provide you with years of reuse. Free fonts are seldom good substitutes: they are likely to have only one or two font styles (bold and italic, if you're lucky), character sets are incomplete, glyphs haven't been designed or their design looks out of place, and the spacing between characters hasn't been considered in context. If you're planning on including photography or illustration in the design (or the designer pitches those kinds of alternatives), don't cheap out.

5.2.2 Critical non-tangibles

Most of the collaborative teams we have worked with were made up of researchers at various points of their career. Some were research assistants funded through scholarships or through our research funds across degree types: from undergraduates to post-docs. We've worked with faculty members who were pre-tenure, those who were academic lifers (like us), and those who were conducting research while working on contract and being paid only for the time they spent in the classroom. We've also worked with industry partners who had full-time careers outside of the academy and were accountable to their employers for time spent with the not-for-profits. Acknowledging these differences is important not just, as we're attempting to argue, because diversity makes for better research. It's important so that we avoid stumbling blindly into a fantasy where everyone has access to the same resources, and is subject to the same pressures and insecurities. More important still, when committing to the wellness of your collaborative teams, is to challenge your own lens of what is important and what is a stressor. This is particularly important when there is a power differential between the various collaborators. Power differentials exist whether we acknowledge them or not – even with the spirit of egalitarianism, unless everyone on the team has the same identity, job security, and social and cultural status, they will have access to different degrees of power.

Please consider the following short (iterative) list of considerations (principles) for feminist collaboration:

1. A project can be considered important while, for a time, taking a back seat to other priorities. Sometimes those priorities are crises of housing, financial security, relationships, or mental or physical health. Other times, while not falling under the crisis heading, those priorities can be life management strategies in order to avoid reaching a crisis state. No one has an absolute right to know what someone else is going through. Your team members may choose to share their stories to some degree they're comfortable with, but don't expect them to. Practice generous assumption – they've missed this meeting because they had to, not because they are incompetent or careless. This is particularly true for projects that run over several years.
2. Avoid assuming that every team member will have the same needs. For example, one of our long-time colleagues who is autistic and has ADHD, recently tweeted about her experience of attending an academic conference, and how the many layers of stress created by the space and its organization impacted her health. Other colleagues who parent small children have faced/face a systemic lack of accommodation with career-altering consequences for not showing up. Consider providing video conferencing opportunities instead of requiring in-person meeting attendance. Plan for affordable childcare access for meetings and conferences, and schedule long breaks for folks to rest or see their kids. Lactating women may need space/privacy to pump or feed. Folks with dietary restrictions need menu options that go beyond lettuce.[1]

3. Certain activities are more likely to result in harm or threat for some team members than others, especially (but not exclusively) with regards to security online. Team members should make their own decisions regarding their safety, and be respected and supported for those decisions, but consider, for example, whether there's a potential power imbalance at play in asking an undergraduate student to pick-up a 'rockstar' academic from the airport.
4. Give particular attention to the realities of your international collaborators since those might be less visible to you. For example, at the time of writing, our Brazilian colleagues are experiencing a high degree of added stress due to a dramatic shift in their country's political climate. International collaborators who have recently or temporarily relocated are also less likely to have an accessible support system, in the form of friends or family, to fall back on in times of crisis.
5. Don't throw away work. The potential for ideas can be (metaphorically) bottomless, but time, energy, and resources aren't. Do your absolute best to respect the work produced by others – respect, in this case, means using it to some benefit.
6. Look for opportunities to publicly acknowledge contribution and expertise, especially for the kinds of contributions that are hard to make fit into a citation format. For example, early on in our careers, we committed to acknowledging designers' contributions with equal emphasis to all others.
7. Ask for and respect everyone's gender pronouns. As a cis-gendered individual, make a point to create a space where visibility and respect of non-binary defaults becomes common practice.
8. Create opportunities for networking and community building that don't centre around alcohol consumption, or always rely on access to the same set of resources (time, money, travel, access to support systems, etc.).
9. Don't assume that you already know all the ways that a team member can contribute. Leave room for shifts in project definition, roles, and responsibilities. Some of our most rewarding projects became unrecognizable to our original intent after three team meetings.

Academic institutions are constructed on assumptions of privilege. Take conference presentations, for example. In order to present your research you need: money to cover registration fees, lodging, flights, and food (that's, on average, at least $1700); ability to get to and from the home airport; child care; visa or passport fees; and ability to take time away from other duties or responsibilities. Recently, such travel may also hinge on having a nationality that isn't under a travel ban.[2] Any expenditures aren't likely to be reimbursed until weeks or sometimes months after the event. This is the way academic institutions have been set up; however, they won't change until we apply pressure for them to do so in order to address the real-world needs of all our collaborators, not just those with privilege of guaranteed, steady salaries and rights of citizenship.[3]

5.3 Project management for interdisciplinary researchers

We have worked separately or together on more than a hundred research projects. Our co-authorship list includes more than 250 different people from over 20 different fields across 18 countries. So, the following observations are based on a reasonably large set of experiences. They are, however, as seen through the subjective perspective of the two of us, so not everyone would agree with the various things we have seen and what we decided they meant, much less the conclusions we have drawn from them. With that disclaimer behind us, let us begin.

Many of our projects have been in the area of humanities visualization, and most involved some form of collaboration between designers and digital humanists. Additionally, we worked with colleagues in computer science, psychology, sociology, city planning, political science, pharmacy, English literature, library and information studies, and chemical and materials engineering. Our research projects have ranged from teams of three or four local members (www.humviz.org) to as many as 50 researchers at seven universities (www.monkproject.org) and 35 researchers across 20 institutions and 21 partner agencies (www.inke.ca). Some of our people come from well-established research disciplines with clearly defined expectations (e.g. psychology), while others are from emerging disciplines where traditions for research methods and publication are not yet firmly established (e.g. visual communication design). Both kinds of researchers constitute a challenge for design research teams, and experience has taught us that it is a useful practice to make all expectations as explicit as possible.

Ideally, of the smaller teams, we believe that no more than three of them should define themselves primarily as interdisciplinary researchers. A project needs some inspiration, a creative force to get it started, and it needs some steady and reliable work. Interdisciplinary researchers are many things, but it is very unusual to find any who are steady and reliable workers. At best, they tend to be sporadic workers who will make a tremendous contribution on the parts of the project that interest them, while being unable to carry out to any satisfactory degree the parts they do not find interesting.

To complicate matters further, it is not always the case that the part of a project that is interesting to an interdisciplinary researcher at the beginning of the project will continue to hold any interest as the project progresses. In fact, it is probably more common than not that the interdisciplinary researcher will lose interest before the project is completed. One of our colleagues has a rule of thumb that the last ten per cent of any project is the hardest to complete, since no one is ever eager to do the hard work of completing that final portion of the work. This is a colleague who has worked with a lot of interdisciplinary researchers over the years.

We believe that this observation stems from the fact that by the time the last ten per cent of the project is left, everyone can now see what the outcome will be. By that point, the interdisciplinary researcher will have been relatively certain of the outcome for some time, and will have gradually been failing to produce work of value as interest wanes.

Given these facts, it might seem like a reasonable question to wonder why it is ever worthwhile to have even a single interdisciplinary researcher on a research team. Why not recruit intelligent hard workers, each with a single, disciplinary focus, and get the job done simply and easily? It is a good question, and the answer is more than that the interdisciplinary researcher will produce insights that would otherwise not be available. The primary reason is that a research project works best when there are a variety of people who have different skills and are able to operate in an environment where the complementary nature of the skills is at a maximum.[4] Interdisciplinary researchers also tend to set the bar of excellent ideas for the rest of the team. It is simply harder to slack off in the presence of an interdisciplinary researcher, because interdisciplinary researchers are inspiring to be around. Second, in interdisciplinary settings, there is always the problem of establishing and maintaining mutual respect across the disciplinary boundaries. It is fairly straightforward to recognize someone who is doing good work in one's own field, but if someone in another field is simply putting in a good effort, it may be more difficult to give credit where it is due. If the person from another field is an interdisciplinary researcher, however, then it is a simpler matter to believe that they are doing good work, even when the person doing the de facto evaluation hasn't really got the expertise to be able to tell.

Managing people by asking them to do only what they are interested in is an approach that makes for a very pleasant working environment in one sense, since you avoid the stress of having to try to coerce people when you have very little actual leverage. It is of course sometimes possible to coerce people to carry out work that they don't want to do, or the industrial economy would never have succeeded. The best method is to have them all report to the same manager, who is also the person who pays them, and to have them share a working space. None of these conditions are typically available in academic research projects, where the team members can be direct colleagues, junior colleagues, or senior colleagues, and may work at other institutions or report to other people. None of these methods works very well in any case with interdisciplinary researchers.

The working environment is at the same time potentially very stressful, especially in the not infrequent case where there is work that falls between the areas of interest of everyone involved. Reducing those empty areas is the reason for including as many as three interdisciplinary researchers on the team. Not only will they produce work that will result in fewer gaps, but they will also each demonstrate excellence in the part of the work they are interested in. Their excellence will inspire the other members of the team to do the best they can in their own areas. Seeing the effort that an interdisciplinary researcher puts into a portion of the project can make the entire project seem more exciting and worthwhile. It is difficult to maintain a belief that something is not worth doing when there are people involved who communicate a fascination with the work whenever you meet them. The reduction in this fascination in the final third of the project is one of the dynamics that requires adjustment if the team is to succeed.

For the project manager, inevitably there will be parts of the work that are not only outside the interest area of the interdisciplinary researchers, but also outside the interests or abilities of the other, disciplinary-focused members of the team. It is possible to try to fill those areas by adding new team members, but there is a limit to how many additional hands a project can accommodate, both in terms of funding and also in terms of other logistical considerations.

Not least of these is the ability to offer co-authorship on presentations or publications. In the academic community, authorship credit is considered by most people to be important, although for senior professors this is sometimes less true than for more junior colleagues. However, while it is not unreasonable to list two or three authors on a paper, and it is possible to list as many as a dozen, the smaller the number, particularly in the arts, fine arts, and humanities, the more prestigious the authorship credit. With larger teams, there are strategies such as naming the team itself as a fourth author, and listing by name only the people who directly worked on a given paper. Then the team members can be named on a website. However, this strategy is less than ideal for faculty members who are working for tenure or promotion and need to be identified as much as possible.

Authorship also raises the simple fact that not all interdisciplinary researchers, even ones that have managed to internalize the academic way of life, are interested in being writers. In fact, the distribution of labour that is the reason for organizing a small research team suggests that it is best not to include more than one or at most two interdisciplinary researcher writers, or else there won't be enough other people doing other parts of the project.

It is possible to have more than one researcher originating from the same field on the same project, but it requires some careful handling. The first thing to keep in mind is that even within the same field, there may be ways to section off the terrain so that there is little or no overlap in the research task. Another approach is to have them work together on a single task, and allow them to figure out the working relationship. We have seen this approach work at the strategic level, where the goal is to discuss the project and determine a vision for the work. However, it has typically failed at the detail level of actually implementing something or carrying out a given piece of work.

What can be done is to adopt the equivalent of pair programming, where two computer programmers are assigned the same task but are only allowed to have one computer. This approach can work not only for computer programmers, but in many areas where expertise is shared. What this can result in is a natural partitioning of the work, where one person is interacting with the computer and the other is stepping back a bit to help consider what needs to be done, or is taking notes, or is assisting in debugging. Pair programming can be very effective but does require the right kind of circumstances and people who can accept this kind of partitioning of the task.

Mixing interdisciplinary researchers with other people also poses its challenges. One of the potential difficulties that can arise is that the other people begin to believe that because the interdisciplinary researchers are only doing work that they love, they are in fact subject to special conditions or some form of preferred treatment. The attitude is basically that 'so and so doesn't ever seem to have to do any of the grunt work around here, and it isn't fair that the rest of us have to pick up the slack'.

One of the easiest ways of forestalling this difficulty is to treat everyone on the team as though they were interdisciplinary researchers, so that you ask them to only do the things that they are interested in doing. There will inevitably be gaps between the tasks that people are interested in, but if everyone has at the heart of their assignment something they love, they will be more willing to volunteer for some additional work that they love less. Every project, no matter how well organized, also has some components that simply no one wants to do. These become the assignment of the project manager, who pays for a smooth-running project by doing the equivalent of washing the dishes and delivering the coffee and pizza.

In terms of the overall size of the research team, it is generally advisable to keep the roster as small as possible, for a variety of pragmatic reasons. Fewer team members means a smaller budget. It means less negotiation about who gets authorship credit and under what conditions. It means less difficulty in coordinating team meetings or conference calls, because there are fewer schedules that have to be accommodated.

But why not, if it is possible, have nothing but interdisciplinary researchers on the research team? Ideally, this may be possible and worthwhile, but in practice, it seldom seems to transpire. When it does, there is always the difficulty that one or more of the interdisciplinary researchers may be in the phase where they are egomaniacal, in which case the working conditions will tend to be subject to implosion. The trajectory that many interdisciplinary researchers have followed through life, or perhaps their natural proclivities, have also tended to render them somewhat eccentric. Working with interdisciplinary researchers requires a certain ability to live and let live, or perhaps to exercise patience as a positive force rather than as a simply passive virtue. That is to say, one is well advised to take a stance of tolerance and acceptance, and learn to work around the results that manifest themselves, rather than attempting to force a path through to a predetermined end.

Providing an environment amenable to the manifestation of results can often be accomplished by establishing a relatively high-level goal for a project, independent of how it may have been described in more formal terms for other purposes. For example, it is not uncommon to chart a path at the beginning that will include one outcome or deliverable for a project, then find that the interdisciplinary researchers on the team have gone hurrying off in every direction, only to return with three or four outcomes, none of which corresponds to the original description.

What we have tended to find is that it is possible to forestall a lot of controversy and even potentially hurt feelings simply by not providing an initial path to an outcome, but rather to describe the project to the research team in terms of the highest level objective. For example, we once did a project where we brought in a dozen senior citizens to try to find online health information, using an existing searchable database and a new visualization prototype. However, in the project meeting, we talked about the objective of the work being to find out whether people who are at risk of failing to successfully use computers will actually be intimidated by seeing thousands of items on the screen at the same time, or whether the presence of those items, combined with tools for manipulating the display, would, on the contrary, be reassuring.

How we moved from a question about the possibility of visual information overload and the details of why it develops to a question about seniors accessing health information is entirely due to the dynamics of the team and the domain interests of its particular members. We could equally well have dealt with any of a hundred kinds of information for a thousand different uses, and still addressed the same larger research objective. What we required was that people who had some trouble with computers try out a system that showed them a lot of data in some area where they were interested in finding data. We learned a great many things from this study, including several fascinating details about the use and also the misinterpretation of our experimental interface. But the main thing we were interested in learning also emerged from the study, namely that this group of people found the conventional retrieval system more frustrating and intimidating than the prototype that showed them all of the data all of the time.

5.3.1 Ways of collaborating

Both designers and digital humanists tend to share a fundamental belief in the extraordinary value of interdisciplinarity, and when collaborating, tend to value the training, knowledge, and expertise brought to the table by the other discipline. However, the practicalities involved in managing and working within a collaborated endeavour can be both challenging and diverse – requiring different strategies from project to project. In this chapter, we discuss a variety of strategies we have developed and/or implemented on past research projects that have involved a collaboration between designers and digital humanists.

5.3.2 Delegation vs. collaboration

There are several models that have been used on interdisciplinary research projects. One is the conventional industrial production line, where a project has been defined by the leaders and is carried out by a series of workers doing each of the steps. We might call this approach Delegation. One advantage of this strategy is that the project, however tedious the work might be, gets done. Another is that the workers develop competence in doing their jobs through repetition, which means in the case of students that they are definitely learning something. A disadvantage is that the needs of the production line can necessitate that the students continue to work long past the time when they are learning. In fact, that is when the production line is at its most efficient. Another disadvantage is that the system is not predicated on the goal of making good use of the interests and skills of the workers.

5.3.3 Cross-disciplinary lessons learned

In addition to disentangling shared vocabulary, learning each other's vocabulary, and mutually benefitting from the history and experience of the other discipline, collaborative research projects between design and DH have also produced a number of insights in the form of cross-pollination of ideas. For instance, design was fairly early to adopt the ecological psychologist J.J. Gibson's concept of affordance, largely due to the work of Donald Norman in the 1980s. In the year 2003, it was still possible to receive reviewer's comments on a DH conference proposal that criticized the author(s) for attempting to coin the term. Ten years later, the concept has been well established in both design and DH. Similarly, the methodological stance of hermeneutic or interpretive inquiry from the humanities or, perhaps more specifically algorithmic criticism from DH, has become increasingly visible as a way of talking about the analysis and synthesis of information in design.

5.4 Managing people who are sensitive to their surroundings

This is a chapter about what it means to work with designers, or with anyone, really, who has not already been ground down by the bastards to the point of no return. Anyone working with designers will soon come to recognize that there is some hype about them being different from other people. But, they get up in the morning and drink ridiculously-priced cold brew like everyone else, and meticulously lace their red sneakers one at a time.

However, there are also some subtle differences that are important. The one we'd like to discuss here is their somewhat unusual hypersensitivity to their surroundings, and how that plays out in everything from a complex relationship with goal-setting to an inability to understand signage.

Let's begin with goal-setting. The idea of the goal is central to human planning, and has been a part of the popular imagination and a subject of research psychology since at least 1935 (Carson et al. 1994). Goals and goal-setting have been baked into corporate culture so thoroughly that they seem to be inextricable from it. However, a goal is an artificial telic construct and as such may have only a limited validity, providing perhaps less utility than is often attributed to it.

Below, we argue that designers tend to have an approach to human activity that is arguably much more deeply rooted in the living of everyday life, and is based on the metaphor of the paramecium. Although only a single-celled organism, a paramecium will attempt to make and maintain effective contact with its environment by moving away from poison and towards nutrient.

5.4.1 Designer as paramecium

Paramecia are members of a genus with several species of single-celled organisms, where mobility is provided by many cilia that sweep in sequence, resulting in a spiral motion through the water (Figure 5.1). Designers are members of a species of multicellular organisms with complex physical, social, and cultural interactions. It would seem at first glance that the metaphoric association of these two creatures may not be robust enough to support much insight, yet the simplicity of the paramecium and its behaviour is in some ways observable in the daily lives of the designer.

In a goal-setting paradigm, the received wisdom is that people do well when they can foresee a possible future accomplishment and plan to achieve it (e.g. Tracy 2010). This telic approach to the world has its virtues, particularly in relatively highly constrained contexts such as manufacturing and retail, where the results can be measured by counting: we produced this many widgets in this amount of time for this cost; we sold this many units over this many hours for this profit.

FIGURE 5.1: Designer or paramecium? Check the shoes.

However, it is a commonplace for self-help systems to encourage people to extend this approach beyond what might be considered its proper scope, and to consider the living of everyday life, the making and maintaining of effective contact with the environment, as a stage upon which to enact the telic strategies of business. We believe this is taking things too far, and that an alternative approach is preferable – that of constantly sampling the environment, and moving away from poisons and towards nutrients.[5]

The paramecium, however, faces several fundamental problems – some of which might be more accurately described as contrary impulses, instead of problems – in carrying out the program of action. These include:

- tenacity;
- repetition;
- comparison;
- community;
- change;
- risk; and
- discontinuity.

We conclude with a few unanticipated side-effects of the paramecium way of life, and with a reality check concerning the typical admixture of poisons and nutrients.

Tenacity, or sticking it out

To be able to ascertain whether or not an environment is poisonous or nutritious can be a matter requiring some sensitivity. Even at the extremes, it is not always clear that the immediate prospects could be better or worse after a few beats of the cilia. To take an example from one of our veteran friends, Tom Nelson, there are times when the walking barrage has exploded beside the landing boat and blasted everyone along with the debris into the ocean. At that moment, it may be pleasant to recognize that one is still alive, and there is perhaps some reassurance in the sense that everyone else in the immediate vicinity is going through a similar experience. Perhaps the best approach is to suck it up and swim to shore, where, admittedly, the machine guns are waiting. Still, since there are a limited number of choices in this environment, and only one of them involves the continuation of the organism, swim, in some senses, it must be.

Or, at the opposite extreme, there are moments when one has just cashed a well-earned paycheque from a job one enjoys and happens to spot a good friend outside a very decent restaurant as the lunch hour approaches, and the tendency may be to feel, not exactly that all is well in this best of all possible worlds, but at least that there are reasonable limits to what can be expected. As the Buddhists point out, living as we do in samsara is itself one of the three forms of suffering, so there is only so much that can be done in the short term.[6] The upshot, of course, is that there is an impulse to carry on as indicated, even though the scope of the activity may not be very wide and the opportunities for articulation may be limited. Some of the specific reasons for this tendency will be discussed later, but at this point it may be sufficient to note that the impulse to tough it out is one of the most inimical impulses that the paramecium faces.

Toughing it out, sucking it up (buttercup is optional), and just keeping your head down are all well and good, but when what you are after is someone who is sensitive to details, putting them into those positions is really acting against your own interests. Take the latte as an example. There is nothing wrong with a good strong cup of black joe designed to melt a spoon, and it may in fact be the preference of some people, including designers. And it is no hardship for anyone to get a free coffee at work. But when one of our colleagues showed up at a symposium with a very large, shiny red Oldsmobile of an espresso machine, the whole experience changed. Excitement was in the air. You never saw a device like that in a place like that. Certainly, the designers benefited, because here was some indication that nutrient was possible, even for the ones who didn't drink espresso. And when the designers benefited, so did everyone else, because the surroundings suggested that somebody cared about somebody else's happiness.

The political right in the United States at one point adopted the term 'snowflake' for people they saw as too delicate for this postlapsarian world. The implication was that they would melt and disappear under the strength of a challenging environment. But, that is not the case. They will not simply disappear – they will change, into people who are not unique and amazing and delicate, but are instead tough enough to survive in a playground world where calling each other names counts as rational discourse. Perhaps we could call them hailstones. And the world has lost another scarce resource, who used to be a person who was sensitive to the details.

Somewhat as an aside, the beauty of the Buddhists is that they believe that something can be done in the long term, and that is to engage in mental exercises that can help transform the experience of samsara into the experience of nirvana. They feel that since it is possible to get better at what you practice, if you practice good causes, you can expect in the long term to get good effects, and in any case you will have had the experience of setting up good causes. In that sense, there is not a lot of difference between the aftermath of a walking barrage and a decent lunch, except insofar as the mind of the person doing the mental exercises is able or not to accommodate the situation and carry on with setting up good causes.

One of the Buddhist saints (or perhaps more properly *bodhisattvas*), Ksitigarbha, is a person who has enough mental stability to spend his time in hell, working to alleviate the sufferings and causes of suffering of the demons. Ksitigarbha is an example of a paramecium who carries his own nutrients with him, which is of course something worth aspiring to. As another Buddhist saying has it, the world is rough and you could try to cover the whole thing in soft leather, but it is perhaps for practical purposes better to put the leather on the soles of your own feet.

What this strategy requires, however, is that several felicity conditions be met. First, the individual in question needs to be able to effect internal change – a capacity that is not really taught to people as an explicit part of current conventional education in the western world.[7] What the Buddhists do, of course, are a variety of mental exercises, strengthening, as it were, the mind's ability to pursue a particular course or to choose among courses the ones most likely to produce benefit. Just as daily push-ups can strengthen the core, daily mental exercises of the right kind can strengthen conviction, tone the thought processes, and produce mental habits that are beneficial.

The second felicity condition is that the environment is not so inimical that it actively interferes with the attempt to produce an internal change. There is a famous image of a Buddha, beyond mundane concerns with either attachment or aversion, and in fact busy with other things, who is

FIGURE 5.2: Here we are with the shoes again (photograph by Olena Tur, n.d.).

accepting with equanimity an acolyte rubbing him with oil and an enemy slicing him with a knife. But for non-Buddhas, either of these experiences can be distracting to the process of producing benefit, or as the designers say, designing.

The third felicity condition is that the coordinating conditions need to be right for the effort to have an effect, whether in the demonstrable present or at a sufficiently close remove that the continued application of the effort does not appear to be done out of sheer perversity. While it is possible to persist when an action is not having the desired results, it is not necessarily commensurate with the best mental practices.

In summary, given the right felicity conditions of internal ability, appropriate environment, and encouraging results, the circumstances can be changed from being a case of 'toughing it out' to one of 'using the opportunity for personal growth'.

However, given that we are generally well advised to improve ourselves whenever possible so that we suffer less in the longer term, there is still something to be said for getting the hell out of Dodge, and for doing it sooner rather than later. If you want designers on your team, you need to consider how your management practices can forestall that impulse.

Repetition: Same shit, different pile

Getting the hell out of Dodge, of course, does not always result in an improvement to the situation, nor is it psychologically always possible to make the move in the first place. The tendency to suffer from a repetition compulsion is not uncommon even among paramecia, with the result that, just as Ksitigarbha carries his own nutrients, lesser creatures may carry their own poisons. Insofar as the response of the paramecium is not entirely to an external reality, but may in some respects be recognized as involving a co-constructed reality that includes the phenomenological experience or interpretation of the viewer, it can be true that the process of sensing the environment and moving accordingly might involve no little degree of construction rather than simply perception and response.

What this implies for the habit of shifting away from poisons is that some introspection might be in order, so that the paramecium can discern to what extent the environment is the source or cause of the poisons, and to what extent the poison is the effect of the paramecium itself. For those situations where the difficulty seems to lie more within than without, it may be the case that some internal modifications will be more effective. On the other hand, it may not. Running away from problems is always worth considering. As our favourite martial arts instructor used to say: 'the first question you should ask yourself in a fight is this: at what point will I be able to successfully run away?' The implication, of course, was that running away before the fight even started was the best course possible.

Another factor worth considering is that the sensitivity of the paramecium may be particularly acute with respect to some specific poison or nutrient, often depending in large part on past experience coming to bear on the present situation. As we say, 'I was chased by it as a child', meaning that it is not unreasonable to expect that we will react strongly because of a previous trauma.

All of which may in fact be moot, since what is important at the end of the day is the experience of the paramecium rather than the roots of that experience; if a situation seems to be poisonous, then that may be sufficient for the purposes of the exercise. On the other hand, the opportunity for change to occur is also central to the metaphor, and if the awareness of the causes of the poisons can help generate plans to alleviate them, then that understanding is perhaps worthwhile.

Comparison: One person's poison is another person's nutrient

Contrary to what may seem to some people at times to be a well-attuned sense of loneliness, one does not live alone on this earth, and given the premise that all comparisons are odious, it is nonetheless incumbent upon the discerning paramecium to learn what can be learned from others. That is to say, life is not just a matter of a single creature in a Petri dish, but instead of an ecology of creatures, many of whom have contributed to the environment one encounters. One of the features of this ecosystem is that the nutrient for one sentient being may very well be the poison for another. Judging the value of a particular environment therefore may involve comparisons against other living creatures who seem similar, but at some fundamental level, the need remains for each person to carry out their own activities of sensing and response.

For example, there is the conventional question of how best to choose a livelihood. The majority of people seem to be more comfortable with regular food and lodging, and the provision of those components of life with some reliability is one of the desired consequences of the daily activity of many. However, there are some basic questions, such as the extent to which the enjoyment of life is either tied to the work necessary for securing life's necessities or is independent of that work. For some people, it appears to be a perfectly satisfactory arrangement that the bulk of their waking life has been pre-purchased by an organization that may or may not have an actual use for the time. For others, however, the idea that their time is under the control of an indifferent force outside their own volition, and therefore even potentially subject to being wasted, is intolerable. Fortunately, many environments support both ways of living, so that there are, for instance, employees and contractors, union members and managers, and even a distinction between functional managers, who keep the lights on, and project managers, who measure their tasks by duration, milestones, and deliverables.

For the paramecium, what this suggests is that the domain of possible choices is not necessarily uniform, but that it consists instead of a number of already existing

FIGURE 5.3: Here, a healthy rat gets bigger on a diet of rat poison: 'Bring it on!' (photo by Shashank Kumawat from Pexels).

structures that can be tested and accepted or rejected, as seems appropriate. To be fair, they are not evenly distributed. However, it is important to have what in some circles they call a right livelihood, by which is usually meant one that leaves the earth better than we found it, but for us involves regular access to very intelligent interlocutors, combined with a lot of flexibility in the daily routine.

We believe that flexibility is important because we like to divide the work according to how smart we are at any given time. Some kinds of work require a lot of mental acuity, while others can be done by a zombie. It is useful in the name of productivity to match the task at hand to the mental capacity available, so that the zombie tasks are not on the docket when the brain is firing on all cylinders, and vice versa. On a similar note, there are times of the day, and they are not necessarily predictable, when a short nap will serve to reset a person's switches and move them from bleary-eyed incompetence to sprightly intelligence. Unfortunately, the conventional work model established with the industrial revolution has not tended to accommodate this perspective.

However, returning our attention for a moment to personal history, whether or not a list of 45 different occupations is reasonable will depend in part on the circumstances and the nature of the given paramecium. We have a colleague who has had only two occupations in his entire life, consisting of a graduate research position and a professorship. He seems satisfied with his occupation and content with his life. We have generally been happy with what we were doing at any given moment, but dissatisfied whenever it seemed that it would continue unabated for any length of time. It was difficult to find what seemed an appropriate combination of freedom of agency, resources for productivity, and brilliant colleagues who enjoyed having us around. Not everyone, of course, places the same value on those aspects of employment as we do. For others, more important factors might include salary, security, respect, a good career path, a company car, a corner office, lack of pressure so there is plenty of time for social media at work, and tolerance for errors brought on by not taking naps when you need them.

Community: A world of paramecia

Unlikely as it may seem, there are also situations under which it is possible that more than one person who behaves like a paramecium will be present, or where there may in fact develop entire ecosystems of people who act like paramecia. These can be strange and heady times, where the range of the possible extends far beyond what would normally be the constraints of the probable. Why precisely this is the case is a bit difficult to determine. It may have something to do with the collective results of attempting in the first place to seek nutrients and avoid poisons, so that paramecia naturally tend to gather where there are more nutrients and fewer poisons. It may also be an outcome of the tendency to attempt to optimize the opportunities in the environment.

It can produce some strange side-effects. For instance, when one of us first arrived at the IIT Institute of Design, a place that we would characterize as an ecosystem of paramecia if ever we've seen one, we noticed a shelf outside the office door. Sitting on the shelf were a set of several coffee machines, all of them disassembled and lying in pieces. There was no obvious place to get a cup of coffee, but if what you happened to be interested in were the component parts and how they had been constructed, you were in the right place (Figure 5.4).

We have seen something similar about the environment itself, which is that in the presence of other paramecia, it tends to be much more physically fluid than is otherwise to be expected. From day to day one will observe spaces being reconfigured for different uses, furniture coming and going, temporary installations emerging, then disappearing. For some months during that first year at the Institute of Design, a car was being mocked up in the common space, and then there was a temporary mock-up at the door into the area, showing what it might look like if there were an additional window, a line on the carpet within which you can be struck by the opening door, and a place to one side where you can set your keys or coffee cup.

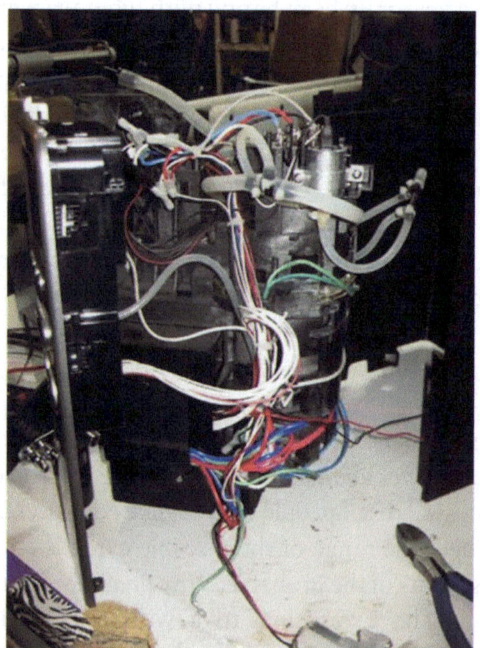

FIGURE 5.4: Disassembled coffee machines: designers must be near.

There is in fact a drawing of a coffee cup on the temporary surface, reminding us of a designer's advice when one of us was making a poster about electronic books. 'Put the word "book" on top of the picture of the book', she[8] said. 'That way people will be less likely to be confused about what you are discussing'. We have subsequently come to believe that you can recognize a designer by the following sequence of events: someone says 'ouch' as they run into something that has been clearly marked with a sign, usually hand-written, after which they mutter 'you call that signage?' The problem they are identifying by crashing into it is that a sign, especially a hand-written one, is typically an attempt to prophylactically repair what was a bad design in the first place, and the designer, like a canary in a coal mine, is reacting to the surroundings as a whole rather than to the patch placed on them.

Changing the world

Can poison change to nutrient? This is the question where the iron enters the paramecium soul. The entire notion of avoiding poison and seeking nutrient is predicated on the premise that the two substances are immutable, or at least immutable for all practical purposes. But what if (1) the abusive spouse has a genuine spirit of amendment, (2) the aggressive boss is looking to transfer out of the unit, or (3) there is a promotion in the offing? Under the right conditions, should not other considerations take precedence, and people (1) make it work for the sake of the children, (2) keep their heads down and wait for a change of leadership, or (3) keep on smiling and hoping for an improvement of circumstances?

Certainly, change is possible. It is in fact an element of faith that causes generate effects, and that the nature of the cause, whether good or bad, equates to the nature of the effect. We wake up every morning and remind ourselves that we want to set up only good causes and get only good effects. However, change can also take time, and if the environment is sufficiently poisonous, the effects on the paramecium can be devastating. In the earliest jobs of one of us, there were five employees and an amount of work that could usually be accomplished by one. This was a pleasure in its way, since it required the bulk of one person's capacity to get everything done. It left the other four free to pursue their own enjoyable hours, which consisted of playing cards, watching television, and reading magazines. However, it was a lonely life, and it was only possible to stay with it for about a year. A healthy paramecium would have left sooner but the pay was good. As soon as something was available with comparable pay but better colleagues, the door, like in the cartoons, had a paramecium-shaped hole in it.

A more robust paramecium, however, or one with different priorities, could very well have made a go of it, and part of that success may have hinged on the poison – in this case, colleagues who were not very interesting to be around – changing to a nutrient. Perhaps they would leave and be replaced by more congenial ones. It was unlikely, since they had been there for ten years and more, and were intending to stay on to retirement. Perhaps they would choose entertainments that might be more interesting to everyone, for example taking up a different kind of card game, or beginning to read books instead of magazines. The odds were not great that this would happen on its own in the foreseeable future, but the paramecium is also able to introduce change, first, for example, by joining the existing card game, then after some period of time, by suggesting alternatives. However, for some people, the persistence of purpose necessary to influence their surroundings, coupled with the odds of the influence successfully improving the situation at the appropriate scale, is such that the exercise is too costly to undertake.

As the Black feminist Audre Lorde so rightly points out, in certain cases profound change might be necessary since the 'tools' of the system cannot dismantle the system itself – the dominant system is so fundamentally toxic that it requires radical dismantling (Lorde, 1984, p.2).

More often, of course, it is the case that some changes are possible while others are not. For instance, while it may not be too difficult to learn to enjoy playing cards, the nature of the job is likely fixed, at least in the short to medium term. In that case, changing jobs is the only viable solution if it is the job itself that constitutes the poison.

It is also possible that the job will change the paramecium, and what seems intolerable at one point will prove in the long run to be tolerable after all. The snowflake, that is, will melt, then freeze into a much sturdier drop of ice. There is, it seems to me, a lot of potential material for writers of tragedies inherent in this observation.

From bad to worse: What if the choice is between greater poison and lesser poison?

To this point, we have described the situation as though the surroundings were divided into two categories: nutrients and poisons. And it does happen, of course, that although the world presents a complex terrain, it can still be understood as a place where nutrients and poisons are indiscriminately mixed. It can also happen that the choice does not involve a nutrient at all, but instead consists of variations of poison. 'Name your poison', they used to say at cocktail parties in the 1950s, and maybe they still say that.

What this difficulty implies for the discerning paramecium is that the environment is not always configured in such a way that there are nutrients present, or at least nutrients that can be discerned, or nutrients that are appropriate for the cooperating conditions. We used to joke about being born as Spider-man on the Prairies – since all of his powers involve tall structures the best he could hope for were a few grain elevators in every town.

Another complicating factor can be summarized with the phrase 'the devil you know', meaning that a paramecium who is thinking about changing out of a poisonous situation might be well advised to figure out whether or not the move will be towards greater nutrient or greater poison. In a conversation with the author Bill Meilen, we suggested that this lifetime had been a hard one, but perhaps the next one would be better. 'But what', he suggested, 'if it turns out that this was your holiday life?'

From good to better: Choosing among nutrients

Just as some environments present themselves as primarily being about variations of poisons, there are certain circumstances when the choice is among variations of nutrients. In conventional terms, we might ask, for example, is it better to be happy or rich? Really, it would be great to be able to face that kind of dilemma. Among biologists, there is a means of distinguishing between the behaviour of different species, where some are characterized as win-shift while others are win-stay. The former strategy works well in situations where a nutrient may turn out to be a trap of some kind, like a poison in disguise, while the latter strategy maximizes on profit because time is not spent looking for the next form of nutrient. Its downside, of course, provides the punchline for the Eartha Kitt song 'Monotonous', where the list of nutrients has only left her exhausted with living (Figure 5.5).

FIGURE 5.5: The incomparable Eartha Kitt performing at Dimitriou's Jazz Alley, in Seattle, Washington. She doesn't look exhausted to us.

Certainly it is possible to get too much of a good thing. It is also true that variety is the spice of life, but the perspective is also valuable from which a person can recognize that having a choice among nutrients is a far more positive situation to be in, despite the inevitable difficulty of having to set some aside in favour of others, than having to choose among a mixture of poisons and nutrients or just among poisons. Plus, one can console oneself with the thought that nothing lasts forever, so that like the king of legend, the slogan 'this too will change' is a useful and valid acknowledgement to make in order to temper the emotional experience of both excessive poison and excessive nutrient.

Discontinuity, or sudden death

A Petri dish typically presents a relatively smooth surface, where the movement of the paramecium can take place across a level terrain. Under those conditions, movement from poison to nutrient may occur along a gradient, with the changes happening gradually. In the world outside the Petri dish, however, the transitions between nutrients and poisons can sometimes be rather abrupt, so that it is possible to be moving along in some confidence that the band of nutrients is holding up well, only to discover that the ground has dropped out abruptly and the nutrients are at their end.

One often wonders, however, when enough will be enough already. As our friend Lorraine once said, 'Adversity builds character, but I can hardly get my character through the door as it is'.

Another alternative, however, presents itself in the context of discontinuity, and that is to treat the existence of discontinuity as an opportunity not just for the experience of positive disintegration, but also as a form of alternative practice within the larger environment. It is just the existence of such discontinuities, after all, between Dodge and other places, that makes getting the hell out of Dodge a possibility.

Unanticipated side-effects

One consequence of the paramecium approach to life is that phenomena that aren't easily recognized as either nutrients or poisons can easily fall through the cracks of perception. We have frequently had the experience often associated with the typical absent-minded professor, where someone will reference an object or even another person in the environment who had simply not registered on our awareness.

There is a similar difficulty with respect to what Gary Kelly[9] has called the 'middle-class concept of the beautiful soul', which suggests that civilization requires a sensitivity to beauty. Not everyone, however, has this kind of sensitivity, even when the surroundings are usually of paramount importance. An effective strategy for these people when it comes to viewing art is to consider all of it under threat, which moves it into the terrain of the perceivable. The formula is to ask yourself what three objects you would choose to rescue if the building were on fire.

Reality check: Taking a few roughs with a smooth

P.G. Wodehouse fans will be familiar with the chef Anatole, whose command of English idioms is imprecise yet evocative. One of his apparent beliefs is that a person needs to accept that no situation is ideal, and that we need, as he says, to take a few roughs with a smooth. It would appear that an element of the Platonic ideal may have slipped into our discussion of the paramecium lifestyle, in the sense that a given situation is usually more complicated than simply having nutrients in one place and poisons in another. While that does happen, it is also true that commonly both the nutrients and the poisons coexist within a single other sentient being or environmental factor.

A paramecium senses and responds to combinations of poison and nutrient, and looks for for a mixture that isn't necessarily one that contains more nutrient and less poison, but instead for one where the nutrients are particularly nutritious, and the poisons are, in comparison with other poisons, more tolerable to the system. In some cases, in relationship terms, that may mean looking for someone who is interested in your becoming a better, stronger, faster, and more adaptive paramecium, and will be interested in supporting that course of action. In terms of poisons, some people might have trouble accommodating someone who enjoyed, for instance, a drink, or who disliked an environment that involved an ever-changing set of experiments. For example, you never know when you may want to grow a massive crop of basil in the living room, or convert the bathroom for a few days into a darkroom, or reinvent the electric motor from first principles.

5.4.2 Conclusion

If our goal is to make and maintain effective contact with the environment, then we can see a way forward in terms of reconciling this paramecium life with the suggestions of the well-intentioned counsellors who advise us that we need to set goals. That is, we could just phrase all the goals as 'to act like a paramecium'.

However, kidding aside, it seems as though the two approaches to living represent considerably disparate locations in the terrain of possible responses to the fundamental question of how best to go about the process of living.

In some respects, we advocate a paramecium approach to life because we have found the general use of goals to not be particularly helpful. On the contrary, persistence in the practice of setting goals and meeting them can tend to render a person insensitive to the demands of the environment, since what is not explicitly related to the accomplishment of the goal is relegated to insignificance, and what is insignificant can safely be ignored. However, it is always a bad idea for scholars to ignore things, since the immersion in visual details is one of the attributes that makes them most effective.

An alternative approach, however, might be to set goals at an appropriate level of granularity so that they include things like getting a decent meal or enjoying a day's work. Certainly, this is not impossible, but it does beg the question of what those kinds of goals accomplish that a paramecium life might not.

It may also be true that not everyone prefers to consider life as taking place on these terms. The necessity for constant or at least regular assessment of the environment may in itself present an insurmountable barrier to participation. However, for those people who are so constituted as to find constant assessment of their perceptions a natural component of the living of everyday life, the paradigm of the paramecium may offer not only some reassurance but also some guidance as to the best way of proceeding. And for the people who are responsible for managing these souls, it may provide some insight into why a coffee machine with free coffee isn't always going to be enough to get them to stay.

5.5 Case study 5: Project charter

In 2005, we began iteratively designing a project charter that spells out the principles under which we operate, as well as the specific policies that are related to each principle. We typically introduce the charter individually to new team members as they are recruited, or else within the first meeting or two of the entire team, then refer to it subsequently as team issues come to light.

We developed the project charter because the researchers we work with come from varying research traditions in the academy. Speaking in broad generalizations that do not always apply, some disciplines, particularly in the humanities, have tended to expect work to be done by a lone scholar, working within a tradition, presenting results to a scholarly community, and training graduate students who will also work alone. Other disciplines, particularly in the sciences and engineering, have adopted instead an apprenticeship model, where a senior scholar manages a lab where junior scholars work. A third model is one in which groups of established scholars work together. They might share a specialized background, or more typically, a disciplinary one. This discipline-based model capitalizes on the benefits of specialization – specialist scholars refine theories, methods, and technologies particular to their disciplines (Seipel 2005).

Interdisciplinary research models build on the strengths of the third, discipline-based model. We define interdisciplinary research as combining two or more academic disciplines that are usually considered distinct in order to reach a common goal. The concept has been further articulated as unidisciplinarity (Hobson n.d.), multidisciplinarity (Wilson and Pirrie 2000), or pluridisciplinarity (Sillitoe 2004), depending on the ways in which the teams functionally interact. We have teams that fall into each of these categories depending on the nature of the project, the experience of the people on the project, and their willingness, need, and ability to work together. For example, in our project on interfaces for visualization of simple decision support systems, the mathematical modelling is handled in a unidisciplinary manner by the project engineers, while the interface design is similarly carried out by a relatively isolated team of designers. In contrast, our project on developing a rich prospect interface for pill identification involved designers, programmers, and information specialists working together at the same table over an extended period, providing each other with relevant literature and insights that crossed disciplinary boundaries.

Genuinely interdisciplinary work is valuable for several reasons. First, it is possible to tackle problems in an interdisciplinary project that could not be dealt with in any adequate way by a single researcher working in the confines of one discipline. As Sillitoe (2004) explains when discussing his interdisciplinary work on poverty, complex research problems often require the cooperation between specialists with diverse backgrounds, in his case, in both the natural and social sciences. Second, the projects themselves can be remarkably fruitful to the researchers involved.

However, although the benefits of interdisciplinary work are significant, it does not come without problems and challenges. To begin with, some disciplines are more open towards interdisciplinary work than others. Therefore, when forming a team, we have had to become conscious that not everyone may have had previous experience working in such a manner. As it often occurs on our projects, some team members come to the table unaware of the methods and processes inherent in each other's research practice. A form of artful integration (Schuler and Clement 2004) is needed – a careful weaving of complementary researchers, methodologies, and practices. In our experience, a project that is made up of a team of researchers who are unknown to one another is particularly challenging. The start of a project does not allow enough time for everyone to become adequately acquainted. By the end of the project, however, our team members seem to gain a substantial awareness of each other's value, particularly if they worked in a pluridisciplinary manner. This knowledge is of great advantage on subsequent projects.

Another challenge occurs when a project begins to go astray. This can occur for a number of reasons, and, as the literature reports, it can take weeks or even months before all of the team members are aware of what has happened (Keil et al. 2004).

Interdisciplinary research requires a combination of new sets of skills and accommodation of other team members in a number of areas where accommodation may not otherwise have been necessary. Hara et al. (2003) outline eight factors impacting collaboration:

- compatibility;
- workstyle;
- writing style;
- work priority;
- work connections;
- incentives;
- socio-technical infrastructure; and
- other forms of compatibility.

In the context of advice for people undertaking interdisciplinary work for the first time, Svensson (2003) has the following list of strategies:

- open yourself up to neighbouring fields;
- map the relevant conceptual territory;
- be prepared to find unexpected connections;
- communicate with people unlike yourself;
- think across boundaries; and
- make sure to introduce interdisciplinary strategies early in the process.

In addition to interpersonal management strategies, several technological solutions for project management have been developed and subsequently adapted to interdisciplinary research management. Microsoft Project Management and the online Basecamp are two popular examples; however, many others exist, each with its own strengths and weaknesses: Asana, Planio, Flow, Paper, Trello, Roadmunk, Jira, and Confluence are a few more recent examples. Research continues in this area with projects such as Zhang et al. (2007), who designed and implemented a research prototype called ACPM (Activity Centric Project

Management). The goal of the system is to make collaborative activities flexible and easier to manage. Their findings indicate that an activity-centred approach could be used to integrate tasks and activities, provide timely activity reports, generate status reports, and allow third-party access to the information, thus helping to manage collaboration.

Finally, no interdisciplinary research project can be expected to succeed unless it has contributions from good team members: 'The most important features of project-relevant skills and knowledge appear to be diversity and complementarity in the skills, perspectives, and knowledge of team members' (Amabile et al. 2001). As one of our colleagues put it during a presentation with seven authors (Wynne et al. 2007), on a good interdisciplinary project, each team member is uniquely valuable – no one is expected to compromise their own expertise. Across its various incarnations, the interface design she was discussing has involved expertise from five disciplines: psychology, humanities computing, computer science, visual communication design, and library and information studies.

> If you let go of your own agenda when coming to the table made up of an interdisciplinary team, more creative 'stuff' tends to emerge. You take true advantage of the interdisciplinary team by not trying to force your own set of values or processes onto them. and, as you've experienced, forcing it doesn't work anyway – they rebel. With interdisciplinary design research you can ask even larger questions, and when you allow those teams to do their own thing, even more creative and unexpected outcomes occur.
>
> (Zimmerman 2003)

Our typical research team involves 3-5 researchers, each of whom sits in a different disciplinary chair. It will occasionally happen that a project requires, for instance, four designers, but most projects will have a designer, a computer programmer or two, a domain expert, and a project manager.

In the standard military model of organization, there would be a hierarchy, where the manager would determine what was going to be accomplished, then divide the work among the others. This form of delegation is not viable for interdisciplinary research, where there are usually no clear lines of reporting that can be used to enforce authority. In different projects the various roles might be filled by colleagues at approximately equal points in their career trajectory, or there may be senior colleagues with junior colleagues, full professors with graduate or undergraduate students, industry partners, faculty members from different departments, and so on.

Under these conditions, delegation from a single authority is problematic, because there is no single authority. It is therefore useful to treat team members as equals, and to attempt to foster a genuinely collaborative management environment rather than adopt a fiction of central control and delegation.

The decision to work collaboratively has significant implications for the direction the project will take. In fact, we have noticed that everything about a project would be different if there were a different person in any of the chairs. Since each chair represents a specialization, the decisions made by each participant will directly influence the way the project proceeds. In general, we typically have a goal for the project before the team is assembled. However, all of the strategic decisions about content, platform, visual language, protocols for user study, and so on are determined by the team members.

This policy on strategic decision-making is an example of the iterative nature of our ongoing Project Charter design process. We only slowly came to the realization that it was a good idea to have our research colleagues determine the project strategy, having noticed that our setting both a goal and a corresponding strategy was inevitably leading after the first few meetings to a point of rebellion, where one or more of the participants would propose an alternative strategy to the one being discussed. It became clear that this key moment in the process was one where additional commitment and motivation were being generated, and we began to start projects without the initial strategy, recognizing that it would be discarded in any case. We wondered at first if discarding the initial strategy was an essential part of creating motivation, but when we removed that step, we found that the moment where participant enthusiasm was generated simply arrived two or three meetings earlier.

Another example of the iterative development of the charter is the policy on publication. We originally were concerned only with presentation at conferences and publication in academic journals, and the policies dealt with the issue of co-authorship. Over time, however, it became plain that we were also tending to adopt online methods of disseminating our work, including websites, blogs, and wikis, and we added a policy so that this form of publication would become part of our early discussions.

Based on these experiences we have come to our own pragmatic understanding of Sillitoe's comment (2004) that interdisciplinary team management is a balancing act between respecting the needs and perspectives of individual researchers on the team and the canons of their disciplines, and supporting the goals of the project.

5.5.1 The project charter

The current form of the project charter contains six major sections, which correspond to the principles under which we carry out our projects. For each principle, there are a number of policies that address specific questions of interpretation. The six principles deal respectively with publication, deadlines, funding, future phases, professional dignity, and goodwill. We do not consider this to be an exhaustive list of principles – it is simply the list we have iteratively developed so far, based on our experiments in project management. This charter is currently on its 14th iteration.

Publication (sharing research outcomes)

Principle: We are interested in disseminating the results of this project as widely as possible, with credit to us for doing it.

The principle of publication may at first glance appear unnecessary, since academics place a high premium on publication. However, for colleagues in the fine arts, publication is not necessarily as important as exhibitions or gallery shows. For colleagues in English Departments, the highest form of publication is the book. For colleagues in Computer Science Departments, conference proceedings are more important than books, because the book is generally considered an archival record of past research, whereas conferences are at the cutting edge. In Humanities Computing, the conferences are often based on abstracts only, rather than full papers; the result is that presentation at even the most venerable Humanities Computing conference is not usually beneficial for Computer Scientists.

In addition to the disciplinary variations in evaluating publication venues, there are also cases where colleagues on a research project are from industry. In these situations, especially if there has been a monetary contribution from the industry partner, it is very important to agree at an early stage about what can be published and when. For colleagues in areas where intellectual property can be valuable, it may also be important to have patent applications in place before results are published to the academic community. Fortunately, interface designs are generally not patentable, which reduces the anxiety somewhat in our field.

Policy: Project members may use any of the work as examples in presentations, papers, interviews, and other media opportunities. They may post any of it to their websites. Wherever possible, they should mention the names of the other project members who were directly involved, as well as the name of the project.

There are many occasions where it is possible to mention a project. This policy encourages our team members to mention our work, even in cases where it is not reasonable to provide a co-authorship credit to every team member. Since the principle is to disseminate our results, these occasional descriptions can have a very beneficial effect.

Policy: The project team will maintain a collaborative project website, which will contain links to all the presentations and publications of the group.

The web is a convenient place for team members to access and to point at whenever someone is interested in our projects. However, setting up and maintaining a web presence is a service load on the project, and needs to be explicitly endorsed or it can easily slip through the cracks. Examples of project sites related to our work include www.inke.ca and www.qcollaborative.com.

Policy: For presentations or papers where this work is the main topic, all team members who worked directly on this subproject should be co-authors. Any member can elect at any time not to be listed, but may not veto publication.

The policy on co-authorship can result in papers with quite a few authors. We now typically have three to five authors on every paper, and our longest list so far includes 17 authors. Multi-authored papers are commonplace in the sciences but still relatively rare in the humanities. In any case, they are a good opportunity for junior colleagues to present and publish. However, on one of our larger projects, we had a team of over 25 faculty members, not including postdoctoral and graduate students. We had deliberately planned the project so that the work would be tightly integrated, which made the choice of co-authors very difficult. For that project, we modified this policy to provide for individually naming the first three authors, then listing the name of the research group as the fourth author. The members of the group can then be listed in a footnote or on the website.

Policy: For presentations or papers that spin off from this work, only those members directly involved need to be listed as co-authors. The others should be mentioned if possible in the acknowledgements, credits, or article citations.

The goal here is to provide a reasonable way to balance the benefit of co-authorship with the possible growth in the numbers of co-authors that begins to reduce that benefit. By suggesting when acknowledgement or citation is appropriate, the policy provides a useful approach to promoting our work without overwhelming the author credits.

Deadlines

Principle: We intend this work to move forward at a steady pace, given due awareness of the vagaries of life.

Deadlines are important to the success of a project, but a positive ongoing relationship between the researchers is also important. It is therefore useful to acknowledge that deadlines are important, but that a steady forward pace is really what is required.

Policy: Project members will make every effort to attend meetings as arranged and to keep in regular contact by e-mail or other electronic means. Frequent absence may result in being warned, then cautioned, then asked to leave the team.

Communication is distinct from the timelines of a project, and people have to be among those present in order to communicate. We generally assume that on interdisciplinary research projects, it is a fundamental fact that people will vote with their feet, and decisions will be made and enacted by the people who are present. However, we also recognize that not everyone can be present all the time. At key points in some projects, when deadlines are tight, we have supplemented this policy with another provisional one, which specifies turnaround time on decisions. Under these unusual conditions, people who don't respond within 24 hours, for instance, are assumed to consent.

Policy: Project members will jointly establish and attempt to meet self-imposed deadlines, in part through providing the project administrator with lists of commitments, so that reminders will be sent out as a matter of routine.

It is not always possible for projects to have an official administrator, and it is a bit of a luxury when they do. However, the strategy of explicitly notifying the other team members of commitments and deadlines can help keep a project moving forward. However, the spirit of this policy needs to be read in the context of the larger principle that allows for the vagaries of life.

This policy is also an example of the iterative development of the charter, which sometimes requires revision to existing policies to accommodate new circumstances. The original form dealt only with self-imposed deadlines, but when we had the opportunity to hire a project administrator, we added the second clause. Although this may seem like a comparatively minor change in wording, in practice it is a significantly different approach to handling communication about deadlines.

Policy: In the event the task is overdue by a considerable amount of time (for instance, whichever is lesser – two months, or double the original timeframe), other members may at their discretion notify the offender that the task will be re-assigned, without prejudice to the constitution of the team or the public credit of any member.

Even given the vagaries of life, it is sometimes the case that a team member simply does not meet deadlines. It is important to be able to re-assign the tasks undertaken by such a person, although it is also worth trying to figure out if there are useful tasks that do not require the person to meet a deadline. There are often tasks that just need to be completed at some point during the process. Examples include writing sections of text for the website or social media, coming up with interesting titles for presentations and papers, carrying out literature reviews and writing up the results, and starting on the next grant proposal.

This policy is another instance where the charter has varied from project to project. On one of the major international projects, the need to coordinate efforts between teams meant that a deadline slipped by two months would be too much, and we not only shortened the duration in the policy, but also wrote the project plan to include monthly updates from the team leaders.

Policy: Project phases will be arranged so as to minimize the need for sequential completion of one phase before another can begin: wherever possible, phases will run in parallel, with communication occurring between people as they work on each phase, rather than waiting to communicate until the end.

Of all the policies dealing with timelines, this one is perhaps the most important. Projects occur over time, which means that they will go through phases. But on an interdisciplinary project, it is a fundamental error to require one group of researchers to wait on output from another group before they can begin. It is one thing to fall behind because your own work is going slower than you'd planned. It is quite another experience to be waiting for months or even years for someone else to give you what you need to start your work.

Funding

Principle: We would prefer for this work to be funded.

Since funding is often quite competitive and is in many cases coupled to the primary research objectives of the principal investigator, it is not always possible to secure research funds for interdisciplinary projects. We have several projects that are being carried out by groups of volunteer researchers who happen to share a common interest. However, in each of these cases we would be able to make faster progress and also provide rewards if some funding could be secured. This principle lets the researchers know that it isn't necessarily neglect that has resulted in a project moving ahead without funding, and that we will do our best to secure funding when we can. At that point, there are additional management considerations, since most agencies will not retroactively fund researchers who have been working as volunteers. One possibility is therefore to use conference travel as a reward that is not retroactive but nonetheless relies on the work having moved ahead to the point where it is ready to present.

Policy: Project members will watch for and notify each other of funding opportunities and participate wherever possible in the writing of appropriate grant proposals.

Given the realities of competitive funding and small pots of money in various locations, academic research can quickly become a never-ending process of writing research grants, some of which can be quite time-consuming. Perhaps not surprisingly, the size of the award does not usually correlate in any meaningful way with the amount of work involved in applying for it. Getting help from other team members in grant writing can strengthen relationships, serve as a learning experience for junior colleagues, and also be used as an early phase in collaborative project planning.

Future phases

Principle: We understand that the work we do on this project may have future phases. Modifications and additions may be made to further the project by other members.

People realize that research has phases that will occur over time. They also know that they may lose interest in the project, or find other projects that are more interesting, or move on to other kinds of work instead of research. However, it is important to have the principle in place so that team members have a chance to acknowledge to themselves that the project may not end with the end of their participation.

Policy: In addition to PDFs or other formats for presentation, project members will keep safe and distribute regularly all native files generated for the project: Photoshop, Illustrator, InDesign, and any other data files or source files. These files will be unflattened and editable. Where copyright restrictions do not apply, fonts should also be included in shared files.

Designers and computer programmers are two groups that are particularly prone to the desire to hold onto their original files and not provide working copies to others. There are a variety of rationales for this undesirable behaviour that all make sense; however, the next policy on this list seems to have made a significant difference in our ability to pry the source files loose from their cold, dead hands.

Policy: As projects progress to new phases, each team member will have the right of first choice over whether or not to continue with the project.

One of the possibilities that can arise in interdisciplinary research is that people decide they would prefer not to work together again. However, if these decisions are too unilateral or too arbitrary, they can poison the communication with worry.

After we stated that people can opt out of future phases, but not be fired without consultation, we suddenly found that many of the reasons for not providing source files simply disappeared.

Policy: Insofar as ethics clearances allow, data backup will be provided through central project servers. Local projects should also make provisions for regular backup of all project files, including versions of files in progress.

Computer scientists are often quite good at managing files on a central server, with version control systems and task assignments that can be tracked towards completion and so on. Other researchers do not necessarily have experience with these kinds of systems, and need to be introduced to the idea that the project archives should be a regular part of the document flow.

Professional dignity

Principle: We wish to communicate in such a way as to preserve professional dignity.

Human beings like to gossip about each other. They like to complain behind each other's backs. Researchers are human beings, and in these respects no different from other people. By stating the principle of professional dignity, we hope to encourage each other to remember that we are working with others who have a professional standing and who deserve respect as colleagues. When tempers flare or pressures are felt, this principle can make a significant difference both in how the situation is discussed and in the eventual outcome.

We had an example of needing explicit reference to this principle in a case where we had a disagreement about the leadership of a subcomponent of one of the projects. The principal investigator and a team leader were not able to successfully negotiate a series of tight deadlines, and a change in team leadership was necessary. The PI had received a number of offline communications from other team members, and by explicitly invoking this principle and its policies, we were able to change the team leadership and still keep a good working relationship with the previous leader, who remained on the team.

Policy: We will strive to maintain a tone of mutual respect whenever we write or meet, and to forgive lapses if they occur.

Like professional dignity, mutual respect may be a hard concept to pin down, but it is relatively straightforward to identify when people are experiencing a lack of it. As with the other charter policies, mutual respect is a best practice we hope to maintain, although in this case we also acknowledge that there may be lapses that will need to be adjusted if they occur.

> *Policy: We will attempt to keep communications transparent, for example, by copying everyone involved in any given discussion, and by directly addressing with each other any questions or concerns that may arise.*

This policy of transparency is another simplifying strategy. If too much back-channel discussion takes place, it can become very difficult for everyone to understand what decisions are being made and why, especially on a geographically distributed team. It is also disturbing to see your name appear in an e-mail thread that never arrived in your inbox, so we feel it is better to err on the side of receiving too many messages and having the problem of sifting through them, rather than dividing the communication between groups. On a typical large research project, we will expect to receive about 2,000 project-related e-mail messages per year.

Goodwill

> *Principle: We would like to foster goodwill among all the participants.*

Enthusiasm and good nature are very beneficial in interdisciplinary research. Situations will inevitably arise where participants will be working under pressure or undertaking tasks that are not congenial. Fostering goodwill can help make the difference, but it requires attention and commitment. As Bennett and Kidwell (2001) point out, interdisciplinary research teams are a form of self-designing work group. Researchers working in this manner always have the possibility to choose whether or not to make an active effort or to withhold effort. Withholding effort can have the consequence of people choosing not to work together again; withholding effort is also often done for emotional reasons involving the relationships between researchers:

> withholding effort occurs in self-designing groups, such as research collaborations, and that the emotional bonds that group members form with colleagues play a key role in whether they decide to work together again, as well as in how they react to perceptions that a coauthor withheld effort.
>
> (Bennett and Kidwell 2001)

Policy: In making financial decisions, we will attempt to allocate resources in ways that indicate commitment to each of the people on the team.

Disputes over the division of financial and other resources can torpedo a project. A colleague who has served as Department Chair once described a choice he made that resulted in a successful and comparatively uncontested allocation of offices. His strategy was to explain a simple principle that incidentally resulted in him getting the smallest office. Disputes subsequently just didn't seem to arise.

Policy: Members will also watch for and notify each other of opportunities for commercialization and licensing. Any commercial agreements or plans will be made so as to include and equally benefit all members of the group.

It is not often the case that commercial benefits are a possibility, but in some disciplines it is becoming increasingly common to explicitly address the issue. How this policy may play out in actual fact remains to be seen, since none of our projects have yet gone on to commercialization. But we currently have three projects that have some potential.

Policy: We will strive to be a group working toward different parts of a larger, coherent, and important whole – one that promises to exceed the sum of its parts.

As with many of our policies, this one might well go without saying. Yet by articulating it as a policy at the beginning of the process, we are able to encourage the participants to watch for opportunities to do more together than they are able to do alone. For those participants who are used to relying on their own resources in a research project, the thought of allowing others to be responsible for some parts of the work does not necessarily come naturally.

In addition to being interdisciplinary, many of our project teams are also inter-institutional, inter-provincial, and international. Canada is a big country, and an inter-provincial project can involve researchers who are thousands of kilometres apart. Not to mention those teams that collaborate across borders. We make use, on different projects, of all the various technologies that are available for meeting at a distance, including project wikis, blogs, websites, collaborative online writing tools, video conferencing, text chats, listservs, and e-mail. In a couple of projects, we've recently added an online project management system, a software version tracker, and a variety of task assignment tools. These technologies allow us to keep the projects moving forward. However, we've found that for periodic leaps forward, it is very useful to collect a group of team members into one location and have them work together for a few days in the same room.

We came across the idea in an anecdote by a colleague, who described going once to a resort hotel with a friend where the two of them sat together over a long weekend and co-authored a paper. Our colleague described it as a very positive experience, so we determined to see if it would work for us. We subsequently met quarterly in this way for the duration of the project. We typically rent cluster housing on campus, where four of us can stay in rooms and share a common working space, or else we take hotel rooms in the same hotel and commandeer one of the public areas. Everyone brings a laptop, and we have multiple people from each role present, so there might be two designers, two programmers, a couple of content experts, and a manager. Our experience suggests that it is useful to have anywhere from four to seven people. We've tried gathering as few as two, but it is not always possible to get sufficient momentum going. We've also collected together as many as a dozen, but they subsequently broke into three sub-groups.

The purpose of these hackfests is not primarily to hold meetings, but instead to work together in the same place, where other team members are available for consultation.

5.5.2 Most recent additions and considerations

Our work with the oil sands and subsequent dive into critical design and feminist HCI impacted our work and perspectives beyond decision support. Intersectionality, as coined and defined by Kimberlé Crenshaw,[10] in particular, has led us to consider simultaneous and intersected oppression and discrimination as likely embedded in our work, and experienced uniquely by those who do not identify with the dominant group's social, biological, and cultural norms (patriarchy, capitalism, and white supremacy). As a first step in recognizing our positions of power, we have committed to acknowledging and welcoming the differences among everyone's situated perspectives, and to working well together, without eliding those differences.

We are also working towards more engagement with the values of speculative design, while acknowledging Luiza Prado de O. Martins's (2015: n.pag.) criticism of its current practice and introduction of the idea of a 'feminist speculative design': 'a strategic approach to addressing issues of systemic gender violence and discrimination within speculative and critical design practices'. We support Prado de O. Martins's engagement of Critical Theory as a useful model for how we can think about the things we are making and the things that have been made.

Specifically, Critical Theory as practised by the Frankfurt School requires us to engage in self-critique, especially with regard to the implicit and explicit power structures inherent in both our design practices and our design products. Any interrogation of an artefact needs to consider its existence as both a collection of multiple, designed parts, and a totality that is something far more complex than the additive nature of its individual components. It should also consider the inherently context-dependent nature of design.

As part of that work, we are considering how the way we manage our projects (not just the work those projects produce) can align with our six principles of feminist critical design:

1. challenges existing practices;
2. aims towards an actionable ideal future;
3. looks for what or who has been made invisible or under-represented;
4. considers the micro, meso, and macro;
5. privileges transparency and accountability; and
6. expects and welcomes being subjected to rigorous critique.

Hence, we undertake the intentional, systemic inclusivity (and promotion) of marginalized voices and contributions. Such inclusivity also means a commitment to the redistribution of power, not just flattening of power. Whenever possible, we will aim to take our designs beyond prototype and, at the very least, leverage gained insights towards improving our world. We will deliberately look outside what's been made (by default) part of the systems and collections we're investigating, inverting them if necessary. We will consider multiple granularities of perspective, and the impact our actions and decisions will have at a micro, meso, and macro levels. We will consider how contributions and commitments to projects can be made more accessible in terms of time and resource commitment. We will ask our team members what transparency and accountability looks like to them, welcome and demonstrate (through action) a welcoming of critique, while noting power imbalances and privilege, and acknowledge and apologize when we've screwed up.

The charter and our related interdisciplinary management strategies have been developed not only by studying the management literature, but also through a process of trial and error on a variety of active research projects. We are also always on the lookout for additional items to include. Rockwell (2007), for instance, pointed out the benefit of explicitly planning for the end of a project, which allows, among other things, for archiving the materials. Early planning can also result in the creation of an archival record, not only of the research results, but also of the research process. Rockwell's advice is to try to save the recipe rather than the cake, since technology changes quickly, and the cake often goes stale. We currently have no principles or policies related to either project archiving or project closure, despite the fact that some of our research funding agencies explicitly request that such archives be created.

We also have additional improvements to make in our quality assurance methods. For example, Cuneo (2003) recommends enlisting the help of outside consultants as adjudicators. To this point, we have relied instead on the reaction of the academic community, but we recognize that more could be done earlier in the process.

5.6 Exercises: Planning

5.6.1 Computer programming project plan

What you'll need

- Place where you can meet and discuss.

Exercise type
Group.

Working in your small group, describe the technical and human resources that you would require to undertake a programming project in an area of interest. You are welcome to choose the kind of project, although avoid choosing a system that consists of a web interface to a database, since the challenge is too simple to provide the necessary level of complexity.

As you go about the process of describing your project, be sure to frame it as completely as possible in terms of the following categories:

- paradigm;
- hardware;
- software;
- project duration;
- personnel (job descriptions, skill sets, % time commitments);
- logistics (timeline, milestones, critical path); and
- risk assessment.

In all cases, be sure to justify your choices by outlining the most obvious alternatives and explaining your rationale for your decisions.

5.6.2 Interdisciplinary research project management

What you'll need

- Place where you can meet and discuss.
- Paper and pens to plan and various software to execute (optional).

Exercise type
Group.

Part 1: Research project, team recruitment, and team justification

Students will recruit a collaborative, interdisciplinary research team consisting of not fewer than three and not more than five members, including the student. Team members may be academic colleagues at the same point in their career trajectory, junior academic colleagues, or senior academic colleagues. The only limitation is that no research team shall include another member of the class.

Students will submit a short description of the research team, including one paragraph describing the project and no more than two paragraphs each describing every member of the research team. The paragraph on the project should outline the research goal. The descriptive paragraphs about the team members should include a very brief description of their expertise, role on the project, relationship to the team leader, and potential strengths and weaknesses. The purpose is to explain their role and justify the choice of including them.

Team members don't need to be perfect matches in order to adequately fill a role.

Part 2: Gantt chart and weekly project reports

One of the goals of this project is to provide hands-on experience in planning and carrying out at least the first phases of a collaborative research activity, such as may be reported at a conference or submitted to a journal. Students will identify an appropriate research topic, divide it into weekly tasks, and create a Gantt chart that includes the first phase of the project, to be completed by the end of the course.

Students will subsequently fill out each week a one-page report, using the following headings: team identification and date, work planned, work accomplished, work planned but not accomplished, work accomplished but not planned, and plans for next week. Regular team meetings should be part of the plans. These sections should include brief explanations. The project reports will be due at the start of class each week.

Part 3: Extended abstract

Each research team will write a short abstract combined with an extended abstract suitable for submission to a conference. The short abstract should be 250–300 words and the extended abstract should be between 750 and 1,500 words in length. Its primary purpose is to explain the project goal, research method, and outcomes.

Part 4: Conference presentation

Students will produce and give a conference presentation consisting of slides, an outline, or a reading script appropriate for a 20-minute talk at a conference. The presentation should relate to the extended abstract. The goal is to be interesting and useful, and to make a contribution to knowledge in the field.

NOTES

1. For more strategies on Making Academia More Accessible, please consult an article of that title by Brown et al. (2018).
2. Culanth has recently offered an alternative model to traditional conference formats. See Pandian (2017).
3. Also consider a deep dive into *Disrupting the Digital Humanities*, edited by Dorothy Kim and Jesse Stommel, first published in 2018 by punctum books, and available through a Creative Commons licence.
4. While this paragraph appears to be focused on diversity in skills, the authors of this text believe that diversity and inclusivity across all spectrums result in more creative, interesting, and compelling work.
5. It is possible to propose the case, as a colleague did recently in conversation, that the paramecium's behaviour is actually predicated on a goal embodied in the species, but we would argue that once the concept of 'goal' is rarefied to that degree, it becomes indistinguishable from related concepts like 'predilection' or even 'biological imperative'.
6. The other two forms are what we normally think of as suffering, and the suffering of change, which can involve any kind of change, including change for the better!
7. H. H. The Dalai Lama made this point explicitly at one of his 2012 public lectures in Chicago.
8. By 'she', we mean Poshen Wong, who was at that point a graduate student with one of us at the University of Alberta. She is now a designer for Johns Hopkins.

9. In your choice of any of his graduate seminars on the Enlightenment, University of Alberta, over the past 40 years.
10. A 'prism from which to view a range of social problems to better ensure inclusiveness of remedies, and to identify opportunities for greater collaboration between and across social movements' (Crenshaw 2008: n.pag.).

6

Our journey continues

As designers working with digital humanities (DH), we have had the opportunity to participate in a number of fascinating projects with varied and brilliant colleagues. An interesting outcome of this work, however, is that many of the models, theories, hypotheses, and methods that we developed and deployed in this context have led us directly into projects that some people (but only a minority) would identify as humanities. Another way to think about these trajectories is that here we have research outcomes from the humanities, informing other disciplines and areas of work.

We present some examples under the headings: Digital to physical, Design for peace and reconciliation, qCollaborative, and Design concepts lab. We believe that this kind of cross-fertilization is another proof of the value of research in the twin interdisciplines of design and DH.

6.1 From the digital to the physical

Graphical and interactive representations of text, data, and text as data can serve many functions. They can serve as effective entry points into complex subject matter. They can provide birds-eye views on large collections (Minard's Napoleon's March to Russia, as discussed in Chapter 4, is one heart-breaking example of a complex, multi-source narrative). Finally, they can help scholars discover patterns and connections between previously (seemingly) unrelated items. But the efficiency that defines graphical data objects also removes critical contexts, and strips away identity through scalable abstraction. Their simplicity – perhaps sometimes even sterility – seldom matches human experience. Worse yet, the decisions that are made based on big data collections and their designed interpretations are anything but sterile. Manufacturers, companies, governments, and institutions use them to make decisions and policies, and to allocate resources. Some of these decisions are made in times of acute stress and within severe time constraints; some have deeply felt impacts on people and the environment, locally, nationally, and across the globe. In their functionality – the kinds of tasks that can be accomplished through them, the data that can be collected and accessed, how that data is represented, and what factors are considered irrelevant or critical – designers (and policy-makers) haven't adequately acknowledged the practical and long-term, as well as ethical and political implications that come at the intersections of design, data, and tech.

Over the past few years, we've shifted our interest away from design for large digital text collections, and towards co-creating new forms of interface that leverage physicality and kinaesthetic intelligence. Through the process of making, thinking, and remaking, we've been attempting to explore the personal, social, and ethical consequences of turning people, environments, communities, or experiences into data, aggregating that data, then abstracting it graphically. Our primary area of concern is with the potential of graphical data visualizations to further the dehumanization and decontextualization of the human experience. We are further concerned that certain individuals, communities, and environments are more vulnerable to what may occur subsequent to such computational translation and abstraction.

In 2016, we began exploring these sorts of questions through a process of thinking through making called materialization. In a series of experiments, we have undertaken turning textual and quantitative data into material builds that generated new data and, more recently, we've started adding a fresh layer of experience through social media and augmented reality. We're using materialization as a form of transmutation: more alchemy than construction, with the results uncertain and in flux.

In 2018, Milena brought 'materialization' into her undergraduate information design classroom. One resulting project, the Wheel of Hypersensitivity, invited passers-by to use differently coloured yarn to map their areas of discomfort. Pre-set categories included feminism, religion, race, Black Lives Matter, abortion, mental health, cursing in public, indigenization, politics, and others. Folks could elaborate on their discomfort paths by leaving explanatory notes (see Figure 6.1).

Another team designed the Tampon project, which asked the campus community to mark their sources and type of shame by dipping a 'tampon' into differently coloured water, then hanging the tampon on a nail, located below one of the display categories: society and media, men, other women, or themselves.

Since many of those who encountered our material data projects did so while going about their regular business, with no previous intent of discussing mental health or menstruation support products, we were able to adopt a 'let's see what happens' attitude to exploring audience engagement. In the context of low fidelity prototyping and a pre-captured audience, we asked, given a particular set of objects and a pre-established content area, what will users do? As a result, the displays were

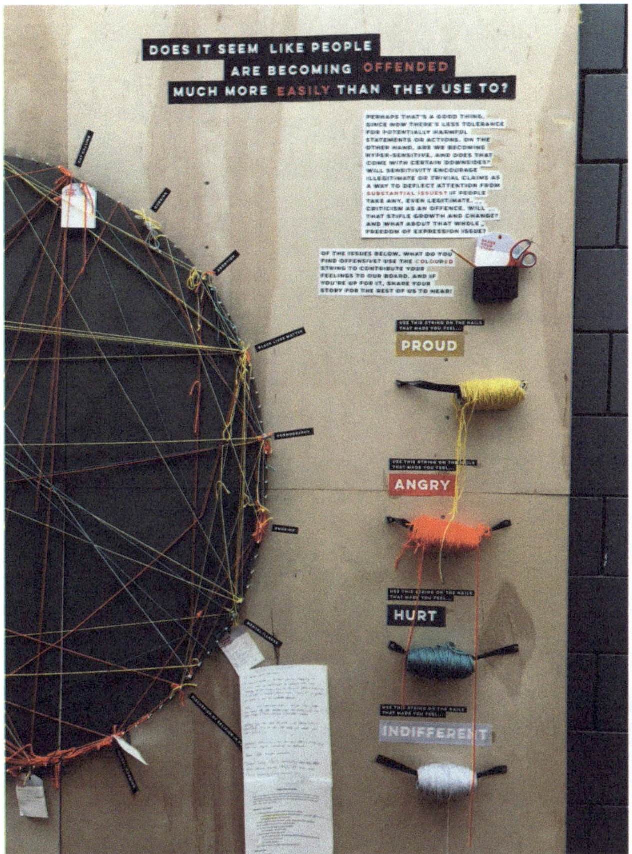

FIGURE 6.1: The Wheel of Hypersensitivity by Danielle Massee, 2018.

more in the spirit of critical design projects than they were of the type of design problem solving that is guided by user-centred processes and ideologies.

What did we learn?

1. In digital making, the resources that are in use often remain hidden – the power that it takes to run our machines, for example, and the environmental consequences of such use. One of the issues that came up early in the tampon project was the ethics of using menstruation-related products as a school project that are, for some, a luxury item. Milena posed this to the students, and their response was to hand-make the 'tampons' from cheaper, more efficient materials.

FIGURE 6.2: *Shame of a Woman* by Kristina Lea, Rosey Eason, and Lauren Ceaser, 2018.

2. Digital making is often a solitary activity – just me and my Adobe. However, these students chose to hand craft each of the 'tampons'. They did so during class while listening to lectures. They created a mini assembly line, where one person was cutting the string, while another was rolling the material around it. They made hundreds of tampons, spending time together building both skills and relationships.
3. Tampons remain a particularly taboo object. Up until very recently, menstrual cycles were depicted using blue dots. The tampon project – successfully – invited physical engagement with tampons. Publically. These tampons were handled, hundreds of times by many dozens of individuals, who encountered them by chance through a central, main campus stairway. Think about that. When was the last time (if ever) that you handled a tampon where someone could see you?
4. The wheel of hypersensitivity offered an unexpected (not pre-planned) window into the human capacity for vulnerability. One student attached a note to the

> mental health segment, sharing their struggle with depression. Another individual attached a long note to the first, expressing their identity as an ally, offering words of support. Yet another person attached a long note to the second, also offering support and a list of on-campus mental health resources.

The main outcome of these projects was a somewhat radical reconceptualization of what it means to consider interaction from the perspective of intersectional feminist design. Unlike digital prototyping, the results were messy and uncertain, and their manifestation leveraged the marginalized, taboo, distasteful natures of their subject matters.

6.2 Design for peace and reconciliation

The Design for Peace project in Colombia brings together a variety of people affected by the war. Some participants may be members of FARC, the guerrilla group demobilized in the 2016 peace agreement with the Colombian government. Others include both local residents and other Colombian citizens, in a design project that seeds reconciliation through collaborative development of small-scale infrastructure improvements. The workshop is the centre of a larger project, whose goal is to establish collaborative prototyping as a viable means of fostering reconciliation by making reconciliation-oriented prototyping methods and examples accessible, intelligible, and teachable in undergraduate and secondary contexts. This project has its home in Colombia, a country on the North-Western corner of South America that has been facing certain critical challenges – after a 50-year civil war, many Colombians are left suffering the effects of living in a post-conflict zone and the consequences of the displacement of over 3 million persons, and the death of 220,000, with four out of the five deaths non-combatant civilians.

The basic premise of the Design for Peace project is that: 'the process of co-design can contribute to reconciliation among the various groups in a post-conflict zone' (Molano et al. 2018: 142). Reconciliation is seeded through the 'close physical, mental, and emotional proximity' required to collaborate in the creation of a prototype, which itself acts as 'a tangible reminder that cooperation can result in mutual benefit' after the fact (Molano et al. 2018: 142). The project uses two principal methodologies. First, it follows the general structure of the IDDS process developed by Amy Smith and the D-Lab team at the Massachusetts Institute of Technology, beginning with a week of orientation, team-building, and skill development; and concluding with two weeks of collaborative prototyping development. Second, it engages the Creative Capacity Building (CCB) methodology, which promotes design by intended beneficiaries and users in order to empower them to be active creators of relevant technologies (Childs 2017).

To date, four workshops have been held, in: San Andrés de Tumaco, Nariño; ZVTN Colinas, Capricho, San José del Guaviare; La Paz, Cesar; and Isla de San Andrés, Archipiélago de San Andrés, Providencia y Santa Catalina. Each workshop is preceded by extensive consultation among FARC and non-FARC community leaders in the relevant region and project leaders based at the Universidad Nacional de Colombia (UNAL), as well as a formal application process for Colombian citizens from elsewhere in the country.

In previous workshop iterations, the Design for Peace project operated on the premise that collaboratively prototyping a product that would help develop infrastructure was sufficient to seed reconciliation. While this approach was demonstrably successful, previous facilitators also noted the need articulated by participants to pursue 'design for benefit' in addition to 'design for profit' (Molano et al. 2018). More specifically, as much as previous workshop iterations tried to empower women in technology-building processes, it remains 'evident that there is still a shade over how the role of women in creating artefacts, creating technologies, creating new ways of interaction, amongst their communities has been invisibilized' (Molano, personal communication[1]). At the 2019 *TaDIC* based in Tumaco,

FIGURE 6.3: A whale made from recycled materials to collect recyclable materials. *TaDIC* Tumaco, Colombia, 2019.

Colombia, we added alternate forms of prototyping, including methods for feminist prototyping and feminist design project management, to the curriculum.

6.3 *qCollaborative*

The qCollaborative undertakes research that uses design to extend and interrogate the lab's commitments within an intersectional, feminist space. Our projects are typically collaborative, paced to encourage reflection, and funded (by grants or industry partnerships). They fall into four research areas:

1. *Feminist placemaking* seeks to better articulate how feminism does and can operate in public spaces through the lens of performative social media interventions. Intersectional feminism, design research, performance, and technology all rest on the basic premise that human beings exist and act only in relation to other humans and non-humans in shared environments and communities; in other words, in publics. We privilege a 'relational' understanding of human existence.
2. *Materializing the digital* uses the process of making, thinking, and remaking to explore the personal, social, and ethical consequences of abstracting people, environments, communities, or experiences into digitally based data. As creatures of embodied cognition, the value of material interaction goes beyond simple understanding into the visceral and implicit forms of knowing and doing. In this area we are interested in strategies for leveraging the power of the digital to inform new modes of physical interaction with customized material cognitive artefacts. Whether taking professional visualization tools for DH into mechanical devices, or developing new analytical tools that exist through physical models, this range of projects interrogates the significance of embodied interaction in ways that challenge the unquestioned hegemony of the digital.
3. Through *remediating experience,* we are considering the nature of spaces co-created by performance, media, text, and interactivity. Our approach is to leverage the history of experience design in corporate settings, both reconceptualizing and re-situating these practices towards design for social good. For example, in our project for the design of experience in liminal spaces such as theatre lobbies, we explored ways of encouraging audience members to expand the interpretive lenses that they were bringing to the performance.
4. *Design for social justice* projects pursue strategies for mending existing social fabrics or creating new ones from whole cloth, whether under conditions such as post-conflict zones in the jungles and coastal towns of Colombia or audience development for justice-oriented arts organizations. Our interests also

extend into the digital where we seek to interrogate the sometimes negative genres of specific technologies that stand in stark contrast to our working list of six foundational critical feminist design practices (Radzikowska et al. 2019) described in Chapter 4:

1. challenge existing methods, beliefs, systems, and processes;
2. focus on an actionable ideal future;
3. look for what has been made invisible or under-represented;
4. consider the micro, meso, and macro;
5. privilege transparency and accountability; and
6. expect and welcome being subjected to rigorous critique.

The qLab intentionally blurs the lines between the academy and activism, provocation, and performance, seeking to disrupt public spaces in ways that will claim room for marginalized and targeted communities. We are committed to challenging and changing unjust behaviours such as racism, colonialism, (cis)sexism, homophobia, transphobia, ableism, classism, and xenophobia wherever they occur, including in academia, in social justice movements, and in ourselves.[2]

6.4 Design concepts lab

The primary goal of this lab is to encourage research by designers into abstract concepts, since from the design perspective, things may look different than they will when they are studied by other fields. The main difference is that the designer is looking not just to understand how concepts are modelled and put to use in the past and present, but also to understand, and maybe intervene into, what they are and how they are used in the future.

The second difference is that the research is carried out using methods related to design, and in particular using experimental prototypes. There is a sense in which all prototypes have an experimental purpose, since they are made to instantiate some features of an artefact that does not yet exist.

However, there is a useful distinction to be made between prototypes in practice and prototypes for research purposes. The latter would be ones that aren't intended to address a problem directly, but instead to learn more about some general principles that could apply not only to the current problem, but also to others.

In all of our projects, we use design research methods involving iterative prototyping – sometimes experimental, and occasionally provocative. We often also do user testing. Finally, for projects where we are developing new theories, we typically use grounded theory creation, following the method by Glaser and Strauss of constant comparison. We are an emerging group of researchers who share a belief that design practice could benefit from better models of abstract concepts. For example, we hear a lot about opinions in the news, but, from the design perspective, what is an opinion? How can we help people form, change, or strengthen their opinions?

6.5 Final thoughts

We have tried to make the case that design and DH have worked together profitably in the past, and that there is an even more glorious future ahead. One thing to consider, as we've mentioned before, is that both DH and design are fields with many sub-disciplines.

DH puts the digital in the humanities, which are themselves a whole lot of scholarly areas. Many universities list more than 15 departments under the humanities, and another dozen social sciences. Within those fields, the interpretative traditions expand still further. In the anthology of literary theories, for example, Rifkin and Ryan list twelve as major topics, with subtopics numbering nearly one hundred. Two of the most well-known DH theories, Moretti's distant reading and Ramsay's algorithmic criticism, aren't even on the list. And, so, the field branches and expands and grows from within, which is exactly what we expect healthy scholarly disciplines to do.

On the design side, we both did our graduate work in a school that had only two departments: visual communication design and industrial design. Graphic design, of course, is a subset of visual communication that emphasizes the illustrative aspect of the work that in its larger context also includes everything from the instructions on pill bottles to web interfaces to digital text collections. One of us now works, twenty years later, in a design school that has only two departments: graphic and industrial.

However, moving beyond graphics and industrial products, people in design now get jobs in a very broad range of activities. As a corrective, we sometimes have the undergraduate students list all the sub-disciplines or focus areas of design they can come up with. Here is a typical list:

1. agriculture;
2. animation;
3. architecture;
4. artificial intelligence;
5. automotive;
6. biomedical;
7. commerce;

8. culinary;
9. curation;
10. data visualization;
11. defence;
12. electrical;
13. engineering;
14. environmental;
15. experience;
16. fashion;
17. graphic;
18. healthcare;
19. industrial;
20. interior;
21. jewellery;
22. landscape architecture;
23. lighting;
24. policy;
25. security;
26. service;
27. signage;
28. sound;
29. strategic;
30. systems;
31. telecommunications;
32. theatre;
33. user interface/user experience;
34. urban planning;
35. visual communication; and
36. web.

As Foucault ([1969] 2004) famously pointed out, categories only exist for as long as someone is willing to put energy and other resources into keeping them. Herbert Simon ([1969] 1996) hoped that designers would try to capture all of creativity. In fact, we have definitely captured graphics and industrial products, but in recent years we have been making headway on a good number of the other thirty-plus items on the list.

DH, however, has for the most part yet to realize this fact. The vast majority of design projects in DH have come from collaborations with either visual communication or information design. Since the growth of the maker movement, a few have involved industrial design. One example is the text analysis milking machine mentioned in Chapter 3 (Radzikowska et al. 2020, n.pag.) where a mixed-up team of friends and colleagues at a women's motorcycle shop built a physical object of arduinos and lumber and sand that served as a re-thinking of the bubblelines interface to comparative search results across multiple documents.

We hope to encounter and engage in many of these kinds of projects in the future and encourage you, our reader, to think beyond communication and information designers when forming your collaborative teams.

Finally, arguments have been made (cf. Ruecker and Roberts-Smith 2018) that there is a role for experience design in collaborative projects between Design and DH. Let's provide an example that we consider successful. Early on in our careers we had the pleasure of making several trips to Washington DC to work on the NORA project. As one would, we took some time from each trip to visit the National Mall. By visit, we mean that Milena dragged Stan on 6-hour treks, up and down the mall, to take photos of all the monuments. Our favourite, by far, was the life-size bronze of President Franklin Delano Roosevelt. It's the one where he's sitting in his wheelchair. One day, while we watched, a group of middle-school children arrived. They took turns sitting in FDR's lap and kissing his cheek. After we left, we noticed that his one leg (the one made better for perching) and one cheek had been rubbed bright by the years of physical attention.

This monument, more than any of the others, embodies the kinds of relationships we hope you'll create both with your project teams and within the projects themselves. Design that has intent and clarity, that's approachable and meaningful, that surprises and, above all else, that resonates.

6.6 Exercises: Intellectual territories

6.6.1 Brief vs. research question

What you'll need

- Space where two groups can gather and discuss together.
- If the activity takes place over an extended time frame, consider supplying large pieces of paper, markers, and tape – to be used as process keepers and displayed in the environment.

Exercise type

Group; works well with students.

Choose a topic area of interest. For example, when we did this exercise in Krakow, Poland in spring 2018 with a group of undergraduate design students, the future of AI was something the students were repeatedly bringing up in discussion. We therefore chose AI as the topic.

Divide folks into groups. For one group, provide a design brief that outlines a problem to be addressed. In the case of our Krakow activity, we assigned them into groups, each one defined by one of Dator's Four Futures: continued growth; sustainability through increased discipline; collapse; and transformation. In a different example of a design brief, we could have suggested that people need to be made aware that the ethical use of AI necessitates that the people affected should be given access to both the training data and the training sequence used. Students could have then designed an information campaign to communicate that message to a particular audience.

For the other group, frame the same project not as a design brief, but instead as a research question. Perhaps the question could be: 'how can a particular audience affected by an AI best be made aware of the ethical necessity of making the training data and training sequence accessible?'

Although the topic is substantially the same, the outcome of the two different starting points should tend to be recognizably different. Have the groups analyse and discuss the differences either at the end of the design process or else at key points throughout.

6.6.2 Operational models

What you'll need

- Space where people can gather and discuss together.
- If the activity takes place over an extended time frame, consider supplying large pieces of paper, markers, and tape – to be used as process keepers and displayed in the environment.

Exercise type

Group; works well with students.

The purpose of this exercise is to introduce the idea of using prototypes as a form of thinking through making, where each prototype is intended to contribute to some aspect of a research question.

To begin, describe how a research question typically involves many aspects, each of which is a candidate to be addressed through prototyping. For example, the MFA students in graphic design in 2018 at the University of Illinois were tasked with developing an operational model of the concept of trust, based on the question: 'what is trust from the perspective of design?' Their first step was to dissect the concept of trust into components to investigate, resulting in a list of more than a dozen items (Figure 6.1).

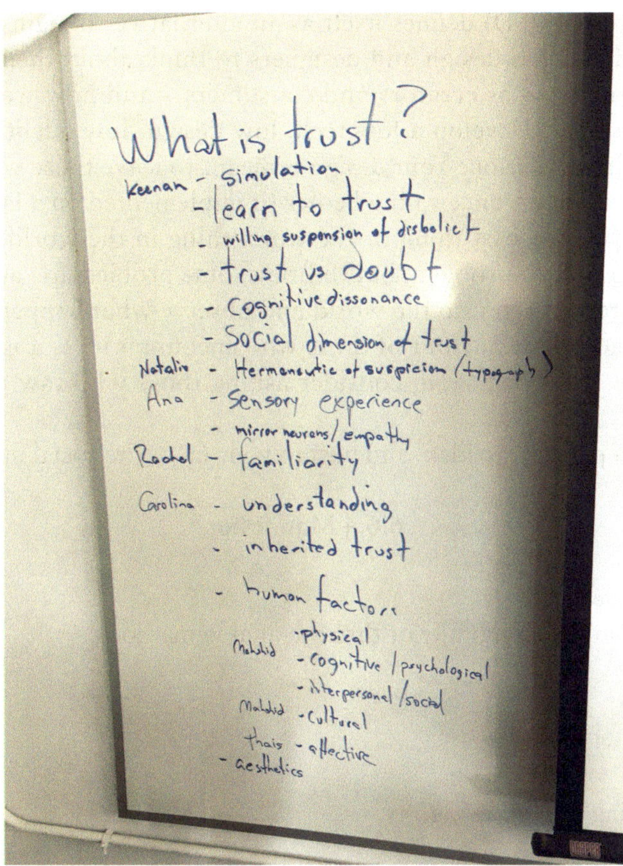

FIGURE 6.4: What is trust? Students list some factors worth considering. (Photo by Stan Ruecker).

People can work on this project individually or in groups. One advantage of the group is that different folks can take on different roles: designer, programmer, UI/UX, writer. Another is that it is possible to involve those who have not yet formulated a research question, since only one is necessary from the whole group.

6.6.3 Micro intervention

What you'll need

- Depends on the intervention.

Exercise type
Group or individual.

Speculative Design (SD) defines itself as an alternative to mainstream design practice. It challenges design and designers to think about their relationship to material culture – as creators and consumers – and how we've made the world worse for it. Develop a low tech, low design, low fidelity,[3] but intentional design intervention. Your design is meant to leave those who encounter it feeling off balance – uncertain whether (if implemented on a large scale) the design would be the best thing or the worst thing in the world. Your design isn't meant to solve a problem, but to bring some problematic aspect to light. Place your intervention into the world and observe what happens. Does your design influence the behaviour of those who encounter it? Is it ignored? Once the design has been removed, consider asking those who saw it about their experience.

Record via photos or video, and post to your favourite social media venue.

6.6.4 Manifesto

What you'll need

- Can be completed digitally or through analog methods.

Exercise type

Group or individual.

Start by reading the following:

- Futurist Manifesto http://www.unknown.nu/futurism/manifesto.html
- First Things First Manifesto 1964 https://maxb.home.xs4all.nl/ftf1964.htm
- First Things First Manifesto 2000 http://www.eyemagazine.com/feature/article/first-things-first-manifesto-2000
- This is not a manifesto – towards an anarcho-design practice http://garagecollective.blogspot.ca/2009/03/this-is-not-manifesto-towards.html

Now write a manifesto for your profession or discipline:

- *interrogate*: Ask questions of yourself and your discipline;
- *examine*: Carefully scrutinize your assumptions and beliefs; and
- *develop*: A new set of rules that will govern your professional practice.

Create a one-page poster that displays your manifesto. Use a compelling title, and try to experiment a bit with typography and layout. Sign this. Include a short statement and a list of 'rules'.

NOTES

1. Professor Hernán Pérez Molano was Coordinator of the Social Innovation Program at UNAL and lead organizer of the 2018 workshop.
2. qLab conveners are Jennifer Roberts-Smith, Shana MacDonald, Milena Radzikowska, Aynur Kadir, Stan Ruecker, and Brianna Wiens.
3. A simple, low technology, and (perceived as) quickly rendered version of a product or design concept.

List of exercises

Design			
Type	**Minimum Name**	**Time**	**Minimum Materials**
Meaning	Metaphors	1 h.	Analog or digital cut and paste
	Object Metaphors	1 h.	Physical objects; camera
	Hindsight is 20/20	5 h.	Access to research resources
	History Down and Across	6 h.	Access to research resources
	Visual Comparison and Contrast	3 h.	Access to research resources
Form	Abstraction Through Reduction	2 h.	Sketching/painting materials
	Abstraction Through Addition	2 h.	Materials for collage
	Unexpected Encounters	2 h.	Camera
	Poignant Close-Ups	1 h.	Camera
	The Black Square Problem	3 h.	Card-stock; black ink pens
	Typographic Portraits	3 h.	Access to a typeface sample; tracing and regular paper; black ink pens
Collections & Territories	Found Arrays	2 h.	Camera; box; method for display
	Tiny Museum	2 h.	Camera; box; method for display
	Mundane Patterns	2 h.	Camera; box; method for display
	Moodboard	3 h.	Access to research resources
	Visual Repertory Grid	3 h.	Analogue or digital cut and paste
Data Visualization	Altered Map	2 h.	Map; mark-making materials
	Stretch Quests	5 h.	Camera

Interface Design	Interface Sketches	6 h.	Sketchbook; ink pens; ruler
	Website Design	6 h.	Access to resource materials; mark making materials
	Experimental Interface	6 h.	Access to resource materials; mark making materials
Intellectual Territories	Micro Intervention	3 h.	Depends on the intervention
Digital humanities			
Text	Deformation	1 h.	Starter textual material
	The Scholarly Edition	2 h.	Manuscript
Collections & Territories	Lives Lived	3 h.	Camera; method for display
Data Visualization	Memory Map	3 h.	Materials for collage
	Walking Map	2 h.	Camera; mark making materials
Interface Design	BigSee or Structured Surface	6 h.	Access to resource materials; mark making materials
	Prototyping for Access to resource materials. Hermeneutic Inquiry	8 h.	Mark making materials
Cross-disciplinary			
Planning	Computer Programming Project Plan	2 h.	Place where you can meet and discuss
	Interdisciplinary Research Project Management.	3 h.	Paper and pens Place where you can meet and discuss
Intellectual Territories	Brief vs. Research Question	1.5 h.	Space where two groups can gather and discuss together; paper and pens
	Operational Models	2 h.	Space where two groups can gather and discuss together; paper and pens
	Manifesto	2 h.	Space where two groups can gather and discuss together; paper and pens

References

Accurate (2018), 'Googssssle news initiative: Building hopes', https://www.accurat.it/work/buildinghopes. Accessed 2 September 2020.

Adams, Hazard (1992), *Critical Theory Since Plato*, rev. ed., New York: Harcourt Brace Jovanovich.

Amabile, Teresa M., Patterson, Chelley, Mueller, Jennifer, Wojcik, Tom, Odomirok, Paul W., Marsh, Mel and Kramer, Steven J. (2001), 'Academic-practitioner collaboration in management research: A case of cross-profession collaboration', *Academy of Management Journal*, 44:2, pp. 418–31.

Antonelli, Paola (2011), 'States of Design 04: Critical Design', *Domus 949* (July/August 2011), n.pag. Accessed 5 July 2015.

Appleton, Jay (1975), *The Experience of Landscape*, London: John Wiley & Sons.

Askville by Amazon (2015), *Number of products in the Amazon inventory*, http://www.amazon.com. Accessed 1 March 2015.

ASM Consortium (n.d.), 'Accidents, although rare, add to costs', Graph, *The ASM Consortium, Abnormal Situation Management Joint Research and Development Consortium*, https://www.asmconsortium.net. Accessed 1 March 2015.

Balsamo, Anne (2011), *Designing Culture: The Technological Imagination at Work*, Durham and London: Duke University Press.

Bardzell, Shaowen (2010), 'Feminist HCI: Taking stock and outlining an agenda for design', In *CHI '10 CHI Conference on Human Factors in Computing Systems*, Atlanta, GA, 10–15 April, New York: ACM, pp. 1301–10, ACM Digital Library.

Bardzell, Jeffrey (2011), 'Interaction criticism: An introduction to the practice', *Interacting with Computers, Special issue: 'Feminism and HCI: New Perspectives'*, 23:5, pp. 604–21.

Bardzell, Jeffrey (2014), 'Design as inquiry: In the loop', *Public lecture delivered at IIT Institute of Design*, Chicago, IL, 9 October.

Bardzell, Jeffrey and Bardzell, Shaowen (2008a), 'Interaction criticism: A proposal and framework for a new discipline of HCI', in *CHI '08 Extended Abstracts on Human Factors in Computing Systems*, Florence, IT, 5–10 April, New York: ACM, pp. 2463–72, ACM Digital Library.

Bardzell, Jeffrey and Bardzell, Shaowen (2008b), 'Problems in the appropriation of critical strategies in HCI', in *HCI 2008: Critical Issues in Interaction Design Workshop*, Liverpool, UK, workshop position paper.

Bardzell, Shaowen and Bardzell, Jeffrey (2011a), 'Towards a feminist HCI methodology: Social science, feminism, and HCI', in *Proceedings of the SIGCHI Conference on Human Factors in Computing Systems*, Vancouver, BC, 7–12 May, New York: ACM, pp. 675–84, ACM Digital Library.

Bardzell, Shaowen and Churchill, Elizabeth (2011b), 'Introduction Feminism and HCI: New Perspectives', *Special Issue: 'Interacting with Computers'*, 23:5, pp. Iii–xi.

Bardzell, Jeffrey, Bardzell, Shaowen, DiSalvo, Carl, Gaver, William and Sengers, Phoebe (2012), 'Panel: The humanities and/in HCI', In *CHI '12 Extended Abstracts on Human Factors in Computing Systems*, Austin, TX, 5–10 May, New York: ACM, pp. 1135–38, ACM Digital Library.

Bardzell, Shaowen, Bardzell, Jeffrey, Forlizzi, Jodi, Zimmerman, John and Antanitis John (2012), 'Critical design and critical theory: The challenge of designing for provocation', *DIS '12 Designing Interactive Systems Conference.* 11–15 June 2012, Newcastle-Upon-Tyne, UK. New York: ACM, pp. 288–97, ACM Digital Library.

Basalla, George (1989), *The Evolution of Technology*, Cambridge, UK: Cambridge UP.

Bass, Gary, Brian, Danielle and Eisen, Norman (2014), 'Why Critics of Transparency Are Wrong, Strengthening American Democracy', Washington, DC: The Brookings Institution, Centre for Effective Public Management at Brookings, white paper, https://www.brookings.edu/research/why-critics-of-transparency-are-wrong/. Accessed 15 March 2015.

Bederson, Benjamin B. (2011), 'The promise of Zoomable user interfaces', *Behaviour & Information Technology*, 30:6, pp. 853–86.

Bennett, Nathan and Kidwell, Roland E. Jr. (2001), 'The provision of effort in self-designing work groups: The case of collaborative research', *Small Group Research*, 32:6, pp. 727–44.

Bhattacharyya, Sayan, Organisciak, Peter and Downie, Stephen J. (2015), 'A fragmentising interface to a large corpus of digitized text: (Post)Humanism and non-consumptive reading via features', *The Future of Reading, Special issue: Interdisciplinary Science Reviews*, 40:1, pp. 61–77.

Birkhoff, George D. (1933), *Aesthetic Measure*, Cambridge, MA: Harvard University Press.

Blandford, Ann Brown, Susan, Dobson, Teresa, Faisal, Sarah, Fiorentino, Carlos, Frizzera, Luciano, Giacometti, Alejandro, Heller, Brooke, Ilovan, Mihaela, Michura, Piotr, Nelson, Brent and Radzikowska, Milena (2012), 'Designing interactive reading environments for the online scholarly edition', *Abstracts of Digital Humanities 2012*, Hamburg, 16–22 July 2012. (ed.) Jan Cristoph Meister, Hamburg: U of Hamburg Press, pp. 35–40.

Blauvelt, Andrew (2003), 'Strangely familiar: Design and everyday life', In A.Blauvelt (ed.), *Strangely Familiar: Design and Everyday Life*, Minneapolis, MN: Walker Art Center, pp. 14–37.

Blythe, Mark, Bardzell, Jeffrey, Bardzell, Shaowen and Blackwell, Alan (2008), 'Critical issues in interaction design', In *Proceedings of the 22nd British HCI Group Annual Conference on People and Computers: Culture, Creativity, Interaction*, vol. 2, Liverpool, UK, 1–5 September, Swinton, UK: BCS-HCI, pp. 183–84.

Boer, Laurens and Jared, Donovan (2012), 'Provotypes for participatory innovation', In *Proceedings of the Designing Interactive Systems Conference (DIS12)*, New York: ACM, pp. 388–97.

Bødker, Susanne (2006), 'When second wave HCI meets third wave challenges', In *Proceedings of the Fourth Nordic Conference on Human-Computer Interaction*, Oslo, NO, 14–18 October, New York: ACM, pp. 1–8, ACM Digital Library.

Bohman, James (2013), 'Critical Theory', Stanford Encyclopedia of Philosophy. (ed.) Edward N. Zalta. Stanford Encyclopedia of Philosophy.

Bradley, John (2005), 'What you (Fore)see is what you get: Thinking about usage paradigms for computer assisted text analysis', *Text Technology*, 2, pp. 1–20.

Bridges, Eileen, Coughlan, Anne and Shlomo Kalish (1991), 'New technology adoption in an innovative marketplace: Micro- and Macro-Level decision making models', *International Journal of Forecasting*, 7:3 (Nov), pp. 257–70.

Bringhurst, Robert (1992), *Elements of Typographic Style*, Roberts, WA: Hartley & Marks.

Brown, Susan (2015), 'Remediating the editor', *The Future of Reading, Special issue: Interdisciplinary Science Reviews*, 40:1, pp. 78–94.

Brown, Susan, Clements, Patricia and Grundy, Isobel (2006), 'Sorting things in: Feminist knowledge representation and changing modes of scholarly production', *Feminisms and Print Culture, Special issue: Women's Studies International Forum*, 29:3, pp. 317–25.

Brown, Nicole, Thompson, Paul and Leigh, Jennifer S. (2018), 'Making academia more accessible', *Journal of Perspectives on Academic Practice*, 6:2, pp. 82–90.

Bruce, Christine and Stoodley, Ian (2013), 'Experiencing higher degree research supervision as teaching', *Studies in Higher Education*, 38:2, pp. 226–41.

Buchanan, Richard (2001), 'Design and the new rhetoric: Productive arts in the philosophy of culture', *Philosophy & Rhetoric*, 34:3, pp. 183–206.

Burnett, Margaret M. (2011), 'What counts as feminist HCI?', *Presentation at ACM CHI Conference on Human Factors in Computing Systems*, Vancouver, BC, 7–12 May, position paper.

Burnett, Margaret M., Beckwith, Laura, Wiedenbeck, Susan, Fleming, Scott D., Cao, Jill, Park, Thomas H., Grigoreanu, Valentina and Rector, Kyle (2011), 'Gender pluralism in problem-solving software', *Feminism and HCI: New Perspectives, Special issue: Interacting with Computers*, 23:5, pp. 450–60.

Bury, Kevin F. (1984), 'The iterative development of usable computer interfaces', In Brian Shackel (ed.), *Proceedings of INTERACT '84 First International Conference on Human-Computer Interaction*, London, UK, 4–7 September, Interaction Design Foundation, pp. 743–48.

Bush, Vannevar (1945), 'As we may think', *The Atlantic Monthly*, 176:1, pp. 101–08, http://www.theatlantic.com/doc/194507/bush. Accessed 10 May 2015.

Butler, Judith (1990), *Gender Trouble: Feminism and the Subversion of Identity*, London: Routledge.

Buxton, William and Sniderman, Richard (1980), 'Iteration in the design of the human-computer interface', In *Proceedings of the 13th Annual Meeting of the Human Factors Association of Canada*, pp. 72–81.

Carson, Paula P., Carson, Kerry D. and Heady, Ronald B. (1994), 'Cecil Alec Mace: The man who discovered goal-setting', *International Journal of Public Administration*, 17:9.

Chandler, Daniel (2007), *Semiotics: The Basics*, 2nd ed., Routledge.

Childs, Toby (2017), 'Creative capacity building in Uganda: Qualitative case research into the impact of CCB on individuals and communities', *International Development Innovation Network*, http://www.idin.org/resources/research/creative-capacity-building-uganda-qualitative-case-research-impact-ccb. Accessed 15 July 2020.

Churchill, Elizabeth (2010), 'Sugared puppy-dog tails: Gender and design', *Interactions*, New York: ACM, 17:2, pp. 52–56, ACM Digital Library.

Clement, J. (n.d.), *Statistics and facts about Amazon (2015)*, Statista, Statista Inc., https://www.statista.com/topics/846/amazon/. Accessed on May 15 2015.

Cockton, Gilbert, Bardzell, Shaowen, Blythe, Mark and Bardzell, Jeffrey (2010), 'Can we all stand under our umbrella: The arts and design research in HCI', In CHI '10 CHI Conference on Human Factors in Computing Systems, Atlanta, GA, 10–15 April, New York: ACM, pp. 3163–66, ACM Digital Library.

Cohen, Dan (2008), *Design matters*, Dan Cohen, https://dancohen.org/2008/11/12/design-matters/. Accessed 12 November 2015.

Crenshaw, Kimberle (2008), 'What kind of ally are you? Or, what is your disaster relief kit?', In *V-Day 10th Anniversary Celebration*, New Orleans, LA, 11 April, Speech.

Coss, Nigel (1982), 'Designerly ways of knowing', *Design Education Special Issue of Design Studies*, 3.4 (Oct): pp. 221–27.

Cuneo, Patrick (2003), 'Interdisciplinary teams: Let's make them work', *University Affairs*, 1:1, n.pag.

Davison, Barbara (2003), 'Management span of control: How wide is too wide?', *Journal of Business Strategy*, 24.4: pp. 22–29.

De la Rosa, Juan (2017), 'Prototyping the non-existent as a way to research and innovate: A proposal for a possible framework for design research and innovation', *The Design Journal*, 20:suppl.1, pp. S4468–76.

De la Rosa, Juan and Ruecker, Stan (2019), 'The nature of design-produced knowledge: The use of prototypes as tools to produce high-resolution maps of possible future states of the system', In *Proceedings of the 3rd International Conference on Design Research (CIDI3)*, Universidad Nacional de Colombia, Bogota, Colombia, 20–22 March.

De la Rosa, Juan, Kolher, Karolina and Ruecker, Stan (2017), 'Prototyping as a resource to investigate future states of the system', In *Proceedings of RSD6 Conference*, Oslo, Norway.

Dempsey, Amy (2002), *Art in the Modern Era: A Guide to Styles, Schools & Movements*, NY: Harry N. Abrams Inc., Pub.

DeRose, Steven J., Durand, David G., Mylonas, Elli and Renear, Alan H. (1990), 'What is text, really?', *Journal of Computing in Higher Education*, 1:2, pp. 3–26.

'Design' (n.d.), *Merriam-Webster's Collegiate Dictionary*, Encyclopædia Britannica.

Dewey, Russell (2007), *Psychology: An introduction: Chapter four – The Whole is Other than the Sum of the Parts*, https://www.psywww.com/intropsych/index.html. Accessed 12 March 2015.

DiSalvo, Carl (2012), *Adversarial Design*, Cambridge, MA: MIT Press.

Dobson, T. M. (2006), 'For the love of a good narrative: Digitality and textuality', *English Teaching: Practice and Critique*, 5(2), pp. 56–68, http://education.waikato.ac.nz/research/journal/index.php?id=1. Accessed 10 October 2006.

Dobson, Teresa, Michura, Piotr, Ruecker, Stan, Brown, Monica and Rodriguez, Omar (2011), 'Interactive visualizations of plot in fiction', *Visible Language*, 45(3), pp. 169–91.

Dobson, Teresa M., Brown, Monica, Grue, Dustin, Peña, Ernesto, Roeder, Geoff and the INKE Research Team (2015), 'The interface implications of understanding readers', Special Issue: Stan Ruecker (ed.), *The Future of Reading, Interdisciplinary Science Reviews*, 40:1, March.

Dormer, Peter (1993), *Design Since 1945*, London: Thames and Hudson.

Drucker, Johanna (2006), *SpecLab: Digital Aesthetics and Projects in Speculative Computing*, Chicago, IL: University of Chicago Press.

Dunne, Anthony (2008a), 'Design for debate', *Neoplasmatic Design, Special issue: Architectural Design*, 78:6, pp. 90–93.

Dunne, Anthony (2008b), *Hertzian Tales: Electronic Products, Aesthetic Experience, and Critical Design*, Cambridge, MA: MIT Press.

Dunne, Anthony and Raby, Fiona (2001), *Design Noir: The Secret Life of Electronic Objects*, Basel, CH: Birkhäuser.

Dunne, Anthony and Raby, Fiona (2012), *United Micro Kingdoms*, London: Design Museum.

Dunne, Anthony and Raby, Fiona (2013), *Speculative Everything: Design, Fiction, and Social Dreaming*, Cambridge, MA: MIT Press.

Dunne, Anthony and Fiona Raby, 'Critical Design FAQ', *Dunne & Raby*, http://dunneandraby.co.uk/content/bydandr/13/0. Accessed 10 February 2014.

Few, Stephen (2004), *Show Me the Numbers: Designing Tables and Graphs to Enlighten*, Oakland, CA: Analytics Press.

Few, Stephen (2006), *Information Dashboard Design: The Effective Visual Communication of Data*, Sebastopol, CA: O'Reilly.

Forlano, Laura (2016), 'Decentering the human in the design of collaborative cities', *MIT: Design Issues*, 32:3, pp. 42–54.

Forlizzi, J., Stolterman, E. and Zimmerman, J. (2009), 'From design research to theory: Evidence of a maturing field', In *2009 Proceedings of the International Association of Societies of Design Research (IASDR)*.

'Form 10-K: Amazon.com, Inc. Annual Report for Fiscal Year Ended December 31, 2014' (n.d.), Electronic Data Gathering, Analysis, and Retrieval (EDGAR), U.S. Securities and Exchange Commission, https://www.sec.gov/Archives/edgar/data/1018724/000101872415000006/amzn-20141231x10k.htm. Accessed 18 March 2015.

Foucault, Michel ([1969] 2004), 'Unities of discourse', in *The Archeology of Knowledge* (trans. A. M. Sheridan Smith), New York: Routledge Classics.

Frascara, Jorge (2004), *Communication Design: Principles, Methods, and Practice*, New York: Allworth Press.

Frayling, Christopher (1993), 'Research in art and design', *Royal College of Art Research Papers*, 1:1, pp. 1–5.

Free Software Foundation (1999), 'Linear programming basics', *LP Solve 5.5 Reference Guide*, Free Software Foundation, http://lpsolve.sourceforge.net/5.5/LPBasics.htm. Accessed 3 February 2015.

Frizzera, Luciano, Vela, Sarah, Sondheim, Dan, Michura, Piotr, Ilovan, Mihaela, Rockwell, Geoffrey and the INKE Research Team (2013), 'Designing for multitouch surfaces as social reading environments', presented at the Digital Humanities, Lincoln, USA: Digital Humanities, http://dh2013.unl.edu/abstracts/ab-318.html

Fuller, Martin (2008), *Software Studies: A Lexicon*, Cambridge, MA: MIT Press.

Galey, Alan and Ruecker, Stan (2010), 'How a prototype argues', *Literary and Linguistic Computing*, 25:4, pp. 405–24.

Garland, Ken (1964), 'First things first: A manifesto', *DesignManifestos.org*. n.p., n.d., https://designmanifestos.org/ken-garland-first-things-first/. Accessed 5 July 2015

Gaver, William (2012), 'What should we expect from research through design?', CHI, NY: ACM Digital Library, pp. 937–46.

Gibson, James J. (1979), *The Ecological Approach to Visual Perception*, Boston: Houghton Mifflin.

Gilbert, Naomi (2014), 'Looking to cite the Johnny Cash Project in my dissertation', email to the author, 5 November, support@thejohnnycashproject.com.

Giroux, Henry A. (1993–1994), 'Consuming social change: The "United Colors of Benetton"', *Cultural Critique* 26 (Winter): 5–32. University of Minnesota Press.

Gosselin, Pierre, Hrudey, Steve E., Anne Naeth, M., Plourde, André, Therrien, René, Van Der Kraak, Glen and Xu, Zhenghe (2010), *Environmental and health impacts of Canada's oil sands industry: Executive summary*, Royal Society of Canada.

Gould, John and Lewis, Clayton (1985), 'Designing for usability: Key principles and what designers think', *Communications of the ACM*, 28:3, pp. 300–11, ACM Digital Library.

Hara, Noriko, Solomon, Paul, Kim, Seung-Lye and Sonnenwald, Diane H. (2003), 'An emerging view of scientific collaboration: Scientists' perspectives on collaboration and factors that impact collaboration', *Journal of the American Society for Information Science and Technology*, 54(10), pp. 952–65.

Harrison, Steve, Tatar, Deborah, and Sengers, Phoebe (2007), 'The three paradigms of HCI', *Proceedings of the SIGCHI Conference on Human Factors in Computing Systems*, April 30–May 3, 2007, San Jose, CA. New York: ACM, pp. 2–18, ACM Digital Library.

Heller, Steven (2003), *Teaching Graphic Design: Course Offering and Class Projects from the Leading Undergraduate and Graduate Programs*, New York: Allworth Press.

Helmer Poggenpohl, Sharon (1999), 'Design moves: Approximating a desired future with users', In *Proceedings of Design and the Social Sciences: Making Connections*, Edmonton, Alberta, Canada, 30 September–3 October.

Heskett, John (2005), *Design: A Very Short Introduction*, Oxford: Oxford University Press.

Hobson, S. (n.d.), 'Case studies in gerontology for the applied health sciences', http://publish.uwo.ca/~shobson/models.html. Accessed 17 July 2007.

Hollifield, Bill, Oliver, Dana, Nimmo, Ian and Habibi, Eddie (2008), *The High Performance HMI Handbook*, Kalamazoo, MI: 360 Digital Books.

Hoover, David (2007), 'The end of the irrelevant text: Electronic texts, linguistics, and literary theory', *Digital Humanities Quarterly*, 1:2: n.pag.

Horkheimer, Max (1990), 'Traditional and critical theory', *Critical Theory: Selected Essays*, New York: Seabury Press, pp. 188–243.

Howard, Amanda (2011), 'Exploring national holidays and suicide rates', Digital Prototype, Calgary, Alberta.

Ichikawa, Tomoko (2016), 'Visualization as experience', *Digital Studies/Le champ numérique*, http://doi.org/10.16995/dscn.32. Accessed 5 July 2017.

Interaction Design Foundation (n.d.), *Gestalt Principles*, Denmark, https://www.interaction-design.org/literature/topics/gestalt-principles. Accessed 15 May 2015.

Ishiyama, John (2002), 'Does early participation in undergraduate research benefit social science and humanities students?', *College Student Journal*, 36, pp. 380–86.

Jansson, Noora (2013), 'Organizational change as practice: A critical analysis', *Journal of Organizational Change Management*, 26(6), pp. 1003–19.

Jones, Heather (2013), 'Why Health Care is So Expensive', Infographic. *Information Is Beautiful Awards*, Kantar, https://healthland.time.com/2013/02/20/what-makes-health-care-so-expensive/. Accessed 4 September 2020.

Kamvar, Sepandar and Harris, Jonathan (2011), 'We feel fine and searching the emotional web', In *Proceedings of the Fourth ACM International Conference on Web Search and Data Mining (WSDM)*, Kowloon, HK, 9–12 February, New York: ACM, pp. 117–26, ACM Digital Library.

Kannabiran, Gopinaath and Petersen, Marianne Graves (2010), 'Politics at the Interface: A Foucauldian Power Analysis', *Proceedings of the 6th Nordic Conference on Human-Computer Interaction: Extending Boundaries*, October 16–20, 2010, Reykjavik, IS. New York: ACM, pp. 1–4, ACM Digital Library.

Karvonen, Kristiina (2000), 'The beauty of simplicity', In *Proceedings of the 2000 ACM Conference on Universal Usability*, Washington, DC, 16–17 November, New York: ACM, pp. 85–90, ACM Digital Library.

Kavakli, M., Scrivener, S. and Ball, L. (1998), 'Structure in idea sketching behaviour', *Design Studies*, 19, pp. 485–517.

Keil, Mark, Smith, H. Jeff, Pawlowski, Suzanne and Jin, Leigh (2004), 'Why didn't somebody tell me?: Climate, information asymmetry, and bad news about troubled projects', *ACM SIGMIS Database: The DATABASE for Advances in Information Systems*, https://doi.org/10.1145/1007965.1007971. New York: ACM, 35(2), pp. 65–84, ACM Digital Library.

Kelly, George A. (1955a), *The Psychology of Personal Constructs, vol. 1: A Theory of Personality*, New York: Norton.

Kelly, George A. (1955b), *The Psychology of Personal Constructs, vol. 2: Clinical Diagnosis and Psychotherapy*, New York: Norton.

Kim, Jinsook (2007), 'Motion gestalt for screen design: Applied theory of grouping principles for visual motion integrity', Ph.D. dissertation, Chicago: Institute of Design.

Kirk, Chris, Kois, Dan and @GunDeaths (2013), 'How many people have been killed by guns since Newtown?', *Slate, Gawker Media.*

Koffka, Kurt (1935), *Principles of Gestalt Psychology*, New York: Harcourt, Brace, and World, Inc.

Kopits, George and Craig, Jon (1998), 'Transparency in government operations', *Occasional Paper 158*, Washington, DC: International Monetary Fund, https://www.imf.org/external/pubs/ft/op/158/op158.pdf. Accessed 5 July 2015.

Krzywinski, Martin (2010), 'Application of Circos to Genomics. Diagram', *Circos*, http://circos.ca. Accessed 5 July 2015.

Krzywinski, Martin, Schein, Jacqueline, Birol, Inanc, Connors, Joseph, Gascoyne, Randy, Horsman, Doug, Jones, Steven and Marra, Marco (2009), 'Circos: An information aesthetic for comparative genomics', *Genetic Research*, 19, pp. 1639–45, CSH Press.

Kumar, Vijay (2013), *101 Design Methods*, Hoboken, NJ: Wiley & Sons.

Kurgan, Laura and Cadora, Eric (2006), *Million Dollar Blocks, New York: Spatial Information Design Lab*, Columbia University. Moma.org https://assets.moma.org/momaorg/shared/pdfs/docs/learn/courses/MillionDollarBlocks.pdf.

Lakoff, George and Johnson, Mark (1980), *Metaphors We Live By*, Chicago: University of Chicago Press.

Landay, James and Myers, Brad A. (1996), 'Sketching Storyboards to Illustrate Interface Behaviors', *CHI '96 Companion*, Vancouver, BC Canada.

Lanzing, Jan (1997), 'The concept mapping homepage', https://research.utwente.nl/en/publications/the-concept-mapping-homepage. Accessed 2 September 2020.

Lea, Kristina, Eason, Rosey and Ceaser, Lauren (2018), *'Shame of a Woman', Paper and Dye*, Calgary, Alberta: Mount Royal University.

Levine, Gregg (2014), 'For $100,000, Susan G. Komen does its bit', *The Scrutineer, Aljazeera America*, 8 October, http://america.aljazeera.com/blogs/scrutineer/2014/10/8/pink-drill-bits-komen.html. Accessed 11 March 2015.

Li, Bocong (2012), 'From a micro-macro framework to a micro-meso-macro framework', In S. H. Christensen et al. (eds), *Engineering, Development and Philosophy: American, Chinese and European Perspectives*, Dordrecht, NL: Springer, pp. 23–36.

Lim, Youn-kyung and Sato, Keiichi (2001), 'Development of design information framework for interactive systems design', in *Proceedings of the 5th Asian International Symposium on Design Science*, Seoul, Korea.

Lima, Manuel (2011), *Visual Complexity: Mapping Patterns of Information*, New York: Princeton Architectural Press.

Lorde, Audre (1984), *The Master's Tools Will Never Dismantle the Master's House*, p. 2.

Lovell, Sophie, Kemp, Klaus and Ive, Jonathan (2011), *Dieter Rams: As Little Design as Possible*, New York: Phaidon Press.

Löwgren, Jonas (2004), *Sketching interaction design*, Talk at Stockholm University, 2 November.

Lupi, Giorgia, Quadri, Simone, Rossi, Gabriele, Ciuffi, Davide, Fragapane, Federica, Majno, Francesco (2013), 'Nobels, No Degrees, Infographic', *Information Is Beautiful Awards*, Kantar, https://www.informationisbeautifulawards.com/showcase/204-nobels-no-degrees. Accessed 21 March 2015.

Lynch, Kevin (1960), *The Image of the City*, Cambridge, MA: MIT Press.

MacDonald, Ziggy (2009), 'Teaching linear programming using Microsoft Excel Solver', *CHEER: Computers in Higher Education Economics Review*, 9:3, n.pag., The Higher Education Academy Economics Network.

Malpass, Matthew (2012), 'Contextualizing critical design: Towards a taxonomy of critical practice in product design', Dissertation, Nottingham Trent University.

Manovich, Lev (2002), *The Language of New Media*, Cambridge, MA: MIT Press.

The Manufacturing Institute (2013), *Untapped Resource: How Manufacturers Can Attract, Retain, and Advance Talented Women*, New York: Deloitte Development LLC.

Maslow, Abraham H. (1943), 'A theory of human motivation', *Psychological Review*, 50, pp. 370–96.

Meggs, Philip (2011), *Meggs' History of Graphic Design*, 5th ed. (eds) Philip B.Meggs and Alston W. Purvis, New York: Wiley.

Mehta, Paras, Stafford, Amy, Bouchard, Matthew, Ruecker, Stan, Anvik, Karl, Rossello, Ximena and Shiri, Ali (2009), 'Four ways of making sense: Designing and implementing searchling, a visual thesaurus-enhanced interface for multilingual digital libraries', Proceedings of the Chicago Colloquium on Digital Humanities and Computer Science, 1:1.

Miall, David S. (1998), 'The hypertextual moment', *English Studies in Canada*, 24, pp. 157–74.

Microsoft (2010–15), Excel Solver, Software.

Milk, Chris (n.d.), The Johnny Cash Project, @radical.media.

'Million Dollar Blocks' (n.d.), *Spatial Information Design Lab*, Columbia University.

MIT SENSEable City Lab (2011), Health InfoScape, Diagram, General Electric: Data Visualization.

Mendaglio, Sal (2008), (ed.) *Dabrowski's Theory of Positive Disintegration*, Scottsdale, AZ: Great Potential Press.

Molano, Hernan, Leon, Farly, Marmolejo, Luis, Rodriguez, Jairo, Ruecker, Stan and Fajardo, Fabio (2018), 'Design for reconciliation: Co-designing a peaceful future in post-conflict zones in Colombia' in S. Ruecker (ed.), *Special Issue: Diseña on Design Research Leading Matters of Concern*, 13, pp. 140–73. English and Spanish.

Monk, Ray (1990), *Ludwig Wittgenstein: The Duty of Genius*, New York: Macmillan.

Moretti, Franco (2013), *Distant Reading*, London: Verso.

Mount Royal University Research Office (2014), 'Faces of innovation', Mount Royal University, Web Application Featuring MRU Researchers, 15 September.

Muller, Michael (2011), 'Feminism asks the "Who" questions in HCI', *Feminism and HCI: New Perspectives, Special issue: Interacting with Computers*, 23:5, pp. 447–49.

Mullet, Kevin and Sano, Darrell (1995), *Designing Visual Interfaces: Communication oriented techniques*, Englewood Cliffs, NJ: SunSoft Press (Prentice Hall).

Muratovski, Gjoko (2016), *Research for Designers: A Guide to Methods and Practice*, SAGE Publications Ltd.

Nieman, Andrea and Dickinson, Jonathan (2013), 'New York City carbon emissions', Infographic, Information is Beautiful Awards, Kantar.

Nightingale, Florence (1858), 'Diagram of the causes of mortality in the army in the East', Diagram, Notes on Matters Affecting the Health, Efficiency, and Hospital Administration of the British Army, London, n.pag., Wikimedia Commons.

Norman, Donald A. (1990), *The Design of Everyday Things*, New York: Doubleday.

NSCAD University (2008), '2008–09 course calendar', http://www.nscad.ns.ca.

Obrist, Marianna and Fuchs, Christian (2010), 'Broadening the view: Human-computer interaction & critical theory', in CHI '10 CHI Conference on Human Factors in Computing Systems, Atlanta, GA, 10–15 April, position paper.

Paley, William Bradford (2008), 'Once more around the sun', Calendar, Information Aesthetics.

Pandian, Anand (2017), 'Call for proposals: Displacements', Cultural Anthropology, https://culanth.org/fieldsights/1168-call-for-proposals-displacements. 2 October.

Papanek, Victor (1973), *Design for the Real World: Human Ecology and Social Change*, New York: Bantam.

Paredes-Olea, Mariana, Ruecker, Stan, Fiorentino, Carlos and Forbes, Fraser (2008), 'Using an affordance strength approach to study the possible redeployment of designs for decision support visualization', Presentation at the 9th Advances in Qualitative Methods Conference 2008. Banff, Canada. October 8–11.

Participants of TaDiC (2019), 'Recycling Whale'. Wire and recycled bottles. Tumaco, Brazil.

Pearce, Laura (2013), 'Feature: Tracing cholera', BlueSci: Cambridge University Science Magazine, Cambridge University Student Union, 25 November.

Pitch Interactive (2013), 'Out of sight, out of mind'.

Plaisant, Catherine, Rose, James, Yu, Bei, Auvil, Loretta, Kirschenbaum, Matthew G., Smith, Martha Nell, Clement, Tanya and Lord, Greg (2006), Exploring erotics in Emily Dickinson's correspondence with text mining and visual interfaces, in *Proceedings of the 6th ACM/IEEE-CS joint conference on Digital libraries (JCDL '06)*, Association for Computing Machinery, New York, NY, USA, pp. 141–50.

Poovey, Mary (2004), 'For what it's worth…', *Critical Inquiry*, 30: Winter, pp. 429–33.

Prado, Luiza and Oliveira, Pedro, 'Questioning the "Critical" in Speculative & Critical Design', Medium. Medium, 4 Febraury 2014, Web. 4 July 2015.

Pytlik Zillig, Brian L. (2009), TEI Analytics: converting documents into a TEI format for cross-collection text analysis, *Literary and Linguistic Computing*, 24(2), pp. 187–92.

Radzikowska, Milena (2011), 'The Paper Drill', Graphic, Stan Ruecker and the INKE Research Group, 'The Paper Drill', in Digital Humanities, 19–21 June, Stanford, CA, n.pag.

Radzikowska, Milena and Ruecker, Stan (2016), 'Materializing text analytical experiences: Taking bubblelines literally', Presentation at the Canadian Society for Digital Humanities/ Société canadienne des humanités numériques (CSDH/SCHN) annual conference at the 2016 Congress of the Social Sciences and Humanities, Calgary, Alberta May 30-June 1, 2016.

Radzikowska, Milena, Ruecker, Stan, Fiorentino, Carlos and Michura, Piotr (2007), 'The novel as slot machine', In *Annual Conference of the Society for Digital Humanities (SDH/SEMI)*, Saskatoon, CA, 28–30 May.

Radzikowska, Milena, Traynor, Brian, Ruecker, Stan and Vaughn, Norman (2009a), 'Teaching user-centered design through low fidelity sketches', In *Proceedings of the 4th Information Design International Conference*, Rio De Janeiro, Brazil, 9–12 September, pp. 744–56.

Radzikowska, Milena, Ruecker, Stan, Bischof, Walter, Annett, Michelle and Forbes, Fraser (2009b), 'Gearing up: Visualizing decision support for manufacturing', *Journal of the 2009 Chicago Colloquium on Digital Humanities and Computer Science*, 1:1, n.pag.

Radzikowska, Milena, Ruecker, Stan, Brown, Susan, Organisciak, Peter and the INKE Research Group (2011), 'Structured surfaces for JiTR', in Digital Humanities Presentation at Stanford, CA, 19–21 June.

Radzikowska, Milena, Ruecker, Stan and Sinclair, Stéfan (2015a), 'From A to B via Z: Strategic interface design in the digital humanities', *Paper presented at IASDR 2015 Congress*, Brisbane, Australia.

Radzikowska, Milena, Ruecker, Stan and Rockwell, Geoffrey (2015b), 'Teaching undergraduate design students using digital humanities research in the classroom', in Aidan Rowe and Bonnie Sadler-Takach (eds), *Design Education: Approaches, Explorations and Perspectives*, Canada: A&D Press.

Radzikowska, Milena, Roberts-Smith, Jennifer, Zhou, Xinyue and Ruecker, Stan (2019), 'A speculative feminist approach to project management', *SDRJ: Strategic Design Research Journal*, 12:1.

Radzikowska, Milena, Kelle, Alyssa and Snell, Madison (2020), 'Prototyping in the Motorcycle Shop: The Milking Machine for Text Analysis', in Roberts-Smith, Jennifer, Ruecker, Stan and Radzikowska, Milena (eds), *Prototyping Across the Disciplines: Designing Better Futures*, Intellect Books.

Rajamanickam, Venkatesh (2005), 'Infographics: Handout', *Seminar at the National Institute of Design*, 1–14. 10 Oct. 2005, Bombay, IN.

Ramsay, Stephen (2011), *Reading Machines: Toward an Algorithmic Criticism*, Chicago, IL: University of Illinois Press.

Rand, Paul (2014), *Thoughts on Design*, San Francisco: Chronicle Books.

Renear, Allen (2004), 'Text Encoding', in Susan Schreibman, Ray Siemens and John Unsworth (eds), *A Companion to Digital Humanities*, Oxford: Blackwell, http://www.digitalhumanities.org/companion/

Resnick, Elizabeth (2003), *Design for Communication: Conceptual Graphic Design Basics*, Hoboken, NJ: John Wiley & Sons Inc.

Rittel, Horst W. J. and Webber, Melvin M. (1973), 'Dilemmas in a general theory of planning', *Policy Science*, 4, pp. 155–69.

Rivkin, Julie and Ryan, Michael (2004), *Literary Theory: An Anthology*, Malden, MA: Blackwell.

Roberts, Lynne D. and Allen, Peter J. (2013), 'A brief measure of student perceptions of the educational value of research participation', *Australian Journal of Psychology*, 65, pp. 22–29.

Rockwell, Geoffrey and Johnson, N. (2007), 'The globalization compendium: Reflecting on contemporary research and online publication', presented at the *Society for Digital Humanities (SDH/SEMI) Conference*, University of Saskatchewan, Saskatoon, 28–30 May.

Rockwell, Geoffrey, Wong, Garry, Ruecker, Stan, Meredith-Lobay, Megan and Sinclair, Stéfan (2009), 'Big See: Large scale visualization', in *Proceedings of the Chicago Colloquium on Digital Humanities and Computer Science, Chicago*, The Illinois Institute of Technology, 14–16 November.

Rodgers, Deborah (2000/2001), 'A grammar for zooming interfaces: Using interaction design strategies to improve user's navigation and spatial awareness', *Information Design Journal*, 10:3, pp. 250–57.

Ross, Shawna (2014), 'In praise of overstating the case: A review of Franco Moretti, distant reading', *Digital Humanities Quarterly*, 8:1, n.pag.

Rottger, Siobhan (2011), 'Exploring art movements', Digital Prototype, Calgary, Alberta.

Ruecker, Stan (2002), 'Carrying the pleasure of books into the design of the electronic book', in William S. Green and Patrick W. Jordan (eds), *Pleasure with Products: Beyond Usability*, London: Taylor and Francis, pp. 135–46.

Ruecker, Stan (2003), Affordances of prospect for academic users of interpretively-tagged text collections, Dissertation, University of Alberta.

Ruecker, Stan (2009), 'Rich-prospect browsing interfaces', in Margherita Pagani (ed.), *Encyclopedia of Multimedia Technology and Networking*, 2nd ed., London: Information Science Reference-IGI Global, pp. 1240–48.

Ruecker, Stan (2012a), 'The perennial and the particular challenges of design education', *Visible Language*, 46:1/2.

Ruecker, Stan (2012b), 'The perennial and the particular challenges in design education', *Envisioning a Future Design Education, Special issue: Visible Language*, 46:1/2, pp. 119–27.

Ruecker, Stan (2018a), Interview of Jorge Frascara and Guillermina Nöel, 'Distributed leadership' in S. Ruecker (ed.), *Special issue: Diseña on Design Research Leading Matters of Concern*, 13, pp. 24–57. English and Spanish.

Ruecker, Stan (2018b), 'Design researchers leading interdisciplinary teams', *Diseña*, Special Issue: 'Design Research Leading Matters of Concern', 13, pp.12–23.

Ruecker, Stan (2018c), 'Distributed Leadership', Interview of Jorge Frascara and Guillermina Nöel, in Stan Ruecker, (ed.), *Diseña, Special issue: Matters of Concern*, 13, pp. 24–57. English and Spanish.

Ruecker, Stan and Radzikowska, Milena (2008), 'The design of a project charter for interdisciplinary research', in *DIS '08 Proceedings of the 7th ACM Conference on Designing Interactive Systems*, Cape Town, SA, 25–27 February, New York: ACM, pp. 288–94, ACM Digital Library.

Ruecker, Stan and the INKE Research Group (2011), 'The paper drill', *Digital Humanities*, Stanford, CA, 19–21 June.

Ruecker, Stan and the INKE Research Group (2015), 'A brief taxonomy of prototypes for the digital humanities', *Scholarly and Research Communication*, 6:2.

Ruecker, Stan and Roberts-Smith, Jennifer (2018), 'Activating interpretation: Experience design in the humanities', in Jentery Sayers (ed.), *Making Things and Drawing Boundaries: Experiments in the Digital Humanities, Debates in the Digital Humanities*, Minnesota: University of Minnesota Press.

Ruecker, Stan, Given, Lisa, Sadler, Elizabeth and Ruskin, Andrea (2005), 'Building accessible web interfaces for seniors: Similarity clustering of pill images', In *Include 2005*, London, UK, 5–8 April.

Ruecker, Stan, Radzikowska, Milena, Michura, Piotr, Fiorentino, Carlos and Clement, Tanya (2007a), 'Visualizing Repetition in Text', *Reassembling the Disassembled Book: Symposium of the Congress of the Humanities and Social Sciences, University of Saskatchewan*, May 2007, Brent Nelson (ed.), *Special Issue of CH Working Papers*. August 2008.

Ruecker, Stan, Sinclair, Stéfan and Radzikowska, Milena (2007b), 'Confidence, visual research and the aesthetic function', *Partnership: The Canadian Journal of Library and Information Practice and Research*, 2:1, n.pag.

Ruecker, Stan, Given, Lisa, Sadler, Elizabeth, Ruskin, Andrea and Simpson, Heather (2007c), 'Design of a rich-prospect browsing interface for seniors: A qualitative study of image similarity clustering', *Visible Language*, 41:1, pp. 4–21.

Ruecker, Stan, Radzikowska, Milena and Liepert, Susan (2008), 'The introduction of radical change in human-computer interfaces', Public lecture delivered at Technische Universität, Berlin, DR, 19 February.

Ruecker, Stan, Radzikowska, Milena and Sinclair, Stefan (2011), *Visual Interface Design for Digital Cultural Heritage: A Guide to Rich-Prospect Browsing*, London, UK: Ashgate.

Ruecker, Stan, Rockwell, Geoffrey, Radzikowska, Milena, Sinclair, Stéfan, Vandendorpe, Christian, Siemens, Ray, Dobson, Doll, Teresa, Lindsay, Bieber, Mark, Eberle-Sinatra, Michael, Lucky, Shannon and the INKE Group (2012), 'Drilling for papers in INKE', *Scholarly and Research Communication*, 3:1, n.pag.

Ruhl, Glenn (2008), 'Merging territories: Creating an Information Design Baccalaureate Degree', In *Proceedings of the Professional Communication Conference*, Montréal, QC, 13–16 July, IEEE International, pp. 1–9.

Sanders, Elizabeth (2004), 'Participatory Designing: Information and Adaptation', Paper presented at the *IIID Expert Forum for Knowledge Presentation*, May 30–31, 2003. Institute of Design, IIT, Chicago, IL.

Schuler, Douglas and Clement, Andrew (2004), 'Artful integration and participatory design: Preface to the proceedings of PDC 2004', in Clement, A., van den Besselaar, P. (eds), *Proceedings of the Eighth Conference on Participatory Design*, 1st ed., pp. v–vi, New York: ACM Digital Press.

Schwartz, Daniel L., Chase, Catherine C. and Bransford, John D. (2012), 'Resisting overzealous transfer: Coordinating previously successful routines with needs for new learning', *Educational Psychologist*, 47:3, pp. 204–14.

Shneiderman, Ben and Plaisant, Catherine (1998), 'Treemap Research at the University of Maryland', http://www.ifs.tuwien.ac.at/~silvia/wien/vu-infovis/articles/shneiderman_treemap-history_1998–2009.pdf. Accessed 15 September 2015.

Sillitoe, P. (2004), 'Interdisciplinary experiences: Working with Indigenous knowledge in development', *Interdisciplinary Science Reviews*, 29:1, pp. 6–23.

Simon, Herbert (1957), *Models of Man: Social and Rational*, New York: Wiley.

Simon, Herbert ([1969] 1996), *The Sciences of the Artificial*, Cambridge, MA: MIT Press.

Sinclair, Stéfan and Rockwell, Geoffrey (2014), *Bubblelines*, Version 01, Voyant Tools, https://voyant-tools.org/?view=Bubblelines. Accessed 1 September 2020.

Small, Hugh (1998), 'Florence Nightingale's statistical diagrams', In *Stats & Lamps Research Conference*, London, UK, https://www.york.ac.uk/depts/maths/histstat/small.htm. Accessed 18 March 2015.

Smith, Kendra S. (2005), *Architects' Drawings: A Selection of Sketches by World Famous Architects through History*, Oxford: Elsevier/Architectural Press.

Snow, John and Cheffins, Charles (1855), *Cholera Map, 1854: Engraving. On the Mode of Communicating Cholera, 2nd. ed.* London, UK: T. Richards, unnumbered plate, Wikipedia Commons, https://en.wikipedia.org/wiki/John_Snow#/media/File:Snow-cholera-map-1.jpg. Accessed 1 September 2020.

Social Science LibreTexts (n.d.), 'Levels of analysis: Micro and macro', *Boundless Learning*, https://socialsci.libretexts.org/Bookshelves/Sociology/Introduction_to_Sociology/Book%3A_Sociology_(Boundless)/01%3A_Sociology/1.04%3A_The_Sociological_Approach/1.4B%3A_Levels_of_Analysis-_Micro_and_Macro. Accessed 10 May 2020.

Stein, Gertrude ([1925] 1995), *The Making of Americans: Being a History of a Family's Progress*, Normal, IL: Dalkey Archive Press.

Stengers, Isabelle (2010), 'Including nonhumans in political theory: Opening Pandora's box?', in B. Braun and S. J. Whatmore (eds), *Political Matter: Technoscience, Democracy, and Public Life*, pp. 3–34.

Sterling, Bruce (2014), 'Design fiction: Speculative everything by Dunne & Raby', Wired Magazine, Condé Nast, https://www.wired.com/2014/02/design-fiction-speculative-everything-dunne-raby/. Accessed 23 February 2015.

Stiemerling, Oliver, Kahler, Helge and Wulf, Volker (1997), 'How to make software softer: Designing tailorable applications', In *Proceedings of the Conference on Designing Interactive Systems: Processes, Practices, Methods, and Techniques*, The Netherlands, http://www.acm.org/pubs/citations/proceedings/chi/263552/p365-stiemerling/. 18–20 August.

Stubblefield, William A. (1998), 'Patterns of change in design metaphor: A case study', In *Conference Proceedings on Human Factors in Computing Systems*, Los Angeles, CA, pp. 73–80, http://www.acm.org/pubs/citations/proceedings/chi/274644/p73-stubblefield/.

Suchman, Lucy A. (1987) *Plans and Situated Actions: The Problem of Human-Machine Communication*, Cambridge: Cambridge University Press.

Suda, Brian (2010), *The Practical Guide to Designing with Data*, Penarth, UK: Five Simple Steps.

Stoicheff, Peter and Taylor, Andrew (eds) (2004), *The Future of the Page*, Toronto; Buffalo; London: University of Toronto Press.

Sullivan, Louis H. (1896), 'The tall office building artistically considered', *Lippincott's Magazine*, March. In public domain, https://ocw.mit.edu/courses/architecture/4-205-analysis-of-contemporary-architecture-fall-2009/readings/MIT4_205F09_Sullivan.pdf. Accessed 1 September 2020.

Svensson, Patrik (2003), 'Interdisciplinary Design Research', In Brenda Laurel (ed.), *Design Research: Methods and Perspectives* (193–200), Cambridge, Mass: MIT Press.

Tracy, Brian (2010), *Goals!: How to Get Everything You Want – Faster Than You Ever Thought Possible*, San Francisco: Berrett-Koehler Publishers.

Tur, Olena (n.d.), 'Amazing View of Angkor Wat', Photograph, Siem Reap, Cambodia.

Twine, France Widdance and Gardener, Bradley (2013), 'Introduction', In *Geographies of Privilege*. (ed.) France Widdance Twine and Bradley Gardener. New York: Routledge, New York, 2013. 1–16.

Vela, Sarah, Frizzera, Luciano, Ilovan, Mihaela, Michura, Piotr, Sondheim, Dan, Rockwell, Geoffrey and the INKE Research Team (2013), 'Manipulating Multiple Editions with the Multi-touch Variorum (MtV) Project', Presented at the *Canadian Society for Digital Humanities/Société canadienne des humanités numériques (CSDH/SCHN) conference (at the Congress of the Humanities and Social Sciences 2013)*, U Victoria, 3–5 June 2013.

Vinson, Norman G. (1999), 'Design Guidelines for Landmarks to Support Navigation in Virtual Environments', *Proceedings of the CHI99 Conference on Human Factors in Computing Systems: The CHI is the Limit*, Pittsburgh, PA USA, May 15–20, pp. 278–85, http://www.acm.org/pubs/citations/proceedings/chi/302979/p278-vinson/.

Watson Boone, Rebecca (1994), 'The information needs and habits of humanities scholars', *Library Hi Tech*, 9:1.

Weitz, Robert (2013), 'Form Follows Function – A Truism That Isn't True', *The Brand Wash*, http://www.thebrandwash.com/2013/03/21/form-follows-function-a-truism-that-isnt-true/. Accessed 21 March 2015.

Whitley, Edward (2011), 'Visualizing the Archive', In *The American Literature Scholar in the Digital Age*, (eds) Amy E. Earhart and Andrew Jewell, Ann Arbor: University of Michigan Press, pp. 185–207.

Willard, Emma (1836), *Picture of Nations*, David Rumsey Map Collection, Cartography Associates, http://www.davidrumsey.com/maps1130446-29401.html. Accessed 5 July 2015.

Wilson, V. and Pirrie, A. (2000), 'Multidisciplinary teamworking indicators of good practice', The Scottish Council for Research in Education Research Report, 77.

Winchester III, Woodrow (2010), '?REALizing our messy futures: Toward culturally responsive design tools in engaging our deeper dives', *Interactions*, 17:6, Nov/Dec, pp. 14–19.

Windsor, Jennifer (2014), 'What is design?', Presentation at the Digital Humanities Summer Institute 2014, Visual Design for Digital Humanists, 5 June.

Winhall, Jennie (n.d.), 'Is design political?' Core77, http://catalinacortazar.com/thesis/wpcontent/uploads/.../IsDesignPolitical.pdf. Accessed 15 July 2015.

Wiseman, Rob and Sless, David (2006), 'Writing about medicines for people: Usability guidelines and glossary for consumer product information', Dept. of Human Services and Health, Australia.

Wittgenstein, Ludwig (1970), *Zettel*, G. E. M. Anscombe and G. H. von Wright, (eds.) Berkeley: University of California Press.

The World Bank (1994), *Governance: The World Bank's Experience*, Washington, DC: The World Bank, https://documents.worldbank.org/en/publication/documents-reports/documentdetail/711471468765285964/governance-the-world-banks-experience. Accessed 10 July 2015.

Wurman, Richard Saul (1989), *Information Anxiety*, New York: Bantam-Doubleday-Bell.

Wynne, Maryanne, Ruecker, Stan, Nelson, Thomas M., Albakry, Waleed, Strong, Michael, Lewcio, Michael and Plouffe, Michael (2007), 'The rich prospect of tension, affiliation and reward: From social capital to image analysis', paper presented at the *Society for Digital Humanities (SDH/SEMI) Conference*, University of Saskatchewan, Saskatoon, 28–30 May.

Yaffa, Joshua (2011), 'The Information Sage', *Washington Monthly* May/June 2011: n.pag., https://washingtonmonthly.com/magazine/mayjune-2011/the-information-sage/. Accessed 5 July 2015.

Yi-Luen Do, Ellen (2005), 'Design sketches and sketch design tools', *Knowledge-Based Systems*, 18:8, pp. 383–405.

Zhang, Shaoke, Zhao, Chen, Zhang, Qiang, Su, Hui, Guo, Haiyan, Cui, Jie, Pan, Yingxin and Moody, Paul (2007), 'Managing Collaborative Activities in Project Management', *Proceedings of the 2007 symposium on Computer Human Interaction for the Management of Information Technology (CHIMIT '07)*. March 30–31, 2007.

Zimmerman, Eric (2003), 'Play as research: The iterative design process', in B.Laurel (ed.), *Design Research: Methods and Perspectives* (176–184), Cambridge, MA: MIT Press.

Index

D

E

F

Design and the Digital Humanities